The Hollywood

MW00784602

The Hollywood Meme
Transnational Adaptations in World Cinema

Iain Robert Smith

EDINBURGH
University Press

Edinburgh University Press is one of the leading university
presses in the UK. We publish academic books and journals in
our selected subject areas across the humanities and social sciences,
combining cutting-edge scholarship with high editorial and
production values to produce academic works of lasting importance.
For more information visit our website: edinburghuniversitypress.com

© Iain Robert Smith, 2017, 2018

Edinburgh University Press Ltd
The Tun – Holyrood Road
12 (2f) Jackson's Entry
Edinburgh EH8 8PJ

First published in hardback by Edinburgh University Press 2017

Typeset in 11/13pt Ehrhardt MT Pro by
Servis Filmsetting Ltd, Stockport, Cheshire, and
printed and bound in Great Britain by
CPI Group (UK) Ltd, Croydon CR0 4YY

A CIP record for this book is available from the British Library

ISBN 978 0 7486 7746 7 (hardback)
ISBN 978 1 4744 4133 9 (paperback)
ISBN 978 0 7486 7747 4 (webready PDF)
ISBN 978 0 7486 7748 1 (epub)

The right of Iain Robert Smith to be identified as author of
this work has been asserted in accordance with the Copyright,
Designs and Patents Act 1988 and the Copyright and
Related Rights Regulations 2003 (SI No. 2498).

Contents

Figures

Acknowledgements

I began the research for this book in 2006 so it would be impossible for me to acknowledge all the countless people who have supported me along the way – I can only do my best to pay tribute to some of the key people who helped develop and refine the ideas contained herein.

This book started life as a PhD dissertation so I want to express my deepest thanks to my supervisors Roberta Pearson and Paul Grainge for their support and unfailing generosity throughout the whole process. My work benefited hugely from the collegiate and supportive atmosphere at the University of Nottingham so I also want to acknowledge the advice from various past and current staff members including Liz Evans, Mark Gallagher, Cathy Johnson, Gianluca Sergi, Jacob Smith, Julian Stringer and Peter Urquhart. For keeping me relatively sane throughout the PhD, I am thankful to my fellow graduate students at Nottingham including Alessandro Catania, Rebecca Cobby, Michael James Collins, Natalie Edwards, Lin Feng, Serena Formica, Fran Fuentes, Kiran Indraganti, Nuno Jorges, John-Paul Kelly, Áine Mahon, Alper Mazman, Anthony McKenna, Matthew Mead, Sinéad Moynihan, Donna Peberdy, Anthony Smith, Alex Symons and Rachel Walls. Moreover, I want to express a special thanks to my flatmates Jack Newsinger, SooJeong Ahn and Nandana Bose for putting up with me over the four years. These were, quite genuinely, some of the best years of my life.

Since completing the PhD, I have been teaching at the University of Roehampton and over my time here I have benefited hugely from discussions with my film colleagues Stacey Abbott, Caroline Bainbridge, William Brown, Michael Chanan, Chris Darke, Deborah Jermyn and Michael Witt. Moreover, I have greatly benefited from the eclectic interdisciplinarity of the department of Media, Culture and Language which allowed me to collaborate with numerous media scholars and translation specialists – most significantly Andrea Esser and Miguel Bernal-Merino with whom I set up the Arts and Humanities Research Council (AHRC) funded Media Across Borders research network – and their keen insights have helped me to broaden out my understanding of processes of cultural globalisation beyond the cinematic.

I am also grateful to the academics and researchers around the world who I met at conferences or conversed with through email. This project would not have been the same without many fruitful discussions with scholars such as Savas Arslan, Irene Artegiani, Eylem Atakav, Colette Balmain, Becky Bartlett, Stefano Baschiera, Melis Behlil, Tim Bergfelder, Will Brooker, Jose Capino, Bertha Chin, David Church, Anna Reynolds Cooper, Corey Creekmur, Rayna Denison, David Desser, David Scott Diffrient, Kevin Donnelly, Kate Egan, Dimitris Eleftheriotis, Darren Elliott-Smith, Elizabeth Ezra, Rosalind Galt, Ian Garwood, Gokay Gelgec, Christine Geraghty, Ed Glaser, Katie Grant, Ahmet Gürata, Dan Hassler-Forest, Daniel Herbert, Will Higbee, Mette Hjort, Matt Hills, Eli Horwatt, Ian Hunter, Russ Hunter, Ekky Imanjaya, Dina Iordanova, Mark Jancovich, Derek Johnston, Nessa Johnston, Bethan Jones, Steven Jones, Shaun Kimber, Mikel Koven, Michael Lawrence, Andrew Leavold, Kathleen Loock, Daniel Martin, David Martin-Jones, Ernest Mathijs, Lucy Mazdon, Mark McKenna, Laura Mee, Xavier Mendik, Renee Middlemost, Lothar Mikos, Stephen Morgan, Lori Morimoto, Lúcia Nagib, Kartik Nair, Kathleen Newman, Gary Needham, Tasha Oren, R. Barton Palmer, Ally Peirse, Emma Pett, Laurence Raw, Steve Rawle, Rashna Wadia Richards, Miriam Ross, Melanie Selfe, Meheli Sen, Deborah Shaw, Neelam Sidhar Wright, Gohar Siddiqui, Adrian Smith, Clarissa Smith, Tim Snelson, Todd Stadtman, Sarah Taylor-Harman, Sarah Thomas, Dolores Tierney, Pete Tombs, Constantine Verevis, Johnny Walker, Yiman Wang, Rachel Mizsei Ward, Tom Watson, Chelsea Wessels and Andy Willis. I am particularly grateful to Austin Fisher with whom I set up the Transnational Cinemas scholarly interest group at the Society for Cinema and Media Studies (SCMS) and who is always ready for a spirited discussion of cinematic transnationalism.

A project of this scale would be impossible without institutional support so I am therefore grateful to the University of Nottingham and the Arts and Humanities Research Council for providing the funding that allowed me to pursue this research, and I am also grateful to the University of Roehampton for providing me with a sabbatical which allowed me to revise and rework the thesis into the book you have before you. Special thanks go to everyone at Edinburgh University Press, and especially to Gillian Leslie and Richard Strachan for their encouragement and patience from the initial proposal to the final proofread. It would not be the book it is today without your support.

Portions of this book have been previously published as articles and book chapters. The sub-section of Chapter 2 in which I discuss *Turist Ömer Uzay Yolunda* appeared in a different form as 'Beam Me

Up, Ömer: Transnational Media Flow and the Cultural Politics of the Turkish *Star Trek* Remake' in *Velvet Light Trap* 61 (2008). Another sub-section of Chapter 2, this time on *Şeytan*, was published as 'The Exorcist in Istanbul: Processes of Transcultural Appropriation within Turkish Popular Cinema' in *Portal: Journal of Multidisciplinary International Studies* 5: 1 (2008). Finally, the sub-section of Chapter 4 on *Ghajini* was published as '*Memento* in Mumbai: 'A Few More Songs and a Lot More Ass-kicking'' in the book *Storytelling in the Media Convergence Age*, edited by Roberta Pearson and Anthony N. Smith. I would like to thank the editors and anonymous reviewers from these publications for their invaluable comments on my work.

On a more melancholy note, the writing of this book was bracketed by two periods of hospitalisation that resulted from my chronic health condition Crohn's disease. Nothing I have done here would have been possible without the unfailing care and support I received at the Hospital Geral de Santo António in Porto, the Queen's Medical Centre in Nottingham, and Charing Cross Hospital in Hammersmith, London. The medical teams at these hospitals supported me through some of the toughest hours of my life and I am incredibly grateful to all of them and to the European healthcare system that supports them.

My parents, Edward and Ailsa, and my younger brother Duncan, have supported my passion for cinema since an early age. Indeed, I can probably trace the initial germ of this book to my mum's decision to allow me to stay up and watch Godzilla films well after I should have gone to bed. It left more of an impression than I think either of us was aware of at the time.

Finally, I would like to thank my wife Cai whom I love with all my heart. We met in the year that I started researching this topic and we were married by the time I finished it. This book is dedicated to you.

Introduction

If there is a [global] village, it speaks American. It wears jeans, drinks Coke, eats at the golden arches, walks on swooshed shoes, plays electric guitars, recognizes Mickey Mouse, James Dean, E.T., Bart Simpson, R2-D2, and Pamela Anderson.

Todd Gitlin (2002: 176)

If Hollywood is indeed the acknowledged dominant cinema in the world, the ways in which minority cultures appropriate and make use of that dominant discourse can prove instructive for both narrative film studies and cultural studies.

Andrew Horton (1998: 173)

While subjected peoples cannot readily control what emanates from the dominant culture, they do determine to varying extents what they absorb into their own, and what they use it for.

Mary Louise Pratt (1992: 6)

On 14 December 2015, the seventh instalment in the *Star Wars* franchise, *Star Wars: The Force Awakens*, premiered in Los Angeles. Highly anticipated as the first instalment since Disney acquired Lucasfilm in 2012, the film was positioned within the wider media discourse as an attempt to reinvigorate the franchise after the relative critical failure of the earlier prequel trilogy. On a budget estimated to be $200 million, considerably higher than the $11 million spent on the 1977 original, the film was a substantial commercial success - grossing over $750 million within twenty days of release, and swiftly becoming the highest-grossing film of all time in North America (McClintock 2016). Nevertheless, while the overall critical reaction was positive, the film received a significant amount of negative criticism focusing on its many resemblances to the first film in the franchise. From *Vox*'s list of 'Five ways the new movie copies the original film' (VanDerWerff 2015) to Geek Crusade's 'Eighteen ways *The Force Awakens* ripped off *A New Hope*' (Jun Heng 2015), there was a considerable amount of online commentary that positioned *The Force Awakens* less as a new instalment in a developing franchise than as a 'rip-off' of the original film. Even director J. J. Abrams acknowledged this reaction, admitting in an interview that 'I can understand that someone might say, "Oh, it's a complete rip-off!"' (McMillan 2016) in reference to the various ways the film paid homage to the George Lucas original. In a year in which the *Spider-Man* franchise is being rebooted for the third time since 2002, and in which presold franchises are becoming an ever more dominant part of the media landscape, it is clear that this reaction to the new *Star Wars* film reflects a wider critical debate about the cultural industries' tendency to remake and recycle earlier texts.

Of course, this is far from a new phenomenon and *The Force Awakens* is certainly not the first film to have been criticised as a derivative rip-off of *Star Wars*. Within America, there have been numerous examples ranging from exploitation films, such as the Roger Corman-produced *Battle Beyond the Stars* (1980), through to the various fan films, porn parodies and other unlicensed adaptations of the franchise that have appeared in subsequent years. Moreover, this phenomenon is not limited to the USA, with a plethora of unlicensed adaptations of *Star Wars* appearing in film industries around the world. In Brazil, for example, Adriano Stuart directed the comedy *Os Trapalhões na Guerra dos Planetas* (The Tramps in Planet Wars, 1978), in which the eponymous 'tramps' are transported into the world of *Star Wars*, complete with a central villain Zuco closely modelled on Darth Vader and a co-pilot Bonzo bearing more than a passing resemblance to Chewbacca. In the same year, Italian director Luigi Cozzi directed *Starcrash*, a space opera that avoided direct imitation of costumes and plot but featured numerous borrowings including an opening sequence that evoked the initial shots of the Imperial Star Destroyer and a central character, Akton, whose preferred weapon was a lightsaber. Meanwhile, within the Japanese industry, *Star Wars* was clearly the model for the Kinji Fukasaku directed *Message from Space* (1978), a relatively high-budget science-fiction film starring Sonny Chiba and Vic Morrow that Toei Studios rushed into production to capitalise on the global success of Lucas's film. Moreover, not only were films being made that resembled *Star Wars* in terms of costume, characterisation and plot, but, in a case that I will discuss in more depth later, there was even a theatrically released film that appropriated actual footage from *Star Wars* – the Turkish film *Dünyayı Kurtaran Adam* (1982). Rather than attempting to recreate the space opera on his rather limited budget, director Çetin Inanç simply took a print of *Star Wars* and spliced its special-effects sequences directly into his own film. As these examples indicate, *Star Wars* was not only the first film in a hugely successful Hollywood franchise but was also the inspiration for a whole series of homages, parodies and 'rip-offs' produced in film industries around the world.

It is important to remember, however, that *Star Wars* was not itself a wholly 'original' text. George Lucas designed the film as a tribute to a number of earlier sources including Flash Gordon and Buck Rogers serials, Hollywood war films such as *The Bridges at Toko-Ri* (1954), and Joseph Campbell's study of mythological archetypes, *The Hero with a Thousand Faces*. Furthermore, *Star Wars* also took inspiration from numerous examples of critically acclaimed world cinema. Most famously, Lucas's original plot outline closely resembled the plot to Akira Kurosawa's *The Hidden Fortress* and this ultimately inspired the strategy to tell the story from the perspective of the film's lowliest characters, C-3PO and R2-D2 (Stempel 2000: 204). Moreover, the iconography of the film was also heavily influenced by German cinema – from Fritz Lang's silent *Metropolis* (1927) through to Leni Riefenstahl's propaganda film *Triumph of the Will* (1935).While I agree with J. Hoberman that *Star Wars* is 'arguably the quintessential Hollywood product' (2004: 319), it is important to note that the film was adapting and reworking numerous elements borrowed from world cinema, and, also, that it would subsequently become the inspiration for films produced in the popular film industries of Brazil, Japan, Turkey and Italy.

This account of cross-cultural borrowings and syncretism points to the deeply interconnected histories of Hollywood and world cinema, yet it is notable that scholarship on Hollywood cinema tends to neglect this wider impact on world cinema while, conversely, scholarship on world cinema tends to neglect the transnational influence of Hollywood. The central argument of this book is that we need to address this interrelationship in order to better interrogate the complex cultural dynamics underpinning the transnational circulation of cinema. Theories of globalisation often position American culture as a hegemonic global force which dominates over local traditions, yet there is a need for an understanding of what precisely happens when these American products are appropriated and reworked by other cultures. There are well-established traditions of adapting Hollywood cinema in the film industries of Turkey, India, the Philippines, Hong Kong, Mexico, Italy, Brazil, Indonesia, Nigeria and Japan, among others – in fact, it is my contention that this process has taken place in nearly every country that has had a thriving popular film industry in the twentieth century. As Ana M. López has argued, 'Hollywood's international presence has had acute effects not only on Hollywood itself – upon its production and textual practices – but on all other filmmaking nations' (2000: 419). From the Nigerian remake of

Titanic (1997) titled *Masoyiyata* (My Beloved, 2003) and the Indonesian reworking of *The Terminator* (1984) titled *Pembalasan ratu pantai selatan* (Revenge of the South Seas Queen, 1989), through to the Mexican version of *Batwoman* titled *La Mujer Murcielago* (The Batwoman, 1968) and the Brazilian parody of Jaws titled *Bacalhau* (Codfish, 1975), there is an extensive history of films produced around the world that rework elements borrowed from Hollywood. It is this phenomenon that I am terming 'The Hollywood Meme' – using the structuring metaphor of the 'meme' to investigate the numerous ways in which Hollywood cinema has been spread and adapted around the world. Yet this syncretic relationship between Hollywood and world cinema has rarely been addressed in scholarship and it is clear that we need to interrogate this further.

This is not to say that scholars of world cinema are unaware of the global presence of Hollywood. Indeed, as Lucia Nagib has argued, world cinema has often been defined explicitly in opposition to Hollywood, with various national cinemas held up as offering alternatives to the dominant American paradigm (2006: 30–1) Moreover, scholars are often making manoeuvres similar to Dipesh Chakrabarty's celebrated strategy to provincialise Europe (2000), in that they are attempting to reframe and refocus our attention elsewhere in the globe. Hollywood is already positioned as the dominant centre within film studies scholarship more broadly, and therefore scholarship on world cinema is often underpinned by a political desire to draw attention to other industries. Bhaskar Sarkar is representative of this gesture when he asks: 'What if Hollywood's hegemony is strategically bracketed . . . so that non-Hollywood cultural circuits come into analytical focus?' (2009: 36).

While I am certainly sympathetic to this desire to bring attention to other cultural circuits, the key question here is whether bracketing Hollywood's global dominance challenges its status or simply recentres it as the unacknowledged standard. This is not a simple question to answer and I acknowledge that the approach I am taking in this book is not without its own drawbacks. To some extent, I am committing the gravest sin that a scholar of world cinema could possibly commit – I am positioning Hollywood at the centre of global film production. I can already imagine the future critiques that see this project as little more than an attempt to recentre Hollywood within discourses of world cinema. There is likely a good reason that such a project has not already been done. Moreover, I am not attempting to argue, as Jane Mills does in her recent book *Loving and Hating Hollywood*, that studying the exchanges between Hollywood and various national cinemas ultimately functions to decentre Hollywood (2009: xii). I acknowledge that the project I am attempting here does

position Hollywood somewhat as a centre. However, it is my contention
that Hollywood *is* a dominant force within global film production and
has had a major impact on filmmaking traditions around the world, and
that despite this, the impact of Hollywood on world cinema is in fact an
understudied phenomenon. Our attempts as scholars to position world
cinema in opposition to Hollywood, or to strategically bracket Hollywood
away from scholarship on other national cinemas, have led us to lose sight
of the overlapping, intersecting nature of world cinema production. It is
not enough to acknowledge Hollywood's dominance and yet neglect the
impact that it has had on world cinema – we need to interrogate what
exactly happens when these Hollywood films become the source texts for
films made in other national cinemas.

Furthermore, there has been a tendency when dealing with Hollywood
to position it as the norm from which all other cinemas deviate – the standard against which other cinemas are defined – and therefore we require
site-specific histories that interrogate exactly how Hollywood has impacted
other contexts. As Mitsuhiro Yoshimoto has argued, 'We need to put the
Hollywood cinema in specific historical contexts; instead of talking about
the Hollywood cinema as the norm, we must examine the specific and
historically changing relations between the Hollywood cinema and other
national cinemas' (Yoshimoto 2006a: 36). This book therefore attempts to
historicise the dynamics between Hollywood and other national cinemas
within specific socio-historic contexts, and therefore to go beyond a conception of Hollywood as the un-interrogated standard. Indeed, it should
be noted at the outset that I do not see Hollywood as simply synonymous
with the district in Los Angeles that has historically been the centre of film
production in America. While the term functions in many respects as a
metonym for popular American cinema, I will be testing the limits of such
a notion throughout this book.

Moreover, there are a number of centres of film production and I am
certainly not claiming that global flows need be associated exclusively
with the spread of Hollywood. As I have discussed elsewhere (Smith
2013), South Korean cinema has recently become the model for a series
of Bollywood adaptations, and there is an extensive history of exchanges
across a range of national film industries. Nevertheless, it is undeniable
that Hollywood has had the most significant global impact of any national
film industry and these processes of transnational adaptation are still
very much structured by broader relations of power. Even if we want to
assert that Bollywood, for example, is at least as significant a centre of film
production as Hollywood, it is nevertheless the case that the Bollywood
industry remakes a significant number of Hollywood films every year,

while the reverse is rarely the case. There are still power differentials shaping these cultural exchanges that we need to address and, while I am sympathetic to attempts to provincialise Hollywood, it is important that scholarship nevertheless interrogates the impact that Hollywood has had for many decades on the popular cinemas of the world.

Rather than treating world cinema as separate from, and opposed to, Hollywood, my aims are to investigate the interrelationship between Hollywood and world cinema. What happens to our understanding of Hollywood when we frame it through discourses of world cinema, and conversely, what happens to our understanding of world cinema when we frame it through its engagements with Hollywood? This book is designed both as an introduction to the global phenomenon of transnational adaptations of Hollywood, and an attempt to theorise the broader implications of this form of cross-cultural exchange. This is not an apolitical gesture. In Edward Said's 2003 introduction to *Orientalism*, he responded to the prevailing climate of fear in post-9/11 America, and proposed that:

> Rather than the manufactured clash of civilisations, we need to concentrate on the slow working together of cultures that overlap, borrow from each other and live together in far more interesting ways than any abridged or inauthentic mode of understanding can allow. (Said 2003: xxii)

In my own small way, I hope that my research here draws attention to the processes of borrowing and exchange through which cultures adapt and live together. Opposing the essentialist positions which envision cultures as 'pure' and under threat of being tainted by the 'other', this book instead argues for a move away from models of cultural globalisation that rely upon notions of dominance and resistance to examine more closely the interstitial processes through which cultures borrow from and interact with each other.

National and Transnational Cinemas

The Hollywood Meme is therefore the first book to offer a sustained examination of the unlicensed adaptations of Hollywood that appear in film industries around the world. Given that this phenomenon stretches from Hong Kong to Mexico, and from Nigeria to Brazil, this book cannot hope to cover everything, so instead it focuses specifically on three case studies: Turkey from 1970 to 1982, the Philippines from 1978 to 1994, and India from 1998 to 2010. The choice of these three national and historical contexts is significant. While I will give a lengthy explanation of the significance of each context in the introduction to their respective chapters, it is worth briefly clarifying that each country had a highly prolific film industry within the period under consideration, and the production of transnational adaptations in particular was intensified. By examining the diverse ways in which Hollywood cinema impacted upon these three industries, the book aims to complicate prevailing models of American cultural domination and provide a more nuanced account of the politics underpinning these global flows and exchanges. Critically, the book draws attention to the overlapping processes of borrowing and exchange through which different national cinemas have interacted with American popular culture. At a time when Hollywood is becoming increasingly dominated by the Marvel and DC cinematic universes, this book draws attention to the neglected history of unlicensed films from around the world that also borrow from Hollywood franchises – from the Filipino comedy *Alyas Batman en Robin* in which Batman and the Joker sing 1950s rock and roll songs, through to the Turkish action film *3 Dev Adam* (1973) in which Captain America and Santo the Mexican wrestler team up to battle against a villainous Spider-Man.

Demonstrating how these popular cultural texts are adapted and reworked in different ways and for different purposes around the world, *The Hollywood Meme* points the way towards a more complex understanding of Hollywood's role within the broader processes of cultural globalisation. Crucially, the book opens up a previously uncharted area of world cinema for academic study and maps out a new direction for studies of global Hollywood. Moreover, *The Hollywood Meme* proposes a new comparative model of adaptation that offers us a critical lens through which to analyse the ways in which American cultural texts evolve and mutate as they are adapted across national borders.

This responds to a broader issue within the study of national cinemas. In his work on Japanese cinema, Darrell William Davis has identified three models of national cinema studies that I think prove instructive for this broader project. First, he identifies the 'Reflectionist: Cinema as Mirror' model in which 'critics look for what is special about a national cinema, its specificity, through the lens of national specificity' (2001: 63). In other words, this method of film analysis is framed through the ways in which a film is said to reflect the national culture in which it was produced. Centrally, this kind of culturalist reading seeks out the various ways in which a film might be said to reflect the local cultural context and treats national cultures as ultimately discrete and bounded. In contrast to this model, an alternative formulation, which Davis titles 'Dialogic: Cinema as Interaction', understands national cinema primarily through its interactions with other national cinemas. Moving away from a conception of cinema as directly reflecting national context, such a model focuses on the relations between industries – often positioning them in a dialectic relationship. While each of these models has the potential to produce invaluable scholarship on national cinema, it is my contention that they tend to treat national cultures as separate and distinct, thereby neglecting the more porous nature of cultural production under the influence of globalisation.

The third model that Davis proposes, and the one that is closest to the position I take in this book, is 'Contamination: Film as Syncretism'. This model is underpinned by the idea that national culture is 'fabricated piecemeal out of various available bits and fragments, often from outside national borders' (Davis 2001: 65). Rather than seeking out the ways in which a film reflects some essentialised aspect of its national culture, or responds in a dialectical fashion to another discrete national culture, this model instead positions all culture as inherently hybrid and focuses on the ways in which cultures intersect and borrow from each other. Through a comparative methodology that I will outline in Chapter 1, this book follows this model of film as syncretism in order to investigate the permeable nature of national culture more broadly.

To a certain extent, then, this book is attempting to answer the call Paul Willemen made in a series of articles in the early 2000s for a comparative film studies (2002, 2005, 2013a, 2013b). Frustrated by the ways in which national cinema histories have tended to reproduce romantically nationalist visions of a unified national culture, Willemen proposes that, 'If we jettison the inherited framework of film history that locates a film at the intersection between "universal values" and "nationalist" specificity . . . it becomes possible to reflect on the ways in which the encounter between "national" histories and the capitalist-industrial production of culture intersect' (2002: 168). Willemen is very careful to avoid equating this 'capitalist-industrial' production mode with Hollywood and while I agree with him that we need to avoid 'falling into the trap of equating American (Western) cultural forms with the forms generated by the industrialization of culture itself' (2005: 103), I nevertheless think that it is important that we do address the impact of the historical dominance that Hollywood has had. Moreover, while Willemen acknowledges that it is 'possible that, in some cases, the Hollywood forms have been taken as the norm to be emulated', he argues that this 'mainly applies to films made for export, that is to say, films expressly produced to try and reap profits in the US market' (2005: 103). As I will demonstrate in this book, this is not an accurate summation of Hollywood's impact on world cinema – indeed, Hollywood films more often function as the model for films produced for the local, domestic market and these films are rarely exported to the US market. So, while this project is undoubtedly indebted to Willemen's pioneering model for a comparative film studies, I believe that my findings here complicate some of the hypotheses he posited that such a model would discover.

Ultimately, therefore, *The Hollywood Meme* fills a pressing need for an analysis of international film production that engages directly with Hollywood's relationship to world cinema. As Tom O'Regan has argued, 'it is in cinema's nature to cross cultural borders within and between nations [and] to circulate across heterogeneous linguistic and social formations' (2004: 262). The challenge is to be able to discuss these border crossings in a way that finds points of difference without exacerbating national stereotypes and finds points of similarity without losing recognition of cultural specificity. In the words of Sonia Livingstone, 'comparative research is challenging because one must balance and interpret similarities and differences while avoiding banalities and stereotypes . . . [and] what is really at stake is a series of epistemological issues which at their most stark pose researchers with the contradiction between the apparent impossibility and the urgent necessity of comparison' (2003: 491).

To balance national specificity with the broader comparative project I am undertaking, I have structured this book into four sections. The first chapter, 'Tracing The Hollywood Meme: Towards a Comparative Model of Transnational Adaptation', describes the worldwide circulation of US film and television and outlines an understanding of global Hollywood that goes beyond existing models of dominance and resistance. Arguing that such processes are significantly context-dependent, the chapter introduces an approach to globalisation that compares the heterogeneous ways in which American popular culture is made use of around the world, and analyses how different strategies are shaped by their respective socio-historic contexts. Specifically, the chapter considers the factors at play within the export of Hollywood cinema and looks at the regulatory frameworks which intercede in the transnational circulation of media. Developing Ien Ang's argument that local responses need to be taken into account if we are to understand the contradictory dynamics of today's global culture – an argument centred on film reception but here applied to film adaptation – the chapter proposes a comparative model that is attentive to the underlying disjunctures and ambivalences within processes of transnational adaptation.

The second chapter, 'Hollywood and the Popular Cinema of Turkey', then uses this model to investigate the boom in adaptations of American popular culture within 1970s Yeşilçam cinema in Turkey. Focusing on films produced between the military coup of 1971 and the subsequent decline of the industry in the early 1980s, the chapter identifies the conditions which helped stimulate a booming industry with an annual production that reached over 300 movies in 1972 yet was so reliant on appropriated material that almost 90 per cent of these movies were remakes, adaptations or spin-offs. The chapter then examines four representative case studies – *3 Dev Adam, Turist Ömer Uzay Yolunda, Şeytan* and *Dünyayi Kurtaran Adam* – and uses them to mark out certain indicative tendencies that contribute to our broader understanding of the factors shaping specific forms of transnational adaptation.

The third chapter, 'Hollywood and the Popular Cinema of the Philippines', builds on the Turkish case study by comparing this to a later production boom in the popular industry of the Philippines in 1978–94. Specifically looking at titles produced subsequent to the Lumauig Bill in 1978, a period in which the cinema of the Philippines began to reach out to an international audience both through the development of new institutions like the Film Academy of the Philippines and through an influx of foreign investment and co-production initiatives, the chapter considers the specific forms of transnational adaptation in this former US colony. Starting with a brief historical account of the development of the film industry, the chapter attends to the considerable tensions and debates surrounding the notion of a 'popular' film industry in the Philippines, and its relationship with the Marcos regime. Developing the comparative aspects of the book, the chapter then interrogates some of the broader structural factors which helped to mould the particularity of the adaptations in this country. These include the colonial history of the country, the co-production strategies with the US, and the level of US media penetration in the Philippines. Focusing on four case studies – *Dynamite Johnson, For Y'ur Height Only, Alyas Batman en Robin* and *Darna: Ang Pagbabalik* – the chapter explores the differences between transnational adaptations produced for the domestic market and those produced primarily for export, a useful contrast to Turkey where this phenomenon was largely restricted to films produced for the domestic market.

Chapter 4, 'Hollywood and the Popular Cinema of India', then complicates the dynamics of power in the previous sections by shifting attention to the ways in which Hollywood is adapted and reworked in an industry which rivals Hollywood's global status: Bollywood. Starting from 10 May 1998 when official industry status was granted to the popular film industry in Mumbai, the chapter explores the factors that have shaped the specific forms of adaptation in this period such as the increasing emphasis on economic liberalisation and the rise of the Hindu right. Historicising the relationship between Hollywood and Bollywood, the chapter attends specifically to the tensions which underlie their respective positions and explores the contextual factors surrounding what Tejaswini Ganti describes as the 'Indianisation' process of adaptation. Identifying some broader indicative tendencies within Bollywood cinema, and focusing on the films *Koi . . . Mil Gaya*, *Sarkar*, *Heyy Babyy*, and *Ghajini*, the chapter asserts that the forms of adaptation utilised in India are considerably different to those employed in the earlier two case studies, and using the comparative model, suggests reasons why this is the case.

Finally, the conclusion brings together the outcomes of each of the case studies in order to suggest some of the predominant tendencies in the transnational adaptation of Hollywood. Given that the book as a whole explores the diverse forms of adaptation in the popular film industries of Turkey, Philippines and India, this chapter offers some conclusions as to the factors which shape the different forms of adaptation encountered in each case, such as the audience awareness of US media, the enforcement of global copyright law and the relative presence of Hollywood studios within the local industry. Ultimately, it will reflect on the utility of the comparative model for studying transnational adaptations and consider how this mode of study can progress in the future.

CHAPTER 1

Tracing the Hollywood Meme: Towards a Comparative Model of Transnational Adaptation

Eclecticism is the degree zero of contemporary general culture: one listens to reggae, watches a western, eats McDonald's food for lunch and local cuisine for dinner, wears Paris perfume in Tokyo and 'retro' clothes in Hong Kong . . .

Jean-François Lyotard (1984: 76)

Motion pictures are the most conspicuous of all the American exports. They do not lose their identity. They betray their nationality and their country of origin. They are easily recognised. They are all pervasive. They colour the minds of those who see them. They are demonstrably the greatest single factors in the Americanization of the world and as such may fairly be called the most important and significant of America's exported products.

Motion Picture Producers & Distributors of
America (quoted in Vasey, 1997 43)

Rambo had conquered Asia. In China, a million people raced to see *First Blood* within ten days of its Beijing opening, and black marketers were hawking tickets at seven times the official price. In India, five separate remakes of the American hit went instantly into production, one of them recasting the macho superman as a sari-clad woman. In Thailand, fifteen-foot cutouts of the avenging demon towered over the lobbies of some of the ten Bangkok cinemas in which the movie was playing, training their machine guns on all who passed. And in Indonesia, the Rambo Amusement Arcade was going great guns, while vendors along the streets offered posters of no one but the nation's three leading deities: President Suharto, Siva and Stallone.

Pico Iyer (1988: 3)

In his travelogue *Video Night in Kathmandu: And Other Reports from the Not-So-Far East*, novelist and essayist Pico Iyer describes such diverse cultural phenomena as mohawk haircuts in Bali, lounge singers in the Philippines and Rambo-inspired musicals made in India. Setting off to explore the impact of American popular culture within Asia, the book tells the story of how Iyer gradually came to find that, 'as I left the realm of abstract labels and generalised forces, and came down to individuals . . . the easy contrasts began to grow confused' (1988: 21). Over the course of seven months, Iyer travelled to Bali, Tibet, Nepal, China, the Philippines, Burma, Hong Kong, India, Thailand and Japan, looking to 'find out how American pop-cultural imperialism spread through the world's most ancient civilizations' and 'what kind of resistance had been put up against the Coca-Colonizing forces' (1988: 4). Yet, while Iyer points to a plethora of examples of the presence and influence of American popular culture in Asia, the book ends with the admission that while Iyer initially thought he would find Western culture in 'conquest of the East', the reality was that the cultural forms had been so adapted and transformed, and were so implicated within the contexts in which they were produced, that 'every one of [his] discoveries had to be rejected or, at best, refined' (1988: 381).

As social anthropologist Arjun Appadurai later argued, Iyer's initial search for examples of America's pop-cultural imperialism throughout Asia was 'in some ways the product of a confusion between some ineffable McDonaldization of the world and the much subtler play of indigenous trajectories of desire and fear with global flows of people and things' (Appadurai 1996: 29). In order to engage with such subtleties, then, this chapter puts forward a comparative model of transnational adaptation that attends to the meaning of these processes of cultural globalisation within their distinct socio-historical contexts. Centrally, the chapter proposes a way to examine more rigorously the structures which underpin the world-wide circulation of American popular culture and the heterogeneous ways in which said culture is made use of around the world.

Initially, this will necessitate an outlining of the prevailing academic debates on cultural globalisation beginning with the critical political economy work of international communications theorists such as Herbert Schiller and Jeremy Tunstall. Their emphasis on macro-level forces which they term 'cultural imperialism' or its corollary 'Americanisation' will then be tempered with the more micro-level work in social anthropology and cultural studies that focuses instead on how cultures receive and transform imported cultural forms. Moving away from notions of cultural homogenisation and dominance, these theorists lay emphasis on processes of localised reception and cultural hybridisation. After pointing to some of the failings in each of these positions, I will employ Marwan Kraidy's notion of critical transculturalism to outline a theoretical model that pays attention to the subtle processes of cultural hybridisation while still retaining the broader concerns of critical political economy around unequal power distribution. Arguing that these processes of hybridisation are significantly context-dependent, I will show how an approach based around critical transculturalism avoids some of the theoretical pitfalls that other models of cultural hybridity have faced.

Secondly, I will outline the contested position of 'Hollywood' within the globalisation debates and illustrate some of the material ways in which Hollywood has gained prominence on the world stage. Discussing some of the drawbacks to solely industry-focused or text-based accounts of Hollywood's position, I will then outline some of the ways in which theorists have attempted to address the transnational reception and subsequent transformations of American cinema, drawing on the ethnographic work of Tamar Liebes and Elihu Katz, and the audience/exhibition studies of Charles Acland and Ien Ang.

Thirdly, given that the films I am dealing with do not license their cross-cultural borrowings, this will further necessitate an understanding of transnational regulatory frameworks and the ways in which they intercede in processes of artistic production, textual circulation and reception. The question of variation in global intellectual property regimes will illustrate ways in which copyright laws not only act to regulate acts of cultural borrowing but actually help shape their meanings.

Finally, the chapter will examine previous academic models of transnational adaptation, looking specifically at the political valence often attributed to such acts. Given the underlying power differentials, transnational adaptation is often framed in terms of resistance in cases where the subaltern adapts from the dominant culture; or exploitation, when the dominant culture adapts from the subaltern. Attempting to move beyond these notions of domination and resistance, I propose a new comparative model of transnational adaptation that is attentive to the social and industrial contexts of transnational adaptations, looking specifically at how the 'characters, plots and textual forms' (Appadurai 1996: 35) of American popular culture are appropriated and re-used in films made around the world. Building on Miriam Hansen's work on 'vernacular modernism' (2000a) and Thomas Elsaesser's notion of 'karaoke Americanism' (2005), I will outline an approach to transnational adaptations that uses the structuring metaphor of the 'meme' to investigate how Hollywood has been spread and adapted around the world.

Processes of Cultural Globalisation

[Globalisation is] a maddeningly euphemistic term laden with desire, fantasy, fear, attraction – and intellectual imprecision about what it is supposed to describe.

Toby Miller et al. (2005: 18)

Globalisation has become one of *the* buzzwords of our time, replacing post-colonialism as the key theoretical prism through which transnational relations are commonly analysed. Yet although – or perhaps, more appropriately, because – the term has attracted so much analytical interest, there is considerable debate as to its nature and its effects. In the late 1960s, the prevailing English-language academic discourse on globalisation was coming out of international communication departments. Rooted in the critical political economy tradition, neo-Marxist theorists such as Herbert Schiller were proposing a vision of transnational relations in which capital, infrastructure and politico-economic power were acting as determinants of international communication processes. Indeed, Schiller's foundational text *Mass Communication and American Empire* envisioned cultural globalisation very much in terms of American cultural imperialism in which 'messages 'made in America' radiate across the globe and serve as the ganglia of national power and expansionism' (1992: 191).

This work was later taken up by Alan Wells in *Picture Tube Imperialism* (1972), which tested the cultural imperialism thesis in Latin America, and Jeremy Tunstall who attempted to interrogate the nature of cultural imperialism in *The Media Are American: Anglo American Media in the World* (1977). While the notion of American cultural imperialism was subsequently 'dismissed as a monolithic theory' by humanities scholars and 'increasingly questioned by empirical research' (Kraidy 2005: 27) the concept still has resonance in the social sciences where the phenomenon of gradual Americanisation has come to be designated with such evocative terms as McDonaldisation (Ritzer 2000), McWorld (Barber 1995), Coca-colonisation (Howes 1996) and Disneyification (Zukin 1995).

By the mid-1980s, a number of scholarly disciplines were offering alternative visions of cultural globalisation, with the rise of active audience theory (see, for example, Ang 1996 laying emphasis on the ways in which American popular culture is received and understood in specific social contexts). Indeed, as John Tomlinson later argued, 'Movement between cultural/geographical areas always involves interpretation, translation, mutation, adaptation, and indigenisation as the receiving culture brings its own cultural resources to bear, in dialectical fashion, upon "cultural imports"' (1999: 83).

The most sustained critique of the cultural imperialism thesis came from a new branch of social science later dubbed 'globalisation studies', gaining prominence in a 1990 double issue of the journal *Theory, Culture and Society* and the following year's *Culture, Globalisation and the World System* edited by Anthony D. King. Moreover, the subsequent decade also signalled an influential shift in the field of American Studies with various collections calling for a move away from the prevailing ethnocentrism towards a global approach that located American culture within the larger processes of globalisation (see, for example, Dominguez and Desmond 1996; Katzmann and Yetman 1993; Wagnleitner and May 2000) Most importantly, these critiques questioned the idea of global cultural uniformity and proposed a way to study the more localised practices of reception and indigenisation. As sociologist Jan Nederveen Pieterse argued, this was 'not to say that the notion of global cultural synchronization' is irrelevant, but that it is fundamentally incomplete and 'downplays the ambivalence of the globalizing momentum and ignores the role of local reception of western culture – for example, the indigenisation of western elements' (2004: 69).

One of the most significant thinkers in these debates was Arjun Appadurai who, in his article 'Disjuncture and Difference in the Global Cultural Economy' and subsequent book *Modernity at Large: Cultural Dimensions of Globalisation*, proposed that 'globalisation does not necessarily or even frequently imply homogenisation or Americanisation' (1996: 14) and that 'the new global cultural economy has to be seen as a complex, overlapping, disjunctive order that cannot any longer be understood in terms of existing centre-periphery models' (32). Offering a highly influential model for exploring such disjunctures, Appadurai proposed a framework for analysing the relationship among five dimensions of global cultural flows that he termed (a) ethnoscapes, (b) technoscapes, (c) financescapes, (d) mediascapes, and (e) ideoscapes (33). Notably, Appadurai's model focused on instability and disjuncture with an emphasis on how transnational cultural flows are circulated and consumed throughout the world in ways unintended by their originators. Significantly for this project, he also drew attention to the ways in which the flows of media and information, or 'mediascapes', 'tend to be image-centred, narrative-based accounts of strips of reality' and 'what they offer to those who experience and transform them is a series of elements (such as characters, plots and textual forms) out of which scripts can be formed of imagined lives, their own as well as those of others living in other places' (35). From such a perspective, the emphasis is not so much on the macro-level study of structural factors such as global economics and media conglomeration, but on the micro-level study of localised reception practices and the ways in which 'characters, plots and textual forms' from cultural imports are utilised and reworked in specific socio-historic contexts.

This work helped to shape the academic field of cultural hybridisation studies which – in subjecting the cultural imperialism thesis to sustained critique – offered an alternative vision of cultural globalisation that emphasised global cultural diversity and processes of transnational adaptation and exchange. Ranging from the theoretical work of sociologists such as Jan Nederveen Pieterse and Roland Robertson to the more anthropological work of Ulf Hannerz and Arjun Appadurai, studies of cultural hybridisation attempted to analyse the diverse ways in which transnational flows of media and culture created new and culturally mixed forms. For Pieterse, while 'the most common interpretations of globalisation are the idea that the world is becoming more uniform and standardised', he instead proposed that we view globalisation 'as a process of hybridisation that gives rise to a global mélange' (2004: 59). Such contributions to the debate, however, were not without controversy, with postcolonial theorist Gayatri Chakravorty Spivak critiquing this 'hybridist post-national talk' which she saw as 'celebrating globalisation as Americanisation' (1999: 361). It should be noted, however, that the focus of Pieterse was less on the spread of American culture than on various hybrid 'phenomena such as Thai boxing by Moroccan girls in Amsterdam, Asian rap in London, Irish bagels, Chinese tacos, and Mardi Gras Indians in the United States . . .' (2004: 69).

Indeed, these phenomena have been discussed variously by cultural hybridisation scholars as forms of 'syncretism, creolisation, mettisage' and 'crossover' (Pieterse 2004: 55). They reflect what Marwan M. Kraidy describes in *Hybridity: or the Cultural Logic of Globalisation*, in that they represent globalisation not as a unitary one-way process of cultural homogenisation, but as an interstitial process through which cultures borrow from and interact with each other. Nevertheless, as Kraidy argues, although these examples point to the hybridising nature of cultural exchange, this does not mean that we should neglect the fact that these processes of hybridisation are highly contingent on structural factors. While most analyses of globalisation that focus solely on cultural imperialism tend to over-emphasise the structural factors of economic power and dominance, and most analyses that focus on processes of hybridisation tend to offer a politically benign vision of diversity, Kraidy offers an alternative framework which he terms 'critical transculturalism' that pays attention to the hybridising nature of cultural exchange and yet still retains the broader concerns of cultural imperialism around unequal power distribution (2005: 9).

More concretely, while cultural imperialism scholars generally focus on the production and distribution stages of the media communication process, and cultural pluralism/hybridisation scholars emphasise the reception, 'critical transculturalism takes a more integrative approach that considers the active links between production, text, and reception in the moment of cultural reproduction' (Kraidy 2005: 149). Such a framework 'focuses on power in intercultural relations by integrating both agency and structure in international communication analysis' (ibid.). This is similar to the position adopted by Dimitris Eleftheriotis in his discussion of spaghetti westerns, asserting that while 'it is beyond doubt that hybrid forms such as spaghetti westerns are the product of cultural interaction and exchange', there is a need for 'a theoretical approach that accounts for the textual specificities of the films and offers an understanding of how these forms relate to a broader field of power relations and to national and international historical contexts' (2002: 101).

This helps overcome one of the central theoretical difficulties in dealing with hybrid cultural forms. For a number of years, discussions of hybridity have been drawing on the pioneering work in postcolonial criticism of scholars such as Robert Young and Homi Bhabha. Heavily influenced by poststructuralist discourse, Bhabha in particular was instrumental in challenging essentialist notions of culture and identity as static and pure with his focus on the interstitial 'in-between-ness' and fundamentally hybrid nature of culture and cultural forms. The problem, as Dimitris Eleftheriotis has correctly identified, was that while the 'tactical emphasis on the hybrid nature of all cultural production that Bhabha and others justifiably and convincingly posit opens up a very important space for politics of identity' (2002: 99), it does not function particularly usefully as an analytical tool for interrogating specific cultural forms. This is because the tactical use of hybridity discourse to challenge essentialist thinking – deliberately unsettling what Pieterse terms 'the introverted concept of culture that underlies romantic nationalism, racism, ethnicism, religious revivalism, civilisational chauvinism, and cultural essentialism' (2004: 82) – tends to conclude that everything is a hybrid which is a conclusion so broad that it can actually function to limit the interrogation of specific instances of cultural hybridisation. As Eleftheriotis observes, the idea that all cultural forms are hybrid 'should not be a point of arrival but a point of departure in the investigation of the different conditions and forms of hybridisation' (2002: 100).

Taking this notion as a point of departure, then, this book attempts to move beyond overly reductive accounts of cultural hybridisation to interrogate more closely the differing conditions and forms of hybridisation. In other words, this is a Gramscian study of 'conjunctures', a mode of study 'which recommends that cultural and social analysis should confront the precise contexts in which [relations of force] . . . have effects and are experienced, even as the contexts themselves are in the process of being made' (Acland 2003: 15). It is necessary, therefore, to make clear at the outset that this will be a 'relational, processual, and contextual approach to hybridity' (Kraidy 2005: xii) that explores film as a particular localised practice. Rather than simply applying theories of hybridity to a variety of cultural forms, the model I am proposing interrogates how these processes of hybridisation relates to their specific cultural context, and it is my contention that this ultimately allows for a more nuanced perspective on the processes of cultural globalisation.

Global Hollywood

As this book deals with the worldwide circulation of American popular culture, the contested position of Hollywood, therefore, is crucial. Within recent academic work on global film culture, there are a number of authors who have attempted to describe and account for Hollywood's international success and popularity. Throughout the varying approaches and methodologies, there are three prevailing strands which have developed: (1) the textualist work that attempts to identify specific textual properties that appeal across cultures; (2) the work in political economy and cultural studies that emphasises the role of industrial processes, transnational corporations and political pressures; and, finally, (3) the more anthropological work which focuses on cross-cultural readings and interpretations of globally exported media.

In textualist explanations of Hollywood's global popularity, the emphasis tends to be on particular textual strategies which are said to be universally popular, from Disney chief Jeffrey Katzenberg's rather glib explanation that the formula for global success is 'a good story, well-executed' (as quoted in Segrave 1997: 247) to the more elaborate discussions of particular textual strategies and forms that resonate across national and cultural borders. One of the most oft-used of these textualist explanations for Hollywood's global popularity is based on the 'cultural discount' thesis – a concept originally employed by Colin Hoskins and Rolf Mirus to explain why a particular text rooted in one culture may have a diminished appeal elsewhere (1988: 500). The work of Scott Robert Olson exemplifies such an approach in his argument that American media texts have a competitive advantage through their use of what he terms 'narrative transparency', defined as 'any textual apparatus that allows audiences to project indigenous values, beliefs, rites, and rituals into imported media' (1999: 5). Asking 'why are movies and television programmes from the United States so popular' (1999: xi), Olson utilises an approach borrowed from Harvard economist Michael E. Porter (1990) which attempts to explain the global success of industries in terms of competitive advantage, and then, accepting that this method

'ultimately proves better in understanding purely industrial products . . .
rather than ones with overt cultural overtones' (1999: xi). Olson attempts
to 'fill in the gaps' (xii) with elements of cultural studies methodology.
Primarily utilising close textual analysis, Olson therefore attempts to
explain the competitive advantage of American films and television programmes through his concept of narrative transparency in which cultural
products are successful primarily because their lack of historical and cultural specificity encourages diverse populations to read them as though
they were indigenous texts.

Olson's work has been roundly and justifiably critiqued for its under-
estimation of the structural factors at play, and the assumption that internationally popular films can be equated with an absence of particularity.
As Charles Acland saliently observed, 'how can we claim, conceptually
speaking, that the specificity of *Titanic* (James Cameron 1997) is nil
and that of *Exotica* (Atom Egoyan 1995) is high?' (Acland 2003: 33).
Nevertheless, such an approach is still worthy of critical attention – if in a
slightly modified formulation – as it does capture 'the kind of knowledge
about international culture produced in the industry itself: a core belief
that the relative mobility of films can be measured or predicted and that
there are cultural forms that transcend specificity' (2003: 34). As we will
see in my later chapters, such a notion of a perceived lack of particularity
in internationally exportable texts often plays a crucial role in determining
the types of transnational adaptation that are produced and the industrial
strategies used to promote and distribute them.

As Paul Cooke has observed, however, while some could argue that
Hollywood is so powerful economically because it simply produces the
most appealing film aesthetics and narrative structures, such a reading
does not take into account 'the effort that Hollywood, along with a variety
of US Governments, have put into gaining global dominance in the areas
of distribution and exhibition' (2007: 4). Through tactical manoeuvring,
such as lobbying for increased global deregulation during the General
Agreement on Tariffs and Trade (GATT) and subsequent World Trade
Organization (WTO) talks, the US government has helped Hollywood to
increase its market share throughout the world and support and nurture
its domestic film industry. Moreover, James Chapman has noted that
Hollywood accounts for 'approximately only 6 per cent of total film
production in the world' (2003: 33) and yet despite this it uses a variety
of strategies to make sure that these films are distributed and exhibited in
cinemas around the world. Within the critical work of political economy,
there has been recent renewed emphasis on these larger political considerations and an attempt to go beyond existing textual explications for

Hollywood's global success. Toby Miller et al.'s *Global Hollywood 2*, for example, proposes that 'the key to the high volume of audiovisual trade is not cheap reproduction, but the vast infrastructure of distribution that secures financing for production' (2005: 295). Furthermore, from a historical perspective this has meant that Hollywood tends to operate in foreign markets through 'distribution cartels' and 'studio partnerships' which 'help maintain the studios' dominance of foreign markets' (Wasko 2003: 179). Nevertheless, as Charles Acland argues, while these economic models offer 'indispensable economic portraits and explanations for US prominence in popular entertainment, [they are deficient] without a theory of consumption' (2003: 37).

Within Acland's own work, there is an attempt to challenge crude forms of political economy and develop an understanding of globalisation attentive to theories of consumption and discourse. In *Screen Traffic: Movies, Multiplexes and Global Culture*, Acland studies these issues from the neglected perspective of exhibition, analysing the ways in which circulating conceptions of movie-going have changed since the mid-1980s. Focusing specifically on the relationships between the US and Canadian national industries, Acland utilises conjunctural critique to challenge notions 'about the homogenisation and levelling down of culture' and 'to identify and dissect the forces and implications of globalising culture, and then to begin to conceptualise how one lives and makes meaning in that context, without judging it as inappropriate, insufficient, or uniform in advance' (2003: 37).

My research in this book is indebted to Acland's approach and also to the more anthropological work of Tamar Liebes and Elihu Katz, who, in their 1993 study of cross-cultural readings of *Dallas*, attempted to challenge received notions of Americanisation. Switching the perspective from the movie studios and distributors onto the audiences themselves, Liebes and Katz sought to 'find out how [these globally popular American films and television programmes] are decoded or, indeed, whether they are understood at all' (1993: 150). Offering an anthropological study of audience responses in the US, Israel and Japan, Liebes and Katz argued that each of the cultural groups under consideration found its own way to 'negotiate' with the programme with 'different types of readings, different forms of involvement, different mechanisms of self-defence, each with its own kind of vulnerability' and that, ultimately, 'we found only very few innocent minds and a variety of "villages"' (xi).

This form of anthropological approach helps us to attend to local responses to, and negotiations with, globally circulating media. While the transnational dissemination of cultural texts can sometimes be perceived as overwhelming or undermining indigenous cultures from a top-down perspective, such bottom-up perspectives to cultural production allow us to attend to the ways in which people utilise imported media in a variety of different ways. As Ien Ang argues, 'these local responses and negotiations, culturally diverse and geographically dispersed, need to be taken into account if we are to understand the complex and contradictory dynamics of today's "global culture"' (1996: 153). There is a necessity, therefore, to interrogate thoroughly the ways in which localised cultures mediate and transform the American popular culture that is circulated around the world. However, rather than offering an ethnographic study of audiences and reception practices – the most prevalent theoretical approach to these local responses and negotiations – this book instead traces the 'global in the local' through an analysis of the ways in which the 'characters, plots and textual forms' (Appadurai 1996: 35) of American media are adapted and reworked in films produced around the world.

Offering a form of reception study that focuses on the practice of adapting material, this book considers the active links between production, text and reception in the moment of cultural reproduction, utilising insights from across political economic, ethnographic, cultural studies and textualist approaches to media. This means an attention being paid not only to the hybrid cultural texts themselves but to the socio-historic contexts in which they are produced and the 'broad range of creative practices which people in different parts of the world are inventing today in their everyday dealings with the changing media environment that surrounds them' (Ang 1996: 148).

With my three case studies dealing with the reworking of American popular culture within three specific contexts – Turkey 1970–82, the Philippines 1978–94, and India 1998–2010 – this book entails not only a discussion of the social and industrial contexts in each of these cases, but an attempt to discover comparatively some of the determinant factors that shape transnational adaptations of Hollywood more broadly. Importantly, however, this book does not claim to be a definitive overview of 'American popular culture abroad' that represents and explains the multitude of ways in which Hollywood has been reworked transnationally, but instead aims to offer a methodology for analysing such transnational adaptations in three specific socio-historic contexts – a methodology that could hopefully be tested and built upon in other later studies. Indeed, the project of this research is not to attach particular interpretive meanings to processes of cultural globalisation in themselves, but to test the limits of totalising theoretical paradigms and suggest ways in which more fluid and interactive approaches can be employed. As Ien Ang has argued,

> It would be ludicrous . . . to try to find a definitive and unambiguous, general theo-
> retical answer to [the question of cultural globalisation] precisely because there is no
> way to know in advance which strategies and tactics different people in the world
> will invent to negotiate with the intrusions of global forces in their lives. For the
> moment, then, we can only hope for provisional answers – answers informed by
> ethnographic sensitivity to how structural changes become integrated in specific
> cultural forms and practices, under specific historical circumstances. (1996: 143)

Processes of globalisation facilitate all manner of borrowings through
transnational media flows. Yet, as I have argued, these processes of
hybridisation are significantly context-dependent; hence, the necessity to
attend to the meaning of these adaptations within their distinct contexts.
In order to attend to this 'slow working together of cultures', I require
a comparative model in order to examine the range of textual strategies
through which transnational elements are reworked, and analyse how
these strategies developed in their specific contexts. Before discussing some possible models for interrogating transnational adaptations,
however, it is important that we address one of the most significant forces
that shape how these processes function – international copyright law.

Regimes of Copyright

> Romantic celebrations of insurrectionary alterity, long popular in cultural studies,
> cannot capture the dangerous nuances of cultural appropriation in circumstances
> where the very resources with which people express difference are properties of
> others. Acts of transgression, though multiply motivated, are also shaped by the
> juridical fields of power in which they intervene.
>
> (Coombe 1998: 10)

It is my position that the very concept of 'culture' rests upon processes of
mimesis in that all cultural works are drawing upon, building upon and
responding to something outside of themselves. As Laikwan Pang argues,
'the act of copying is perhaps the single most important cultural activity'
and, by extension, 'copying and culture cannot be separated; cultural
boundaries can never be rigidly drawn because culture is necessarily transformed by copying, which takes place everywhere all the time' (2006: 5).
Yet, while all art involves borrowing and adapting earlier material, there
is often a line drawn between an acceptable level of borrowing and what is
defined as unacceptable plagiarism. Indeed, this distinction, as Ian Condry
argues in *Hip Hop Japan: Rap and the Paths of Cultural Globalisation*
(2006), necessarily varies from culture to culture, and from time to time.
Therefore, in this section, I will outline some of the contemporary debates
on copyright and the ways in which global regimes of intellectual property

intercede in processes of transnational adaptation. In other words, what happens when you have disjunctions between different national conceptions of intellectual property? How does this affect the 'right' to copy?

To address this question, let us turn back to the Berne Convention for the Protection of Literary and Artistic Works from 1886, the first international treaty of copyright law. The Berne Convention was developed at the instigation of authors in France, most notably Victor Hugo, who were concerned that their works were being 'pirated' in other countries with no legal recourse. Prior to the adoption of the Berne Convention, nations rarely granted copyright protection to foreign nationals, and it was only with the said convention that copyright protection was extended to works by nationals from all Berne signatories. As Pang notes, 'Berne for the first time introduced copyright to an international scope' (2006: 17).

Significantly, this served the purposes of those, who as Eva Hemmungs Wirten notes, 'can be seen as exporters/producers of assets deemed intellectual property, and not the interests of the importers/consumers of the same assets' (2004: 40). This meant that, from the very beginning of international treaties of intellectual property, being an exporter rather than an importer offered a competitive trade-related advantage. In this sense, the expansion of copyright protection around the world can be read in terms of what Peter Drahos calls 'regulatory globalisation' (2002: 161). As Drahos notes, the movement of intellectual property rights has broadly been from developed to developing countries, in that the laws on copyright and intellectual property are based on European models which have then been exported around the world through 'processes of empire building and colonisation' (164). Hence, for net 'exporting' nations, the aim was generally to expand the breadth of intellectual property rights in order to gain the 'maximum return from the trade in intellectual property rights and the goods and services to which they relate' (163). On the other hand, for net 'importing' nations, the emphasis tends towards resisting these controls and we can see this in the negotiations surrounding the agreement on Trade-Related Aspects of Intellectual Property Rights (TRIPS) and General Agreement on Tariffs and Trade (GATT). Moreover, within Ronald V. Bettig's study of copyright and the political economy of intellectual property, he claims that some of the factors which contribute to video piracy in Asia and the Middle East are:

lack of IP laws and weak enforcement of existing laws; minimal participation in bilateral and multilateral international IP agreements; a proliferation of recording technologies; underdeveloped local production industries; and public demand for content resulting from screen quotas, state controlled broadcasting or censorship. (Bettig, as summarised in Wang 2003: 30)

In this way, we can see some of the ways in which Western models of ownership come into conflict with alternative models of intellectual property in other parts of the world; and the ways in which this reflects wider power differentials. Moreover, following Pang, it would appear that the global expansion of copyright

> is connected to the political economy of capitalist development in general and the United States' national interests in particular. If the United States is the cultural Empire, this Empire is maintained largely through the global copyright regime's ensuring that all players in the culture industry comply with its rules, thereby guaranteeing profits from the exportation of copyrighted property around the world. (2006: 10)

Of course, these global regimes of copyright do not exert true global control as the practices of piracy and plagiarism proliferate throughout the world. Furthermore, the concept of cultural expressions being effectively regulated and owned is being fundamentally challenged given that, as Pang notes, 'It is the wide transcultural copying of expressions, more so than ideas, that defines our global cinema' (2006: 48).

It is these transnational copies of expressions that forms the basis of this book. Looking at the myriad ways in which copyrighted materials are borrowed, adapted and reused on a transnational level, this book attempts to get to grips with the politics of these borrowings. Consequently, this is a study of the ways in which the 'expressions' of American popular culture – the plots, the characters, the music, the footage – are adapted and made use of in other national film industries. Moreover, I interrogate just how this extensive copying of expressions, which Pang describes, relates to differentials in national context; from competing regimes of copyright control, to governmental policy, and to industrialised modes of production. Given this wider political context, acts of appropriation are frequently, if not inevitably, positioned as political acts. As Julie Sanders argues,

> the study of appropriations in an academic context has in part been spurred on by the recognized ability of adaptation to respond or write back to an informing original from a new or revised political and cultural position, and by the capacity of appropriations to highlight troubling gaps, absences and silences within the canonical texts to which they refer. (2005: 98)

This sense of the 'empire writing back' has informed much of the debate on transnational adaptation to date. As we will see in the following section, this approach is certainly politically useful, but in many ways is actually quite a limiting model of transnational interactions.

Previous Models for Studying Transnational Adaptation

The appearance of 'our' signs in 'their' lives was long a commonplace of an inverted culture shock in which the anthropologist professed his or her own bemused innocence. Too often the Adidas T-shirt on the native was figured as the sign of tragic cultural decline, the sure mark of worldly sophistication, or . . . the romantic expression of a resistant agency.

Rosemary Coombe (1998: 19)

Throughout the late twentieth century, much of the discussion of transnational adaptation has centred on the relations of power such borrowings indicate. One of the most relevant models for understanding the implications of transnational adaptation within cinema has been that offered by Joao Luiz Vieira and Robert Stam in their discussion of Brazilian parodies of US cinema. Looking specifically at the films *Bacalhau* (1976), a Brazilian soft-porn parody of *Jaws* (1975), and *Costinha e o King Mong* (1977), a low-budget parody of *King Kong* (1976), they argue for parody as occupying a special role in the context of asymmetrical arrangements of power:

> By appropriating an existing discourse but introducing into it an orientation oblique, or even diametrically opposed to that of the original, parody is especially well suited to the needs of the oppressed and the powerless, precisely because it assumes the force of the dominant discourse, only to deploy that force, through a kind of artistic jujitsu, *against* domination. (Vieira and Stam 1990: 84)

Drawing on Bakhtinian theories of the carnivalesque, Vieira and Stam point to transnational adaptation as a way to direct cathartic laughter against dominant cinema, a way to overturn – however, briefly – the hegemonic power exerted over marginal filmmaking practice. Yet, these examples also indicate some of the problems in using this kind of model to understand processes of transnational adaptation. While suggesting the possibilities for carnivalesque parody as a subversive form, Vieira and Stam ultimately lament that these particular parodies do not live up to their subversive potential. Rather than being the 'springboard for a devastating critique of the shallow factitiousness ultimately conveyed by the increasingly sophisticated mimesis of contemporary dominant cinema' (1990: 95), these films eventually offer a

> 'last laugh' at Brazilian cinema. The filmmakers regard themselves as aliens in the 'higher' world of true cinema; the laughter provoked by the parody rebounds against themselves and the audience. Rather than question spectatorial identification with the foreign model, *Bacalhau* fosters uncritical admiration. (93)

To some extent Vieira and Stam are lamenting the ways in which *Bacalhau* fails to achieve the political resonance which their parodic model suggests, but I would contend that it also points to the more ambivalent nature of transnational adaptations of Hollywood in general. While the model that Vieira and Stam offer, of parody as a form of Bakhtinian carnivalesque, is certainly politically attractive, it actually neglects 'the subtler play of indigenous trajectories of desire and fear with global flows of people and things' (Appadurai 1996: 29) that other models may be able to interrogate. Therefore, while we should be attentive to the political motivations lying behind *some* acts of transnational adaptation, the reliance on dominance/ resistance models can actually neglect the much more ambivalent nature of many of these borrowings. As we will see when I turn my attention to the films themselves, they exhibit subtle and complex relationships to their source texts; a relationship that is not addressed in models that are reliant on concepts of politicised resistance to the hegemon.

In this way, I am reluctant to build my comparative model of trans-national adaptation around conceptions of 'writing back to the centre' or 'resistant jujitsu'. One could quite imagine a study of transnational adap-tations of Hollywood in terms of a subversive resistance to US hegemony, the Empire Writing Back through appropriating the very cultural artefacts which embody this hegemonic force. Positioning Hollywood as a form of cultural imperialism, such a model would read these films as a form of postcolonial resistance, but, as I have outlined, this would be a problem-atic formulation. While some of these adaptations show potential to be read as critical, subversive or parodic, we need a model for understanding transnational adaptations which is attendant to the more general ambiva-lences and complexities.

Moreover, this kind of model can only function on a case by case basis – using close analysis to test to what extent a particular film resists Hollywood hegemony – and it is important that we are also able to engage with cultural interactions on a larger scale. For example, Paul S. N. Lee, in his 1991 article 'The Absorption and Indigenisation of Foreign Media Cultures', moves away from questions of resistance to imported culture to instead offer up a taxonomic model of the myriad ways in which foreign media cultures are absorbed and indigenised into Hong Kong popular culture. Examining three forms of popular culture – music, cinema and television – Lee identifies four key modes of absorption which he charac-terises utilising biological metaphors.

First, we have the 'Parrot' pattern which is a 'wholesale adoption of foreign cultural forms and contents, just like a parrot imitating the human voice in both form and content' (Lee 1991: 64), and illustrated simply by the example of foreign television programmes such as *Cheers* playing on Hong Kong television. Secondly, we have the 'Amoeba' pattern which 'keeps the content but changes the form, just like an amoeba which appears different in form but remains the same in substance all the time' (65). Lee illustrates this with the example of the American television show *That's Incredible* being played on Chinese television but with the addition of local hosts who are there to 'make the show look less foreign' (65). The third pattern is 'Coral' which 'keeps the form but changes the content, just like the coral which maintains the coral shape after it has died' (ibid.). For this pattern, Lee suggests the example of Cantopops which are pop songs that utilise foreign melodies but replace the words with Cantonese lyrics. Finally, we have the 'Butterfly' pattern which 'absorbs and indigenises foreign cultures to an extent that one can hardly distinguish the foreign from the indigenous' (65). Lee characterises this pattern as a particularly long process, hence the metaphor of a butterfly developing from a larva, and offers up certain kung fu films which 'could be considered partly as a metamorphosed version of Bond films without the sex and sophisticated weapons, but with fists and primitive skills' (65).

While this is certainly a useful model in terms of indicating the differing extents to which content is changed when it is imported, it sadly tells us little about how the content itself is actually changed. As a model primarily describing cultural 'absorption' rather than adaptation per se, it is only the Coral and Amoeba patterns which really get to grips with how elements change and, even then, they do little to explain the textual features which such patterns of absorption indicate. So, while the use of biological metaphors certainly has an aesthetic appeal, the model itself cannot adequately explain the processes of transnational adaptation that I am examining. Nevertheless, one way in which my approach is certainly sympathetic to Lee's is in the attempt to describe the wider cultural factors contributing to the emergence of these patterns. Offering up a model that attempts to identify trends and tendencies, Lee points towards an understanding of transnational relationships that addresses the contextual determinants that shape these cultural borrowings.

An alternative taxonomic model is offered by Tom O'Regan in his discussion of *Australian National Cinema*. Developing Yuri Lotman's theory of cultural transmission – which itself came out of a study of Russian cultural history in the eighteenth and nineteenth centuries – O'Regan offers five stages that a national cinema must go through in order to move from being a receiving culture to a transmitting culture (1996). The first stage is where, 'The texts coming in from outside keep their "strangeness". They are read in the foreign language (both in the sense of natural language and in the semiotic sense' (Lotman 1990: 146). The second stage is 'where the imported text and the home culture . . . restructure each other' (146) and it is this stage that is most germane to the processes investigated in this book. In this stage, 'translations, imitations and adaptations multiply' (O'Regan, 1996: 218), leading to cultural productions being dismissed simply as pale imitations of the 'original' works. Thirdly, we have a situation whereby the home culture's product is re-evaluated 'in a situation of assumed international comparison' (220). For O'Regan, 'the fourth stage assimilates the imported matrices making them entirely its own' (221), and so describes the moment when the texts produced are no longer derivative copies but begin to provide original structural models for their genres. Finally, the fifth stage is where 'the receiving culture . . . changes into a transmitting culture and issues forth a flood of texts directed to other, peripheral areas of the semiosphere' (146). As I have written about elsewhere (Smith 2015c), these stages emphasise the agency of the receiving culture, offering a model of transnational adaptation that is focused less on the concept of imitation and more on the notion of transformation and negotiation. Indeed, these examples push O'Regan to postulate that the distinctiveness of Australian national cinema may rest less in some notion of separate Australian-ness but rather 'may be found in its negotiation of cultural transfers' (1996: 219).

Both O'Regan and Lee's models describe processes of cultural transmission and absorption. While this is certainly useful for a meta-level overview of processes of transnational adaptation, it is generally less useful for examining specific texts and interrogating their complexities. Before I propose my own comparative model, therefore, I would like to move back to the textual level by introducing two approaches to Hollywood cinema that I believe are particularly useful for interrogating processes of transnational adaptation, and which partly inspired my own approach in this book.

First, I would like to look at Miriam Hansen's work on cinema as a form of 'vernacular modernism' (2000a; 2000b; 2009). In her article 'The Mass Production of the Senses' (2000a), Hansen argued against neoformalist accounts of classical Hollywood cinema in order to suggest that that the global success of Hollywood was less about the supposedly universal narrative organisation of the films than the result of its ability to provide an experience of capitalist-industrial modernity and modernisation. Showing how a mass cultural form such as cinema could be considered modernist, Hansen complicated the prevailing accounts of classical Hollywood cinema and suggested a new way of approaching the circulation of cinema worldwide. Most importantly, Hansen took this model and subsequently applied it to Chinese cinema – discussing Shanghai silent cinema of the 1920s and 1930s as an instance of 'vernacular modernism' and positioning it in negotiation with the American cinema of the period. Such an account, therefore, offers a promising model for interrogating the transnational and translatable resonance of Hollywood worldwide. On the other hand, Hansen's model is very much focused on the relationship between classical Hollywood cinema and modernity in the first few decades of the twentieth century whereas my project is focused on a post-1960s era framed by postmodernity, and associated with a postclassical Hollywood. To some extent, therefore, my project in this book is a study of vernacular postmodernism – a study of the 'global post-modern' to use Stuart Hall's terms (1991: 32) – that builds on Hansen's work to examine a later period in the history of Hollywood's global circulation.

Secondly, I am drawing on Thomas Elsaesser's concept of 'karaoke Americanism' (2005: 317). In his book *European Cinema: Face to Face with Hollywood*, Elsaesser outlined some of the common oppositions used between European cinema and Hollywood where 'Europe stands for art, and the US for pop; Europe for high culture, America for mass entertainment; Europe for artisanal craft, America for industrial mass production.' (300). Elsaesser argues that while European discourses on American cinema often display some level of anti-Americanism based around such an opposition, there exists another discourse that he terms 'karaoke Americanism' which evokes the way that 'Europeans love to play at being American' (317). While this was a relatively brief observation in Elsaesser's argument, Jaap Kooijman has subsequently developed this concept further in his book *Fabricating the Absolute Fake*. Kooijman uses the concept in order to frame Dutch pop culture artefacts not 'merely as imitations of the American original, but as cases of active cultural appropriation' (2008b: 15). Placing emphasis on the performative nature of this process, Kooijman asserts that karaoke 'implies an active performance of mimicking and mockery . . . [while] also paying tribute to the original in a specific local or national manner' (117). As we will see when I turn to my own analysis of local interactions with American popular culture, this conception of a karaoke Americanism has numerous resonances with the processes I am describing.

Nevertheless, while karaoke Americanism is a useful model for exploring specific instances of cross-cultural borrowing, it is less useful as a way of grasping the larger flows of culture that shape these instances. For the purposes of my study, here, we need a concept that is scalable – that can describe both the macro-level of the global spread of Hollywood, and the micro-level of specific instances of transnational adaptation. To achieve this, I am proposing a comparative model of transnational adaptation based around the structuring metaphor of the 'meme'.

A Comparative Model of Transnational Adaptation

Stories, great flapping ribbons of shaped space-time, have been blowing and uncoiling around the universe since the beginning of time. And they have evolved. The weakest have died and the strongest have survived and they have grown fat on the retelling.

Terry Pratchett (2002: 8)

Coined by biologist Richard Dawkins in his 1976 book *The Selfish Gene*, the term 'meme' was designed to be a cultural equivalent of the biological gene, and was defined as 'a unit of cultural transmission, or a unit of imitation' (1989: 192). It has since been widely embraced as a way of discussing the circulation of concepts and ideas, especially in online media. In a manner analogous to genetics, the meme is a unit of culture which spreads and replicates, transforming itself to fit with whatever new habitat it finds itself in. For Dawkins,

Just as genes propagate themselves in the gene pool by leaping from body to body via sperms or eggs, so memes propagate themselves in the meme pool by leaping from brain to brain via a process which, in the broad sense, can be called imitation. (1989: 189)

It is important to note, however, that I am not basing my work on the science of 'memetics' in which scholars such as Richard Brodie (1996) have attempted to take Dawkins' concept and build a scientific evolutionary model of cultural transfer. I am not convinced that memes actually propagate themselves by leaping from brain to brain in the manner Dawkins describes, but rather I am using the concept metaphorically for the purpose of investigating processes of transnational adaptation.

As Robert Stam (2004) and Linda Hutcheon (2006) have argued, the model of the meme is very useful for tracing adaptation across cultures. Stories travel around the world and are adapted to their new environments through processes of mutation in ways analogous to genes, with some dying out and others flourishing. Breaking us away from the stranglehold of fidelity discourse which still dominates much scholarship on adaptations, the concept of the 'meme' allows us a way to consider how and why films are adapted and reworked in contexts far removed from their source.

Of course, part of the challenge in using a memetic model is in how we define and delineate an individual unit of cultural transmission that we can then trace. Throughout this book, I generally use the concept to describe an individual film which is spread and adapted as it travels, although it is important to note that a film may then be broken up into many smaller individual memes and their individual processes of adaptation can then be traced and followed. Meanwhile, the concept is sufficiently scalable to then refer to the much broader collection of memes that make up Hollywood as a whole, and, consequently, provide the title of this book. In other words, the meme can be used all the way from a micro-level investigation of the spread and adaptation of specific individual elements such as a character or piece of music to a macro-level investigation of the ways in which an industry such as Hollywood has been spread and adapted around the world.

Of course, it is not a perfect concept. Henry Jenkins et al. (2013) have recently criticised the notion of the meme for stripping aside the concept of human agency. Unlike genes, they argue, culture is not self-replicating and it has a reliance on people to borrow, rework and maintain it. It is their suggestion, therefore, that the biological metaphor which sees the 'meme' as a cultural analogue to the 'gene' is misleading. Attempting to avoid metaphors of viral infection and contamination to describe these processes, Jenkins et al. instead propose the notion of spreadable media in which consumers play an active role in 'spreading' content rather than being 'carriers' of viral media. While I am sympathetic to this attempt to shift more attention to human agency, I actually think that the concept of the 'meme' is already more attentive to agency than this critique allows for.

At the core of the concept is an emphasis on mutation and adaptation – with ideas not only spreading virally but also adapting and evolving as they travel. It is the evolutionary nature of this metaphor which is especially useful for this book as I am seeking to explore how the Hollywood meme travels to different contexts and is then adapted to these new environments, with some memes dying out while others flourish. As a structuring metaphor for the processes of adaptation that I am discussing, this therefore allows me to consider the factors which lead Hollywood texts to be taken up in a variety of different ways and for a variety of different purposes. This allows for a comparative model to be developed that maps the proliferation of a meme from one context, and then traces how it spreads and mutates as it travels to other contexts. In this way, the model helps us to consider which memes are flourishing in which locations, how they are being adapted for local (or indeed global) audiences, and to what purpose.

While this study will be necessarily attentive to the specificity of each example of transnational adaptation, it will also attempt to address the myriad contextual factors that shape different modes of borrowing. In other words, there will be an attempt to explore the possible determinant factors that shape different forms of adaptation. Why is one form of adaptation proliferating within a specific context? How do governmental policy and industrial conditions affect the modes of adaptation used? How does this relate to tensions in global copyright agreements? What meanings do these adaptations have in their contexts of production and reception? Taken together, this comparative model offers a method for tracing both the large-scale circulation of cultural forms, and the smaller-scale adaptation of specific elements within local contexts. Moving us away from models of dominance and resistance, therefore, this model allows us to interrogate the syncretism underpinning the circulation of global Hollywood and transnational processes of cultural exchange more broadly.

CHAPTER 2

Hollywood and the Popular Cinema of Turkey

In the two centuries leading up to World War II, the ongoing attempts at westerniz-
ing Turkey were modelled on European patterns and precedents. By the mid-1940s,
however, Europe was in ruins. At least for the time being, it could no longer act as
the object of fascinated desire it had previously been. The United States inherited
this mantle.

Nezih Erdoğan (2004: 121)

Our school is foreign cinema, I'd like to stress that. We learnt the profession first of
all through observation.

Tevfik Fikret Ucak (2006)

Every act of borrowing is in effect a reinvention

Peter Metcalf (2002: 16)

In the Turkish sci-fi comedy *G.O.R.A.* (2005), writer/star Cem Yilmaz
thoroughly lampoons many of the Americentric traditions of Hollywood
science fiction. After the film opens on a space station in which all the
characters are speaking English, one character points out the anomaly,
pleading, 'Can we not have it in Turkish?'. The film then restarts, only
this time with everyone – including the alien races – 'conversing in the
Turkish language and using Turkish lira to trade. In this alternate universe, it is not America that has colonised the peoples' consciousness – to
paraphrase those infamous words of Wim Wenders – but Turkey. This
pointed inversion of the Americentrism in Hollywood science-fiction
narratives, however, is balanced with an obvious affection for those same
films, with *G.O.R.A.* also offering loving homages to such iconic US films
as *Star Wars* (1977) and *The Matrix* (1999).

This tension between oppositional critique and mimetic reverence
illustrates one of the many layers of ambivalence that lie at the heart of
transnational processes of cultural exchange. While the film is undoubtedly offering a critique of the Americentrism in science-fiction narratives,
it is also drawing upon and imitating elements from those same cultural

products. Indeed, these processes of borrowing and adaptation are not solely a contemporary phenomenon. Transnational adaptation has a long history within Turkish popular culture, ranging from the literary borrowings of the *Edebiyyât-ı Cedîde* (New Literature) movement in the early twentieth century through to the more recent musical reworkings of bands like the Dolapdere Big Gang. This tendency is particularly evident in those cycles of popular cinema from the 1960s, 1970s and 1980s that are known within Turkey as *Yeşilçam*. Literally meaning 'green pine', Yesilçam is the name of a street in the Beyoglu area of Istanbul in which most of the Turkish film studios had their offices. In fact, the name has come to signify 'Turkish popular cinema' in a manner similar to the way 'Hollywood' acts as a synecdoche for 'American popular cinema'. Steeped within what Nezih Erdoğan terms 'mimicry beyond innocent inspiration' (2003: 166), Yesilçam films of this period self-consciously appropriated elements from US popular culture, often taking characters, plots and music, and recontextualising them within films produced in the local industry.

In this chapter, I utilise my comparative model of transnational adaptation in order to analyse the specific nature of these cultural borrowings and relate this to the socio-historical context in which they were produced. Focusing on films produced between the military coup of 1971 and the subsequent decline of the industry following a further coup in 1980, the analysis will identify the material conditions that helped to shape the Turkish film industry at this crucial historical conjuncture. By 1972, the industry had an annual production of over 300 movies, yet was also reliant on appropriated material to the extent that 'almost 90 per cent of these movies . . . were remakes, adaptations or spin-offs' (Gürata 2006: 242).

As Turkish cinema is still largely unexplored in English-language criticism, the chapter will necessarily begin with a brief outline of the history of this national cinema to help to contextualise the specific industrial developments of the period. Crucially, this will be a narrative that attends to the underlying tensions and contestations surrounding the establishment of a thriving popular film industry in the country. This broad overview will then be nuanced with close contextual analysis of the specific material conditions in which Yeşilçam cinema developed, paying attention to the governmental and industrial policy decisions that helped shape this particular mode of popular film production. Building on these contextual accounts, I will then offer a close textual analysis of four specific cases of transnational adaptation within Turkish popular cinema. The first case study will be *3 Dev Adam* (1973), in which the characters of Captain America, Santo the Mexican wrestler and Spider-Man are transposed to modern-day Istanbul. Secondly, I will examine the insertion of the local character Turist Ömer into a recreated episode of *Star Trek* in *Turist Ömer Uzay Yolunda* (1974). My third case study will be *Şeytan* (1974), an unofficial, unlicensed remake of *The Exorcist* (1973) in which the prevailing Catholic iconography is replaced with that of Islam. And finally, my fourth case study will be *Dünyayi Kurtaran Adam* (1982) in which footage from *Star Wars* (1977), along with music from various titles including *Raiders of the Lost Ark* (1981), was appropriated and used within special-effects sequences in a largely unrelated narrative.

Utilising my comparative model within a framework of critical transculturalism, I will interrogate how each of these texts specifically reconfigures and recontextualises its source texts with a particular emphasis on the processes of transposition. As I outlined in the previous chapter, these case studies of hybridisation are significantly context-dependent so careful attention will be paid to the ways in which each of these borrowings mediates the conditions of its production. This chapter will ultimately mark out certain tendencies within the Turkish popular film industry that contribute towards our broader understanding of the determinant factors shaping specific modes of transnational adaptation.

Yeşilçam: The Golden Age of Turkish Popular Cinema

The cinema is a discovery so important that one day it will change the face of the world's civilisation much more than the discoveries of gunpowder, electricity, and the continents. Cinema will bring about, for all men on this earth, the possibility of knowing one another, of approaching and loving one another . . . Cinema will eliminate divergences of view among men and will be of great value in realising the humanist ideal. We should accord cinema the importance it deserves.

Mustafa Kemal Atatürk (as quoted in Dorsay 1989: 22)

When Mustafa Kemal Atatürk came to power and founded the Turkish Republic in 1923, he instituted Westernising reforms aiming to break away from the Ottoman legacy and to orientate Turkey decidedly towards Europe (Chaudhuri 2005: 67). Inspired by the European republican model and the writings of Muslim secularist Ziya Gökalp, Atatürk brought in a number of key reforms designed to radically alter the shape and structure of the society. Symbolised in the six arrows of his party's emblem – populism, republicanism, nationalism, secularism, statism and reformism – these reforms included such symbolic changes as the banning of the fez in 1925, the introduction of a new code of law in 1926, the replacement of the Ottoman script (based on Arabic with Persian influences) with the Latin alphabet in 1928, and a series of state programmes which discouraged Ottoman cultural forms in favour of imported Western and folk traditions.

The position of cinema within these reform programs is significant as this was a medium that many commentators initially perceived as a Western form of entertainment (Erdoğan 1998: 259), and, furthermore, as we can see in the quotation above, was promoted as a tool of modernisation by president Atatürk himself. In recent years, this broader narrative of modernisation has come under stringent attack from scholars who have attempted to problematise the notion of Turkish modernisation as a 'disciplined and unambiguous process' (Bozdoğan and Kasaba 1997: 23). Pointing to the complexities and ambivalences underlying any such ideas of enlightenment and progress, scholars such as Deniz Kandiyoti and Ayse Saktanber have suggested that we need to explore further the tensions which complicate the prevailing streamlined versions of Ottoman/ Turkish history (Kandiyoti and Saktanber 2002). Until now, however, there has yet to be a sustained analysis of the complex and fluctuating relationship with imported Western – and specifically American – cultural forms that underpin some of these tensions. Through an analysis of the films produced in the Turkish popular film industry which rework elements from American popular culture, this chapter will show how this functions as a privileged site for exploring the underlying tensions and contestations around notions of modernisation and the place of transnational adaptation therein.

To begin, therefore, we must return to the years immediately following the founding of the Turkish Republic in 1923. As a number of scholars have noted (Dorsay 1989; Erdoğan and Gokurk 2001; Arslan 2011), cinema production during Atatürk's presidency was still very much in its infancy and there was little that could be called a 'film industry' per se. During this period, the central figure was the appointed director of the municipal theatre of Istanbul, Muhsin Ertuğrul. Often derided in histories of Turkish cinema for being overly theatrical and not sufficiently cinematic, Ertuğrul's films were predominantly literary adaptations and utilised casts made up of theatre actors. As we can see in the following quote from Atilla Dorsay, this was not without controversy:

> In general, he perceived filmmaking as the mere placing on film of theatre productions and was thus content to film his greatest successes on stage, using the actors, decors, costumes and technicians of his theatre. He cared little for creating a uniquely cinematographic language. (1989: 22)

While it could be argued that such accounts actually misrepresent the plurality of styles and themes within Ertuğrul's cinema (see, for example,

Onaran 2013), it is nevertheless true that his films were produced within an artisanal mode of production that emphasised small crews, static cinematography and plots primarily based on theatre and literature. Indeed, during this period he was the only filmmaker producing feature-length films and for this reason Ertuğrul has come to dominate accounts of the early years of the Turkish film industry. In subsequent years, other directors began producing features, such as Faruk Kenç who made *Yilmaz Ali* (The Indomitable Ali, 1940) and Adolf Körner who produced *Duvaksız Gelin* (The Unveiled Bride, 1942). This went hand in hand with the establishment of new production companies such as Halil Kamil Films and Ses Film which helped to broaden the range of cinematic production in Turkey. Nevertheless, there was still little resembling an industrial framework for film production in Turkey and, despite Atatürk's protestations above that, 'cinema is a discovery so important that one day it will change the face of the world's civilisation much more than the discoveries of gunpowder, electricity, and the continents', there was very little state support to help develop the local industry.

This all changed in the years following Atatürk's passing in 1938 as his presidential successors Mustafa İsmet İnönü (1938–50) and Mahmut Celal Bayar (1950–60) oversaw a number of governmental changes that affected Turkish film production and laid the groundwork for the boom that was to come in subsequent years. The first major change came, in 1945, with the establishment of the Association of Film Producers to bring together all the film producers of Turkey and lobby for more favourable industrial conditions. This tactic came to fruition in 1948 when the Istanbul municipal tax on movie tickets was reduced by half for Turkish films (to 25 per cent), and this move was soon followed by similar measures in other cities around the country (Dorsay 1989: 24). This protectionist form of subsidy contributed towards an economic climate in which the number of Turkish films rose from an average of 1.46 films per year during 1916–44 up to an average of 56.7 in the years 1950–9 (ibid.).

Secondly, as Nezih Erdoğan and Dilek Kaya have argued, the devaluation of the Turkish lira during subsequent years inadvertently led to 'a severe reduction of foreign film imports starting in the mid-1950s' (Erdoğan and Kaya 2002: 51). As Turkish film importers were not able to pay their accumulated debts to American distributors, they were therefore unable to afford to distribute new releases. This became more serious when, in 1958, Turkey devalued its currency from 2.82 to 9 lira per US dollar, thereby tripling the debt of the film importers and forcing them to cancel most of their planned releases. Not only that, but the United States Information Agency (USIA), which sought to 'control the construction of the American image in foreign countries' (2002: 51), used this extra leverage to bring Turkey into its Informational Media Guaranty (IMG) programme which allowed the producers a certain flexibility in paying off their debts but also meant that only those American films approved by the USIA could be imported. As Kerry Segrave notes, this created a blacklist of films which were refused distribution including *Written on the Wind* (1956), *The Blackboard Jungle* (1955), *All the King's Men* (1949), *All Quiet on the Western Front* (1930), *Sweet Smell of Success* (1957) and others (1997: 204). The combination of subsidised exhibition for Turkish films and a parallel fall in US imports led to a significant boost in the numbers of films being produced by the local industry. Together these changes created a positive socio-economic climate for Turkish film producers who were subsequently able to release their own products to fill the gaps left in the schedules. Most significantly, these changes were heralded for allowing the industry to 'finally free . . . itself from the yolk of the theatre' (Dorsay 1998: 24); in other words, the changes in governmental policy and economic context helped to develop an industry that was not only more productive but also produced a wider range of genres and modes of filmmaking.

As Nezih Erdoğan has argued, the years post-1945 were further marked by an increased engagement with US culture. While the predominant model for Atatürk's reform programmes was Europe in the years preceding World War II, the subsequent years marked an increasing relationship with America both politically and culturally. This new political relationship was cemented through symbolic acts, such as in 1946 when the American battleship Missouri sailed to Istanbul to return the body of the Turkish ambassador Munir Ertegun, and through more reciprocal arrangements such as the rise in US economic aid after Turkey joined NATO in 1952. As Nezih Erdoğan and Dilek Kaya note,

> During this time, along with a government which enthusiastically announced America as 'the major friend' of Turkey mainly for its economic and military aid, popular magazines introduced the American way of life to Turkish society. America was constructed as an object of desire and the American way of life as the narrative of a social fantasy which has lasted to the present. (2002: 47)

What is significant here is how this 'object of desire' helped to shape the mode of production which proliferated in the Turkish film industry in the subsequent years. While many other small national cinemas embraced the state-supported model of European art cinema, the Turkish industry followed a rather different path. As Savas Arslan has noted, the Turkish film industry relied on private entrepreneurship rather than state support, a model that encouraged a popular film industry to develop and stood in stark contrast to the art cinema traditions which flourished in many of its European neighbours (2011: 10). Moreover, there are a number of parallels with the popular European cinematic traditions of the period, especially that of Italy. With a number of production companies founded in 1960, including Saner Film, Yerli Film, Erler Film and Kurt Film, all housing their offices on Yeşilçam Street in the Beyoglu area of Istanbul, the Turkish industry moved towards an industrial mode of filmmaking that became synonymous with low-budget, quickie production methods and popular generic modes including variants on the melodrama, comedy and the historical epic.

Indeed, such was the emphasis on this popular mode of filmmaking that a group of filmmakers and intellectuals surrounding the film magazine *Yeni Sinema* proposed a counter tendency called 'Yeni Sinema', an art cinema movement opposed to the values of Yeşilçam. As we can see in Table 2.1, there were a number of structuring oppositions underlying this movement that will prove instructive for understanding what was at stake in the development of Yeşilçam cinema in Turkey.

The notion of a domestic Yeşilçam cinema is significant as these films were primarily intended for distribution within Turkey only. Relying upon the Bölge İşletmeleri ('regional system'), producers would raise their financing through advance sales made to seven separate distribution areas: İstanbul (Marmara region), İzmir (Aegaean region), Ankara (Middle Anatolian region), Samsun (Black Sea region), Adana (Mediterranean region), Erzurum (East Anatolian region) and Diyarbakir (South East Anatolian region). Such a system laid the emphasis on a domestic capitalist mode of production rather than a state-funded art cinema movement, with the flourishing industry built around what was generally referred to as 'quickies' – low-budget films that were shot and edited in a matter of months and primarily funded through pre-sales to

Table 2.1

Yeni Sinema	Yeşilçam
Western	Domestic
Art cinema	Popular cinema
Model: European art cinema	Model: Hollywood
To create	To produce
Auteur policy	Star system
Alternative modes of production	Capitalist mode of production
Festivals, competitions	Production-distribution-exhibition

(Erdoğan 1998: 262)

distribution companies (Arslan 2011: 109). This meant that leading stars would often make more than twenty films a year, working on several productions at the same time and functioning within a star system where the advance sales made to the distributors would often rely upon the name of a well-known star. Furthermore, as producer Nusret İkbal explains, by the 1960s the emphasis on 'quickies' led to a perceived emphasis on quantity over quality:

> The number of original movies are very few. We plagiarise photography, artifice, mise-en-scene as well as the plots of foreign movies. Earlier, Turkish cinema imitated German and Arab films, now we are dealing with cheap imitations of American, Italian and French cinema. And we describe this as 'influence'. This is rather deceptive. However, everyone has to plagiarise while we are producing 150 movies each year. In these circumstances no single filmmaker can create an original piece. Because s/he lacks both time and creativity. (İkbal as quoted in Gürata 2006: 243)

For İkbal, the motive behind the prevalence of remakes was the assembly-line production system that limits the time and effort spent on each production. The question here is not whether it truly is less *creative* to remake a movie than to write a new script – it could be argued that both expend significant amounts of creative energy – but to recognise that producers such as İkbal were feeling that the distinct mode of production was impacting on the types of film they were able to produce in this system. Moreover, the industry was reliant on just three screenwriters – Safa Önal, Bülent Oran and Erdoğan Tünaş who wrote the scripts for a significant proportion of the films produced each year – and the emphasis was on producing scripts very quickly to respond to whatever was popular at that moment.

Most significantly, Erdoğan's chart (see Table 2.1) suggests that the implied 'model' for Yeşilçam was Hollywood cinema rather than the European art cinema model represented by the Yeni Sinema movement. This can be seen both in terms of the industrial models that I have been describing but also in the significant number of films which were adapting material from Hollywood itself. As we will see later in my case studies, this was not an insignificant amount and relied upon a conception of copyright law that did not require studios to acquire the property rights of the earlier films and TV shows that they wished to adapt. While the boom period came to an end in the years following a military coup d'état in 1980 and the subsequent decline of the film industry, this quick and economical mode of production meant that throughout the 1960s and 1970s, Turkey was the third most productive film industry in the world (Evren 2005). This leads to a significant question: if Turkey was third only to America and India in the size of its film industry, why has so little been written

about this so-called 'golden age' of Turkish cinema? Why are the popular
cinema traditions of Yeşilçam elided in the few histories of Turkish cinema
that exist in the English language (such as Dorsay 1989 and Kaplan 1996)?
While this situation has improved somewhat with the publication of Savas
Arslan's excellent *Cinema in Turkey* (2011), it is nevertheless the case that
Yeşilçam is still very much neglected within academic scholarship.

Certainly one of the reasons for the neglect of these traditions is the very
fact of their being 'popular'. As Dyer and Vincendeau note in their book
on *Popular European Cinema*, 'The popular cinema of any given European
country is . . . generally marginalised in favour of the often little seen but
critically acclaimed art film traditions' (1992: 1). While the productivity of
the industry throughout the 1970s is occasionally referred to in historical
discussions of Turkish cinema, the films themselves are generally ignored
in favour of the arthouse works of filmmakers such as Yilmaz Güney and
Ömer Kavur. Of course, while this may be partly due to a certain level of
disdain towards popular cinematic traditions, it is significant that these art
films were also shown at film festivals and through subsidised international
exhibition circuits while the domestic Yesilçam productions were rarely
seen outside of the country and generally without any subtitles. Moreover,
while their popular nature may be part of the reason for this particular
elision in histories of Turkish cinema, another more telling explanation
is the hybrid nature of the films themselves. Yeşilçam was a cinema profoundly influenced by other cinemas, producing unlicensed remakes of
films from around the world. As Dimitris Eleftheriotis has argued, 'Such
forms are traditionally excluded from national cinema studies as being
either too complicated or too contaminating of the hegemonic understanding of the "national" as "essential" and "pure"' (2006: 226). With a
cinema so heavily invested in intertextual reworkings of media from other
cultures, the search for an essentialised notion of Turkishness within these
forms of Turkish cinema becomes deeply problematic. It is my contention
that it is primarily for this reason that Yeşilçam has been all but ignored in
discussions of Turkish national cinema. Yet, conversely, it is for this very
same reason that Yeşilçam is so rich for analyses that focus on the transnational flows of media and culture. Rather than problematically utilising a
few privileged examples that attempt to show some pure or unified sense
of national identity, this book instead follows the work of Ahmet Gürata
and Nezih Erdoğan in engaging with the 'multiple modalities of numerous popular but profoundly impure films, genres and narrative strands'
(Eleftheriotis 2006: 224).

Within this context, Savas Arslan has recently introduced the term
'Turkification', which usefully evokes such a transformative notion of

cultural exchange. Reclaiming the term from its use as derogatory slang, Arslan uses the term to describe the various practices of translating and transforming Western cinemas in Turkey. Importantly, rather than seeing these transformations in terms of two discrete national cinemas coming into contact, Arslan lays emphasis on the fluidity of these cultural formations and their overlapping, intersecting nature:

> The translation of the West implicit in Turkification does not simply take place between two languages, but also through other elements of cultural multiplicity. It is not reducible to a transfer from one set to another, each clearly coded and decodable. Here the West and the East are not identifiable totalities with a firm set of elements; they are surfaces on which various particularities float. (2011: 83)

Therefore, rather than trying to separate out the essential 'Turkish-ness' or 'American-ness' of these Turkish adaptations, as if these were notions that could be anything other than deeply problematic, this chapter will instead situate these films within the socio-historic context from which they arose, approaching these borrowings as privileged insights into the dynamics of transnational flows of media and culture. Let us turn now to an industrial account of the various cycles which proliferated within Yeşilçam cinema, and a broad overview of the prevalence of adaptation and reworking therein.

Remakes, Adaptations and Spin-offs within Turkish Popular Cinema

> In 1978, me, my dad and mother went to Paris. *Superman* was in the cinema then. We went and saw the movie. When the film ended and we were getting out, my father looked at me and asked me, 'Why don't you make a *Superman* too?'
> Kunt Tulgar (2007)

Here we can see the rather matter-of-fact approach that director Kunt Tulgar took in his decision to produce a version of Superman for Turkish audiences with the film *Supermen Dönüyor* (Superman Returns, 1979). A low-budget adaptation of the Superman story, capitalising on the hype surrounding the previous year's Richard Donner film, *Supermen Dönüyor* transposed the character to Istanbul, utilising elements from the Donner film, the earlier 1940s serials, and the comic books themselves. Indeed, Kunt Tulgar's father Sebastian had made a similar decision twenty-seven years earlier when he established Millet Film and decided to make a Tarzan film capitalising on the interest surrounding the European release of *Tarzan's New York Adventure* (1942) by producing *Tarzan Istanbul'da*

(Tarzan in Istanbul, 1952). Utilising footage shot at a local zoo along with stock footage from documentaries and even other Tarzan films, Tulgar had created his own version of the Tarzan tale for Turkish audiences.

This was part of a broader trend for features to draw on foreign sources, as we can see in another 1952 film, *Drakula Istanbul'da* (Dracula in Istanbul), which transposed the character of Dracula to Istanbul in its adaptation of Ali Riza Seyfi's novel *Kazikli Voyvoda* (Vlad the Impaler), a novel that was itself an adaptation of Bram Stoker's 1897 *Dracula*. Produced by Turgat Demirağ, the film has some historical significance in that it was one of the first films to make clear the relationship between the fictional Dracula and his historical antecedent, the fifteenth-century nobleman Vlad the Impaler (Scognamillo and Demirhan 1999: 434). More importantly for our current concerns, these two films also triggered a cycle of similarly themed productions in which an imported character becomes 'Istanbul'da', such as *Görünmeyen Adam Istanbul'da* (The Invisible Man in Istanbul, 1955), *Fantoma Istanbul'da Buluşalim* (Fantômas: Appointment in Istanbul, 1967) and *Süper Adam Istanbul'da* (Superman in Istanbul, 1972).

By the mid-1960s, there had arrived a large number of low-budget quickies that utilised heroes from comic books and the black and white American serials of the 1930s and 1940s like Flash Gordon, Zorro and Captain Marvel. One of the most significant features in this cycle was actually not a Turkish production but an Italian one – albeit one shot in Turkey. The feature *Kriminal* (1966), based on a popular comic book, was shot in and around Istanbul and offered inspiration to filmmakers such as Yilmaz Atadeniz who watched the production and decided to make a feature based on the similar Italian comic character Killing – *Killing Istanbul'da* (Killing in Istanbul, 1967). As Pete Tombs attests, 'within a month it had made more than three times the normal profit for a low budget movie' (1998: 106) and this helped to trigger a cycle whereby rival production companies attempted to produce similar comic-book and serial-style action features including *Örümcek Adam* (Spider-Man, 1966) and *Baytekin Fezada Çarpişanlar* (Flash Gordon: Battle in Space, 1967).

One of the most significant of these comic book transpositions was the 1973 film *3 Dev Adam* (Three Mighty Men) which transposed the characters Captain America, Santo the wrestler and Spider-Man to modern-day Istanbul within an action melodrama narrative. Through a close analysis of this film that teases out the specific ways in which director Tevfik Fikret Ucak utilises these borrowed elements, I will now interrogate the cultural meanings invested in this transnational adaptation.

3 Dev Adam (1973) / Spider-Man

Superheroes exist in their previous forms in graphic novel collections of comic books, DVD collections of television series, and internet recreations of superhero stories that reinterpret 'canonical' superhero mythology outside the boundaries of copyright law. Consequently, superheroes exist within a fascinating cultural dialectic . . . [Yet] While this dialectic results in part from media conglomerates striving to keep their properties consistent and yet relevant, the superheroes exist only partially within the control of companies that own them.

Terrence R. Wandtke (2007: 15)

In recent years, a number of scholars have attempted to get to grips with the cultural life of superhero characters, offering a serious analytical look at the ways in which characters change and adapt through different political and socio-economic periods. Probably the most significant text in legitimising the study of superheroes would be Umberto Eco's seminal 'The Myth of Superman' (1979a), but it is two more recent works that I think are most useful in framing the various ways in which superheroes have transformed over time: Terrence R. Wandtke's *The Amazing Transforming Superhero!* (2007) and Roberta Pearson and William Uricchio's *The Many Lives of the Batman* (1991). By drawing on the specific models that they each propose for understanding the 'migrations of a shifting signifier' and utilising these to address the transnational dimension of such transpositions, this section will tease out the implications of transposing Captain America, Santo the wrestler and Spider-Man to Istanbul in the film *3 Dev Adam* (Three Mighty Men, 1973).

In his introductory essay to *The Amazing Transforming Superhero!*, Wandtke critiques those models of transformation that see superheroes as evolving in a controlled and coherent manner over time, and instead proposes a model based around revisionism. Utilising a taxonomy of four types of superhero revisionism, Wandtke argues that superheroes are revised and transformed through different historical periods and within different cultural contexts, and we therefore need to 'more clearly define the types of revision that we see in superhero narratives in order to fully encourage the debate on superheroes as pervasive global tropes' (2007: 15). First, Wandtke proposes the notion of *additive* revisions which are 'seemingly minor additions that can be read as the logical outgrowth of the basic premise established within a superhero narrative' (15). Within this mode, the revisions are incremental and do not radically revise or alter the fundamental characteristics that we attribute to certain superheroes. The second type are *fundamental* revisions which are 'major changes which signal a departure from what has been presented before in a specific superhero narrative' (17) such as when the character Captain America returned in the late 1960s in a much darker, less jingoistic incarnation. As should be obvious, these are differences of degree with the attendant difficulty that there can be difficulty in differentiating whether any such revisions are suitably major enough to qualify as *fundamental*. Thirdly, we have *conceptual* revisions which 'rewrite the basic ideas not of a superhero but of the superhero as a general idea with wide-ranging social impact' (19) which is a mode exemplified by Alan Moore's *Watchmen* in which the very conception of what constitutes a superhero comes under scrutiny. Fourthly, and finally, we have *critical* revisions which 'operate outside the mediums typically associated with superhero narratives such as comic books, animation, and film' and are instead 'interpretive positions taken by critics of popular culture who study superheroes . . . that ultimately have an impact on the way that superhero stories are told' (22).

While there are problems with this taxonomy – not least that Wandtke only has two categories which deal with tangible revisions of particular superheroes – this model will still have use in our discussion of the revisions of superhero characters we find in *3 Dev Adam*. Although Wandtke's model is not explicitly transnational, such a model will prove useful once grounded in the cross-cultural dynamics I am describing, and will allow for a more nuanced analysis of what is at stake in this form of transnational adaptation. To achieve this goal, however, this work also needs to be brought together with Pearson and Uricchio's chapter 'I'm Not Fooled by that Cheap Disguise', in *The Many Lives of The Batman*, which attempts to identify key components of the Batman character and thereby helps us to identify more precisely the nature of any revisions made and the constraints under which these function. Suggesting that five key components constitute the core character of the Batman, Pearson and Uricchio offer a model for studying the extent to which the character is transformed in different time periods and across different media, and they argue that 'without the presence of all five key components in some form, the Batman ceases to be the Batman' (1991: 187). These are shown in Table 2.2.

Utilising Wandtke's model of revisionism and Pearson/Uricchio's analysis of core components, I will now examine in more detail *3 Dev Adam*. Directed by Tevfik Fikret Ucak in 1973, *3 Dev Adam* was produced by Tual Films and was part of a cycle of comic-book adaptations and masked superhero films in which superhero characters were transposed to modern-day Istanbul and engaged in distinctive forms of action melodrama. Indeed, the film was later hailed by author Pete Tombs as a film which comes 'closer than most to being a real "comic strip on film"'

Table 2.2

Traits/attributes	Wealth, physical prowess, deductive abilities and obsession
Events	Divided into fixed and accruing events such as the origin story, and iterative events, that is repetitive, non-identical and non-accruing events, most of which involve crimefighting
Recurrent characters	Commissioner Gordon, Robin, Alfred, Joker etc.
Setting	Batman/Bruce Wayne lives in Gotham City
Iconography	The Batman's costume (cape, cowl, gauntlets and logo) with an abundance of bat-shaped objects.

(Table adapted from Pearson and Uricchio 1991: 186)

Figure 2.1 Spider-Man planning his smuggling operation in *3 Dev Adam* (dir. T. Fikret Uçak, Turkey, 1973)

(1998: 107). The film opens with a young woman buried up to her neck in sand, while Spider-Man and his gang sadistically use the propeller from an outboard motor to slash her face. As we can see in Figure 2.1, this is a Spider-Man character who shares much of the same iconography (red masked costume with spider logo on the chest) as earlier incarnations, yet here is adapted into a villainous criminal who throughout the narrative leads an antique smuggling operation, commits a series of sadistic crimes and murders a number of residents of Istanbul.

As should be obvious, this is not the Spider-Man character we recognise from the comic books created by Stan Lee and Steve Ditko. If we use the Pearson/Uricchio model, we will recognise that the traits we broadly associate with Spider-Man (such as an ability to cling to walls, superhuman strength, and a sixth sense for danger), along with the setting, events and recurrent characters from the comic books, are simply not present in this incarnation of Spider-Man. Indeed, the only recognisable aspects of

Spider-Man which persist from earlier incarnations are the costume and the name Örümcek Adam itself. This would of course qualify as a 'fundamental revision' according to Wandtke's model, but what is significant here is less the ways in which Spider-Man differs from earlier incarnations, but rather how this transposition of the Spider-Man character then functions within the film. As the film progresses, we learn that the bloodthirsty 'Spider-Man' gang from the Far East are smuggling historical artefacts through the country in order to sell them to antique dealers in America as part of a larger money-laundering operation. Chief Orhan of the Istanbul Police Department decides to bring in Captain America and Santo the Mexican wrestler from their respective countries in order to track down Spider-Man and take down his operation.

This perfunctory narrative serves to facilitate an action crime drama in which the masked superhero characters face off against various criminal gang members until a final showdown in which all three superhero characters come together for an extended fight sequence in which Spider-Man is eventually apprehended. Indeed, this has many similarities to the other superhero crime dramas of the period which are based around fast-paced action, one-dimensional characterisation and extended scenes of fist fighting such as *Killing Istanbul'da* and *Casus Kiran* (Spy Smasher, 1968). For director Ucak, the move towards action and drama movies was a reaction to the predominant mode of theatrical-style cinema being produced in the country: 'Our group always had fantastic movies and themes in mind' (Ucak 2006).

Nevertheless, what is significant here is that these superhero characters do not display any 'superhero' traits – i.e. superpowers – and are instead positioned as archetypal melodramatic heroes and villains who merely happen to utilise the iconography of foreign superhero characters. Moreover, this fits within a broader trend for crime dramas in Turkey in which the traits of the masked 'superhero' characters are grounded in the everyday world. This is reflected in a conversation early on in *3 Dev Adam* when Chief Orhan asks the Captain America character, 'Why do you put on masks and outfits during duty?', and he explains that this is a ploy to capture Spider-Man who is a 'child-minded lunatic' who attacks anyone else who wears a mask. Quite apart from whether this is a convincing sequence, it illustrates the emphasis being placed on verisimilitude in the narrative whereby the use of superhero costumes is explained rationally as a method for crime prevention – in other words, we are not watching 'Captain America' in Turkey but rather a police chief who is dressed in that costume in order to capture a criminal. Indeed, as we can see in Figure 2.2, it is clear that these characters are portrayed as ordinary men

Figure 2.2 Captain America getting into costume in *3 Dev Adam*

who are simply wearing superhero costumes rather than characters who retain the superpowers we associate with them.

Taking the Pearson/Uricchio observation that 'without the presence of all key five key components in some form, the Batman ceases to be the Batman' (1991: 187), I contend that the absence of the familiar character traits attributed to Spider-Man, Captain America and Santo the wrestler (aside from their iconographic costumes) means that this is such a fundamental revision of the characters that they are no longer the superheroes they resemble. In this sense, the filmmakers are not so much transposing the characters into Istanbul as they are transposing the iconography we associate with those characters – an important distinction.

To further understand the ways in which these superhero characters were adapted, we need to address the industrial conditions of the time, which shaped the production. As I outlined earlier, the mode of production in Yeşilçam cinema laid emphasis on quickie productions that were shot on very low budgets and funded through pre-sales to distribution companies. Through utilising the recognisable characters of Spider-Man, Captain America and Santo the wrestler, Ucak and his team were able to associate their product with the well-known comic-book and serial characters and thereby utilise this fact in their pre-sale arrangements. As I have argued elsewhere in relation to the low-budget spoof genre (Smith 2011), this model of adaptation utilises a form of 'associative commercialism' in which the appropriation serves to draw consumer attention to the product through an implicit relationship with a well-known franchise. Political economy scholars such as Eileen Meehan have addressed the ways in which superhero franchises function through cross-promotion in which

the film per se becomes only one component in a product line that extends beyond
the theatre, even beyond our contact with mass media, to penetrate the markets
for toys, bedding, trinkets, cups and other minutiae comprising one's everyday life
inside a commoditised, consumerised culture. (1991: 49)

Each product helps to produce intertextual associations and consumer
awareness which can then feed into interest in the other products available.
While this is an important intervention, these elements are only part of the
picture. These large transmedia franchises do not simply offer an oppor-
tunity for corporations to generate merchandise and exploit commercial
intertexts but also provide a web of intertextual associations around the
said product that can then be appropriated and used by filmmakers to bring
attention to their products. The result is that filmmakers are then able to
draw attention to their low-budget products by parasitically feeding off the
commercial value of their intertextual relationship to a blockbuster franchise. While the corporate world which Meehan was describing was the
furore around the 1989 *Batman*, characters such as Spider-Man, Captain
America and Santo had a significant level of popularity within the Turkey
of the 1970s through widely distributed comic books, photo novels, serials
and, in the case of Santo, movies. This was a consumer knowledge that
director Ucak was attempting to associate with *3 Dev Adam*; as he himself
explained, 'We wanted to draw all the young people of Turkey into the
movie houses' through bringing together 'my childhood heroes' Captain
America, Santo and Spider-Man (Ucak 2006).

What this relationship rests upon, furthermore, is a conception of
copyright in Turkey which allowed for the utilisation and reworking of
copyrighted characters without any form of licensing or payment to the
copyright holders. In the US the legal perspective on a character such as
Batman is that the DC legal department hold the trademark for 'Batman
and all related characters, the distinctive likenesses thereof and all related
indicia . . .' (Pearson and Uricchio 1991: 193), meaning that permission
must be granted to use Batman images on other products or in other
publications ensuring 'a uniformity of iconographic and narrative depictions of the Batman and prevents dilution of the trademark' (ibid.). In
Turkey this was not the case, and this allowed filmmakers to freely utilise
characters such as Spider-Man, Captain America and Santo without
any fear of reprisals. While I will go into further detail on the specific
nature of Turkey copyright law in my next section on *Turist Omer Uzay
Yolunda*, it is important to note that the freedom to rework trademarked
characters such as Captain America and Spider-Man allowed for a much
more fundamental form of revisionism than we find in the official texts

produced for the US market. These revisions go far beyond those that would normally be allowed by the Marvel legal department and are less about self-consciously reworking earlier incarnations than about utilising the iconography of these characters as 'exploitable elements' which help bring attention to a low-budget production within an economic market that does not allow for large marketing budgets or expensive promotion. Indeed, the tactic was something of a success as the film did relatively well at the Turkish box office and, more significantly, managed to get foreign distribution deals within Libya, Morocco, Egypt, Tunisia and Tanzania – something that was extremely rare in Turkish cinema of the period.

Turist Ömer Uzay Yolunda (1974) / Star Trek

Television came to Turkey in 1968. Its influence really began to be felt in the early 1970s. The Government-controlled TRT began national broadcasting in 1973 and there was an almost immediate effect on the cinemas. Audiences began to desert them in droves. From 3,000 cinemas in 1973, the number fell as low as 334 in 1992: that's one cinema for every 200,000 people.

Pete Tombs (1998: 112)

While many commentators consider television to be one of the major causes of the sharp decline in Yeşilçam cinema in the 1980s, the introduction of national broadcasting by Turkish Radio and Television (TRT) in 1973 led to a number of feature films which were themselves heavily influenced by television programming. These include *Tatli Cadi* (Sweet Sorceress, 1975) and its quickly produced sequel *Tatli Cadinin Maceralari* (The Adventures of the Sweet Sorceress, 1975) which both reworked elements from the TV series *Bewitched*, and the film *Turist Ömer Uzay Yolunda* (Tourist Omer in *Star Trek*, 1974), which borrows elements from the TV series *Star Trek*. In this section, I will analyse the ways in which tangible elements from the US TV series *Star Trek* are appropriated and reworked in the film *Turist Ömer Uzay Yolunda*, and I will then locate this within wider debates on the relationship between Turkish cinema and the US media that was entering the country at the time.

During the height of Yeşilçam production, the Turist Ömer series appeared, a series of popular comedy films directed by Hulki Saner and featuring Sadri Alişik as the title character 'Turist Ömer'. At the time, Saner was one of the most prolific filmmakers in Turkey, having produced a number of melodramas such as *Tatli Günah* (Sweet Sin, 1961) and *Çifte Nikah* (Two Marriages, 1962) and some of the later instalments in the long-running *Ayşecik* series. It was this collaboration with Sadri Alişik, however, that was to be his most successful and popular film franchise running to seven instalments. According to Saner's biography, the character of Turist Ömer was inspired by his uncle, a man whom he describes as 'a traveller, a lovable person, friendly, chatty, bohemian, but principally a traveller' (Saner 1996: 67). This emphasis on travelling would have the most resonance with the character, with the nickname 'Turist' being added after Saner observed tourists in Istanbul whom he saw wandering idly around the city: 'Omar hasn't got anything to do either. He wanders around idly so we called him a tourist. And then the name just stuck' (68).

The original *Turist Ömer* film appeared in 1964, in which Ömer, a poor, rural character, travels to Istanbul and finds himself like a 'tourist' in the urban sprawl of the city. Commenting on the changes that were taking place in Turkish society, and indeed drawing much comedy from the resultant conflict between notions of 'tradition' and 'modernity', Turist Ömer spends the film offering his irreverent observations on the peoples and places he encounters (Arslan 2011: 169). The following films in the series continued to draw currency from this 'fish out of water' narrative by moving Ömer further afield, introducing him to high society in *Turist Ömer Dümenciler Krali* (1965) where he is mistaken for a foreign prince, and then allowing him to comment on the situation of migrant workers when he travels to Germany in *Turist Ömer Almanya'da* (1966). In the three subsequent films, he travels to Arabia (*Turist Ömer Arabistan'da*, 1969), Africa (*Turist Ömer Yamyamlar Arasinda*, 1970) and Spain (*Turist Ömer boga güresçisi*, 1971) respectively, although his position as a tourist commenting on the strange peoples and customs he encounters leads to some moments of rather xenophobic 'comedy'. *Turist Ömer Yamyamlar Arasinda*, in which he travels to Africa, actually translates as 'Tourist Ömer among the Cannibals', signalling the crude stereotypes contained within that particular narrative. Indeed, Saner's biography notes that they had to 'black up' some of the actors in Turkey to play the cannibal roles after they returned from location shooting in Africa.

After travelling to all these disparate places, and commenting on the strange peoples and customs he encounters, the final film in the series, *Turist Ömer Uzay Yolunda*, sees Turist Ömer travel into outer space. Furthermore, rather than an unspecific generic 'space', he travels into the world of the American TV series *Star Trek*. Although the original *Star Trek* series had begun transmission in the US in 1966, it was not shown in Turkey until 1973 when the government-controlled TRT began broadcasting the series. While television penetration had not yet reached significant levels, especially in the more rural areas of the country, the series gained sufficient circulation that by 1974 director Hulki Saner and his team decided to set the final *Turist Ömer* film in the world of *Star Trek*.

This was the first *Turist Ömer* film to deal with an explicitly fictional world – although, of course, the representations of the other locations are certainly 'fictions' in their own way – and it is significant that Ömer himself does not show any prior knowledge of *Star Trek* or draw attention to the fictionality of the world in which he finds himself. There are no winks to camera when Ömer meets Spock and Kirk, or when he boards the bridge of the Starship *Enterprise* (here titled the Atilgan, Turkish for 'enterprising'). Moreover, this is made all the more remarkable in that not only is Ömer entering the world of *Star Trek*, but he is actually entering into the specific episode 'The Man Trap'. Hulki Saner and his team recreate the costumes, sets and much of the dialogue from this particular episode, with the primary difference being that Turist Ömer is now inserted into the story. While the recreation of the plot and characters from an episode of *Star Trek* could be read as merely derivative of the TV show, the following analysis will pay attention to the specific ways in which the film utilises those appropriated elements and suggest a more nuanced reading of the film.

It is my contention that the insertion of the local character Turist Ömer into the world of the US TV series *Star Trek* allows the filmmakers to comment playfully upon the relationship between their film and the source text, and by extension comment upon the American popular culture that was entering the country at the time. Of course, this does not mean that we should necessarily interpret the film as a form of resistant critique aimed at *Star Trek* or its US creators. As I discussed in Chapter 1, analyses of transnational adaptation which rely upon a model of domination and resistance actually serve to obfuscate the subtler relationships which underlie these borrowings. Therefore, in my analysis, I will first address the ways in which *Turist Ömer Uzay Yolunda* recreates 'The Man Trap' episode of *Star Trek*, paying particular attention to the ways in which this reflects specific practices in the Turkish film industry of the period. Secondly, I will move onto the role of Ömer within this narrative and outline the ways his presence impacts this form of appropriation. Then thirdly, and finally, I will discuss how the processes of hybridisation contained within this text reflect on wider issues surrounding the transnational flow of media into Turkey. While the filmmakers were not making an explicit parody of *Star Trek* or, by proxy, a critique of the American media entering the country at the time, there is much to suggest a more dialogic relationship that reflects the hybridising nature of cultural exchange.

First of all, as we can see in Figure 2.3, the *mise en scène* of the Starship *Enterprise* is closely recreated both in terms of set design and through the use of actors who physically resemble the characters from the original

Figure 2.3 Recreating the Starship *Enterprise* in *Turist Ömer Uzay Yolunda*
(dir. Hulki Saner, Turkey, 1974)

series. Even the distinctive costumes are replicated, complete with
stylised arrowhead on the left breast, and coloured shirts designating
rank – albeit with Spock wearing a gold shirt signifying command rather
than his usual blue science/medical shirt. What is most significant here is
that these replications are done without any form of licensing from Gene
Roddenberry or the studio NBC. Indeed, one of the most significant
contextual factors shaping this particular adaptation of *Star Trek* is that
of copyright.

The freedom to utilise elements from *Star Trek* without any form of
licensing was quite specific to Turkey, as Ahmet Gürata argues:

> the notion of plagiarism in Turkey was not identical with that prevalent in the
> West . . . While both adaptation and remake are usually defined by their legally
> sanctioned use of material (whose rights the filmmakers should have purchased), in
> Turkey that was not the case. (Gürata 2006: 242)

In fact, the freedom to 'plagiarise' from *Star Trek* actually reflects an
alternative conception of intellectual property rights within Turkey of
that period. While Turkey had implemented aspects of the 1948 version
of the Berne Convention into law in 1951 (Law No. 5846), the law was
rarely used and it was only when the possibility of media reproduction on
a large scale became a reality (as with VHS and cassette tapes), and exter-
nal political pressure was exerted, that Turkish law began to move more
in line with Anglo-American models of copyright protection. Moreover,
it was not until 2001 and heated negotiations with the EU that the law was
substantially revised and specialist courts were set up specifically to tackle
copyright infringement.

As I discussed in Chapter 1, international treaties on copyright protection tend to serve the purposes of those who are exporters of content rather than those who are primarily importing content from elsewhere. In the case of 1970s Turkey, a net importer of such assets, the incentive was not there to expand copyright protection to the media texts entering the country, and this contributed to the cultural climate in which *Turist Ömer Uzay Yolunda* was able to replicate much of the *Star Trek* episode 'The Man Trap'. Conversely, as this film was never exported to an international audience – the current circulation of the film relies upon grey-market bootlegging – there was little incentive for the US producers to sue for copyright infringement. Indeed, as the film was only circulated to the domestic market, it is highly unlikely that Gene Roddenberry and his team were even aware of this Turkish remake.

The process of replication was not limited to *mise en scène*, as the film also uses the credit sequence and theme song from the original series, albeit with its own titles superimposed on top. This opening sequence actually comes to be representative of the processes of the film as a whole, in that Turkish elements are overlaid on top of a detailed recreation of the US series. Evoking Gerard Genette's conception of a palimpsest – an ancient scroll that has been written on, scraped off and then written on again – *Turist Ömer Uzay Yolunda* draws attention to its status as a 'hypertext' writing on top of its earlier 'hypotext' *Star Trek*. Furthermore, this is not the only unattributed use of music in the film. Both the Ventures' cover of 'The Twilight Zone' theme, and the Pink Floyd song 'Echoes' are also used. The employment of unlicensed music from foreign media texts was a tendency very much prevalent throughout the Yesilçam industry.

After this opening, the plot of the episode 'The Man Trap' is then closely recreated using much of the same dialogue, characters and plot points as the original series. Known among *Star Trek* fans as 'The Incredible Salt Vampire' episode, 'The Man Trap' follows the *Enterprise* on a routine mission to an alien planet to conduct a medical examination on Dr Crater and his wife Nancy. Soon after arriving, crewman Darnell is discovered dead with strange red marks on his neck. After he has been taken back to the ship, further tests show that his salt levels have fallen to zero. The plot then continues with the discovery of further dead bodies until it is unravelled that Nancy has been replaced by a shape-shifting alien that requires salt for sustenance, even if that means sucking it from the bodies of the ship's crew.

This plotline is closely followed in *Turist Ömer Uzay Yolunda* albeit with a number of deviations reflecting the differing mode of production within the Turkish film industry. While *Star Trek* is very much a studio-based television series, recreating alien planets within the studio, *Turist Ömer Uzay Yolunda* was – like the majority of Yeşilçam films – primarily shot on location. This means that the alien planet is now depicted using the ancient ruins of Ephesus. While the location shoot was primarily a budgetary decision, reflecting the lack of large-scale studio facilities in Istanbul, the use of Ephesus reflects what Savas Arslan terms 'Turkification' in that the text is transformed through its translation for the Turkish context. Depicting this alien planet using the location of one of the seven wonders of the ancient world offers up a quite different aesthetic from the studio-bound depiction we found in the original episode. In many ways this is an inversion of the palimpsest tactic I described earlier, with the world of *Star Trek* here being written onto the site of Turkish culture, rather than the other way round.

Interestingly, unlike other Yeşilçam remakes produced in this period, the shooting style does not differ greatly from the series it is drawing upon. For Nezih Erdoğan,

> Plagiarism, of which Yeşilçam has often been accused, is by no means a simple issue. The technical and stylistic devices of Yeşilçam differ radically from those of Hollywood and European cinema. Lighting, colour, dubbing, dialogue, shooting practices, point of view shots and editing create a very specific cinematic discourse in even the most faithful of adaptations. (2003: 266)

Yet the style of this particular transnational adaptation is remarkably similar to the *Star Trek* series it is drawing upon. While the mode of production in the Yeşilçam industry, which attempted to meet the demand for over 200 films a year by keeping to very low budgets and short shooting schedules, could not imitate the more expensive technical and stylistic devices of Hollywood, the mode of production in US television was similarly economical at the time. Even though *Star Trek* was technically in the action/adventure genre, it was dialogue scenes that dominated and these could be closely recreated by Hulki Saner and his team. Nevertheless, even in these dialogue scenes, the use of a trope characteristic of Turkish cinema, in which characters speak facing the camera rather than each other, lends the scenes a distinctive quality. This was partly a result of the conditions of production, as Nezih Erdoğan has noted:

> In trying to meet a demand for 200 films a year, production practices had to run at great speed . . . To save time and money, shot/reverse shot and other point of view shots were avoided as much as possible. This meant the domination of front shots: characters mostly performed facing the camera and did not turn their backs to it. (2003: 266)

The difference between a forty-seven minute television episode and a seventy-one minute film also necessitated some expansion and embellishment of the plot of 'The Man Trap'. Drawing from a variety of other *Star Trek* episodes, the filmmakers utilised iconic scenes from 'What Are the Little Girls Made of' through the addition of an army of androids controlled by Dr Crater; 'Arena' through the addition of an alien creature which fires at them from a rocky outcrop; 'I, Mudd' through the addition of female android servants; and finally 'Amok Time' through an evocation of the infamous battle between Kirk and Spock, in this case caused by the shape-shifter taking the form of Spock's long dead lover from Vulcan.

Throughout these narrative additions and stylistic deviations, however, the emphasis is still very much on recreating the world of *Star Trek*. Where the film moves from this imitative mode into something more parodic is through the insertion of the character Turist Ömer. As with the tradition established in his previous films, he acts as a 'fish out of water' offering jokes and witty asides at the expense of the strange and unfamiliar locales which he encounters. The fact that he is entering into this US TV show, and is poking fun at the world of *Star Trek*, suggests a level of engagement beyond that of simple imitation. This is most apparent in the relationships he develops with the other characters, and most specifically with Spock.

We are introduced to Ömer at a literal 'shotgun wedding' in Istanbul where he is being forced to marry a pregnant young girl. After praying to God to escape this fate, he finds himself transported onto an alien planet by the mysterious Dr Crater, and into the plot of 'The Man Trap'. He is then taken by two scantily clad robots to meet the Doctor and asks him, 'Where is this strange place? Is it near Kasimpasa [a district in Istanbul]?'. Crater, a little bewildered by this question, tries to explain, 'It is 3 million light years from Kasimpasa'. Ömer, still not understanding the situation, asks again, 'So are we close to Taksim [again in Istanbul]?'. As this sequence continues, Dr Crater becomes increasingly bemused by Ömer's questions and simply gives up trying to explain. This early exchange illustrates a theme running through the film in which Ömer's use of local reference points clashes with the interstellar world in which he finds himself.

Significantly, it is his use of urban slang from Istanbul and constant use of local reference points that causes friction with the crew of the Starship *Enterprise*. After the plot of 'The Man Trap' is underway, and the shape-shifter Nancy starts killing off members of the *Enterprise*, Ömer is brought onto the ship for questioning. Since he is initially thought to be a representative of an underdeveloped 'alien' race, Dr McCoy takes him into the medical bay to do some scientific tests. After declaring that he hardly has

Figure 2.4 Ömer joking with Spock in *Turist Ömer Uzay Yolunda*

a brain, the crew conclude that he could not be the mysterious murderer, with Spock concurring, 'He doesn't have the attributes of a monster. There are no monsters that stupid!'

Part of the reason for this dismissal is that Ömer is constantly making fun of the order and the rationalism of the crew, bringing anarchic comedy through his observations and interactions. This is most clearly present in his relationship with Spock who, even in the original series, came to represent logic and rationality in the face of the illogic of the human race. Constantly joking with Spock, whom he terms Kabakulak (literally, 'rude ear'), Ömer repeatedly distracts him from his investigation and upsets his sense of rational order, as we can see in Figure 2.4. This is exemplified by a running joke in which Ömer often goes to shake Spock's hand, but then pulls it away using the slang expression 'zit yazaneye gel' – a meaningless slang expression of disdain – taunting Spock's sense of rationality and decorum, and leading him to declare to Kirk, 'You see Captain, it is an illogical creature'. Later, in an exchange that further heightens the tensions underlying this relationship, Spock attempts to explain to Ömer why he is having problems understanding him, 'On my planet, rationality is every-thing, logic comes first'. Ömer replies, 'Well, don't forget, on my planet, food comes first. Zit!', again playing on his irrational need to upset Spock. Indeed, when Spock attempts to ask the computer what this 'zit' phrase means, the computer proceeds to cackle to itself manically, explaining that it cannot answer this strange request. As Savas Arslan has argued, Ömer's presence on board not only leads to many changes to the original episode, it also frames Ömer as an 'Eastern character "beyond reason"' (2011: 174).

While this could be read as simply reinforcing Orientalist (and indeed Occidentalist) stereotypes, it is important to recognise that this relationship draws on traditional forms of comedy in Turkey, most specifically the shadow plays featuring Karagöz and Hacivat. Derived from the shadow puppet theatre of China, Indonesia and Egypt, the Turkish karagöz plays were developed in the late sixteenth century and centred on two friends: the rowdy, tactless, ill-educated Karagöz and the more refined, educated Hacivat. Identified as a member of the lower classes, Karagöz would use his wit and tenacity to outdo Hacivat at every turn. As James Smith has argued, although 'Karagöz is not an entirely flattering reflection', his 'power to rule over upper-class characters like Hacivat gave the audience a sense of power' (2004: 190). The Turist Ömer series fits within this tradition, focusing on a male comic character who is from the lower classes, and showing how he is able to overcome the difficulties of his situation through wit and tenacity. In this light, Ömer's playful jokes at the expense of Spock – the more logical and level-headed of the two – can be read as engaging in this popular tradition of comedy in Turkey, one in which this anarchic lower-class hero is able to poke fun at the world of the logical, well-educated Spock. Moreover, this is a relationship that takes on an extra resonance when we consider the national associations which underpin this relationship between Ömer and Spock.

By the end of the film, the roles are somewhat reversed, and Spock, who has always been serious and rather staid throughout, jokingly pulls away his arm after Ömer attempts to shake it, exclaiming 'Zit' and playing off the earlier scenes where Ömer did this to Spock. And when Ömer is transported back to the marriage ceremony in Istanbul, he remarks on finding that his ears have become pointed, 'Hey Mr Spock, you are a great guy. You've given me ears like yours!' before using the Vulcan nerve pinch to escape his captors and make his exit. Each has taken on characteristics of the 'other', with Spock now seeing the pleasures of a little irrationality, and Ömer now able to escape from his situation using his new-found Vulcan powers. These moments are quite literal illustrations of the processes of hybridisation I have been outlining, even if admittedly the hybrid could most accurately be described as Turkish/Vulcan rather than Turkish/American.

Ultimately, this is a narrative that deals with 'alien' cultures coming into contact, initially fearful and mistrustful but finally finding commonalities and exchanging traditions and ideas. This is reflected in the ways in which Spock and Ömer are initially antagonistic, but both come away having learnt from and borrowed elements from the other. This aspect takes on added significance in light of the ways that Ömer is positioned very much as the sole 'Turkish' character in the world of *Star Trek*. While everyone in the film speaks Turkish – hardly surprising since the film was produced by a Turkish production company, using Turkish actors, and aimed at the Turkish market – what is significant is that Turist Ömer is the only character acknowledged within the film to be 'Turkish'. In this way, he comes to evoke the position of the Turkish filmmaker coming into contact with *Star Trek*, appropriating some of the characteristics of the US media text and mixing these with styles and traditions from the local industry. As I have argued, this hybridised relationship is not one of resistant critique, much less an inauthentic imitation, but a playfully palimpsestuous adaptation that both engages with the US media entering the country at the time and asserts the agency of the Turkish film industry writing on top of it.

Şeytan (1974) / *The Exorcist*

In the Turkish-German documentary *Crossing the Bridge: The Sound of Istanbul* (Fatik Akin, 2005), the record label bosses Ahmet Uluğ and Cem Yegül comment on the interstitial status of Istanbul:

Cem Yegül: Istanbul is Asia and Europe. It's East and it's West.
Ahmet Uluğ: But actually that's an advantage. We try to be European, but at the same time we're open to the East. That's a part of us too. We're open to both sides.

The film goes on to illustrate this thesis with a focus on Istanbul's varied musical culture, which ranges from traditional Arabesque singers such as Orhan Gencebay through to contemporary acts, such as the rapper Ceza and the neo-psychedelic rock group Baba Zula. Exploring the ways in which Turkish musicians have borrowed and adapted elements of musical traditions as diverse as hip-hop, fusion and post-rock, *Crossing the Bridge* lays emphasis on the idea of Istanbul as a 'bridge' between Europe and Asia both geographically and culturally.

This idea of Turkey as a 'bridge' recurs throughout much of the academic writing on Turkish culture although in recent years a number of scholars have attempted to interrogate the tensions beneath this notion of a 'bridge' – focusing specifically on the tensions between secularism and Islamism within modern-day Turkey. While this is a hugely divisive topic – and one to which this chapter certainly could not do justice – it will prove useful as a background to my analysis of the film *Şeytan* (1974), an unofficial, unlicensed remake of *The Exorcist* (1973), in which I pay specific attention to the ways in which this remake replaces the prevailing Catholic iconography with that of Islam. Reading the film through the ways in which elements are translated for the Turkish cultural context,

I will illustrate how this remake of *The Exorcist* offers us an important insight into the cultural changes that were happening at the particular socio-historic moment in which it was produced.

There have been some important developments in remake theory in recent years (for example, Mazdon 2000; Verevis 2005) that have attempted to move beyond reductive value judgements and stale conceptions of textual fidelity to analyse remakes through the 'material, historical and political conditions which surround and penetrate the moment of production and subsequent moment(s) of reception' (Mazdon 2000: 26). Utilising this approach, I will first interrogate the status of Turkey within contemporary political debates, critically examining the debates around Turkey as a country bridging East and West. Secondly, I will then outline some of the recent work on Turkish cinema of the 1970s and 1980s which attempts to identify tensions between the centralised Kemalist programme of secularism and the rising Islamist sentiment in this period. Thirdly, I will offer a close textual analysis of *Şeytan* which attends to the ways in which this remake transforms elements of *The Exorcist* and the contextual factors that shaped these changes. Finally, the chapter proposes an understanding of this film which lays emphasis on the potential for subtle forms of political commentary being evoked through transnational adaptation.

To help to situate this analysis, I will first turn to one of the major political debates of the past two decades. Following the collapse of Marxist-Leninism and the end of the Cold War, Samuel P. Huntington famously predicted a 'clash of civilisations' between 'Islam' and 'the West' (1993). According to this model of international affairs, the fall of the Berlin Wall signalled the end of the mutually supportive security ties between the US and Muslim states, and a subsequent shift in power within many Muslim countries towards more anti-Western political parties. Without the common enemy of the Communist USSR, previous alliances would gradually fall away and international conflict would become less about ideology or economics and more about opposing cultures and civilisations.

As Edward Said later argued, such a model of transnational relations is fundamentally reductive and incomplete. Huntington's thesis centres on the interactions of eight major civilisations, of which 'the West' and 'Islam' take up the structuring opposition. Such a model reduces the dynamics and plurality of these civilisations to essentialised blocs, which, as Said argues, paints the world, 'as if hugely complicated matters like identity and culture existed in a cartoonlike world where Popeye and Bluto bash each other mercilessly' (2001: 1). Significantly, when Huntington deals with Turkey's position in this global model, he attempts to undermine the prevalent model of Turkey as a cultural bridge, painting it instead as a 'torn' country:

> Turkish leaders regularly described their country as a 'bridge' between cultures. Turkey, Prime Minister Tansu Çiller argued in 1993, is both a 'Western democracy' and 'part of the Middle East' and 'bridges two civilisations, physically and philosophically' . . . A bridge, however, is an artificial creation connecting two solid entities but is part of neither. When Turkey's leaders term their country a bridge, they euphemistically confirm that it is torn. (1998: 149)

Huntington's model relies on a binary opposition being made between East and West, Asia and Europe, refusing to acknowledge the dynamic interdependency and heterogeneity of these cultural blocs. Stretching his thesis to fit a country that pointedly refuses to fit such a binary, Huntington falls back on an empty rhetorical flourish rather than addressing the fundamental difficulties such a model faces when discussing a nation such as Turkey. This is a country that is both Muslim and secular; a country that is both European and Asian. Istanbul, the only metropolis in the world that straddles two continents, has at one time served as the capital city of the Roman Empire (330–95 CE), the Byzantine Empire (395–1204 and 1261–1453 CE), the Latin Empire (1204–61 CE), and the Ottoman Empire (1453–1922 CE), its cityscape extending on both the European side (Thrace) and the Asian side (Anatolia) of the Bosphorus Strait. Designating Turkey as a 'torn country' presents the world in terms of monolithic blocks far removed from the dynamic interactions of culture that such a history indicates. Moreover, it is worth noting that the Ottoman Empire was itself very much part of Europe and European history, as well as Asian/Middle Eastern history, in both a geographical sense (at its zenith, the Empire reached to the 'doors' of Vienna) and a more metaphorical sense (the values of 'Christian' Western Europe were partly constructed in opposition to their Ottoman 'other' in the East).

As I argued earlier, when Mustafa Kemal Atatürk came to power and founded the Turkish Republic in 1923, he instituted Westernising reforms aiming to break away from the Ottoman legacy and to orientate Turkey decidedly towards Europe. Most controversial of all Atatürk's reforms were those related to secularism, including the abolishment of the caliphate – the supreme political office of Islam worldwide – the disestablishment of the state religion and the removal of all Islamic practices from public life. Underlying this was a sense of Turkish nationalism and a desire for Turkey to reject its Ottoman history and become a new 'nation-state'. As Nezih Erdoğan and Deniz Göktürk note,

After the founding of the Republic in 1923, a nationalist discourse that had already been gaining power in the final years of the Ottoman Empire was disseminated directly by the state, aiming to legitimise a transition from ummet (from umma, meaning the Islamic community or population) to millet (from mille, meaning nation). (2001: 534)

With the traditional association between state and religion having been dissolved, the nation-state became an instrument in what Nizayi Berkes calls 'the real aim of the Turkish transformation' (Berkes 1997: 510): modernisation and economic development. Of course, we should not neglect that this embrace of secularism in the name of modernisation was itself heavily politically charged. As cultural anthropologist Yael Navaro-Yashin argues in *Faces of the State: Secularism and Public Life in Turkey*, 'Secularism is not a neutral paradigm, but a state ideology as well as a hegemonic public discourse in contemporary Turkey' (2002: 6).

Within studies of Yeşilçam cinema, a number of scholars have attempted to tease out the ways in which these underlying tensions are reflected in the films that were produced in the country. Most famously, Kevin Robins and Asu Aksoy argue that the 'deep nation' – the Turkish form of nation-building which involved an idealisation of collectivity – was gradually unravelled throughout the secularist/Islamist conflict in late twentieth-century Turkey, and that the story of Turkish cinema 'can be told in terms of the progressive disordering of the ideal of the Kemalist nation' (2000: 215). Within their article, they then go on to identify the various ways in which the popular cinema of the period reflects this disordering through reflections of 'traditional, usually folk-Islamic, values' (209) far away from the Republican ideal of the nation.

As Deniz Kandiyoti has argued, this is a 'frozen mammoth' approach to cultural production in which items of popular culture are treated as 'eruptions of the marginal and the repressed into the realm of cultural expression' (2002: 10). While a number of scholars have identified the ways in which the Kemalist reform programmes were seen to remove Islam from public life, Robins and Aksoy's analysis of Turkish cinema lays emphasis on the ways in which popular Islamic forms of cultural expression slowly re-emerge in the 1970s and 1980s. In the context of these cultural shifts, I will now turn to the film *Şeytan*, a Turkish remake of the US horror feature *The Exorcist*, and a film that was produced during this time of rising Islamic consciousness.

Şeytan marked a collaboration between two of the key figures in Turkish cinema history: producer Hulki Saner and director Metin Erksan. Saner, one of the most successful and prolific filmmakers in Turkey, began the project after seeing that *The Exorcist* was courting media attention and inciting controversy around the world. At a time when censorship of US films was still commonplace – *The Exorcist* was not to be officially released in Turkey until 1982 – Saner decided to capitalise on this public interest by producing a Turkish version of the film for the domestic audience. Indeed, Saner, who had previously achieved success with both the *Turist Ömer* and *Ayşecik* series, resolved to make this a prestige project, hiring acclaimed director Metin Erksan to helm the film and giving him a relatively large budget for a Yeşilçam production.

Erksan himself was already a celebrated filmmaker, one of the figureheads of the social realist movement in the 1960s, and winner of the Golden Bear at the 1964 Berlin Film Festival for the film *Susuz Yaz* (Dry Summer, 1964). While he is generally seen to have gradually abandoned the social outlook of his earlier works, moving towards a more 'popular' mode of film production, Erksan was a filmmaker of considerable weight and stature to bring to this Yeşilçam project. While it would be easy to position this remake as an unoriginal copy of the prior film, this study will follow Lucy Mazdon's work on remakes, looking less at questions of 'origins' and 'authenticity' and more at the intertextual dynamics that underpin this exchange. As Mazdon argues,

> Rather than a search for origins (the linear causality of the relationship between the 'original' and the 'copy') a study of this kind involves a description of exchange and difference; the unbroken vertical axis which leads from the 'original' text to the remake as 'copy' is replaced by the circles of intertextuality and hybridity. (2000: 27)

Furthermore, the prevailing critical mood to condemn remakes for their supposed lack of originality neglects the ways in which elements are appropriated and transformed within a particular socio-cultural context. To explore this issue further, I will now discuss the ways in which cinematic censorship operated within Turkey and relate this to the discussion in hand. As Nezih Erdoğan has argued, 'Censorship in Turkey has been a matter of policing from the very beginning and it has been one of the major ways in which the state has intervened in the distribution and exhibition of films' (Erdoğan and Kaya 2002: 53).

The central law governing censorship within Turkey was established in 1934 – the Regulation about the Control of Films and Film Screenplays – and was executed with minor revisions until 1977. Of course, as Chris Hellier has argued, 'political limits are still being imposed on Turkish filmmakers and, despite the lifting of many restrictions since Turkey's return to civilian government in 1983, there are Turkish films which cannot be shown in the country' (1997: 123). The original law focused on ten criteria which a film should avoid:

1. the political propaganda of a state
2. degrading an ethnic community or race
3. hurting the sentiments of fellow states and nations
4. propagating religion
5. propagating political, economic and social ideologies which contradict the national regime
6. contradicting our national and moral values
7. opposing the military forces and reducing the dignity and honour of the military forces
8. being harmful to the discipline and security of the country
9. provoking crime
10. attacking the state. (Erdoğan and Kaya 2002: 54)

Most interesting here is the fourth criteria which said that a film could be banned for 'propagating religion'. As a consequence, the majority of Turkish films that dealt with religion were not explicitly celebratory or propagandist but instead cloaked their politics within more subtly allegorical tales. It is my contention that the adaptation of *The Exorcist* allowed for a subtle form of political commentary on the status of Islam within Turkey which may have run into trouble had it been approached directly.

Şeytan, as in *The Exorcist*, opens on an archaeological expedition in the Middle East where an elderly man discovers various historical artefacts signifying the devil. We then cut to a domestic scene featuring Ayten (Meral Taygun) and her twelve-year-old daughter Gul (Canan Perver). During the subsequent scenes, the theme from *The Exorcist* (Mike Oldfield's 'Tubular Bells') is repeatedly used to set tone and suspense. Until this point, the film is a close recreation of the plot and characters of *The Exorcist*. Significantly, however, the replacement of Father Karros with the secular writer Tugrul Bilge (Cihan Unal) represents an important moment of translation. Bilge is a journalist who is researching the ancient notion of demonic possession from the perspective of mental health. The film offers a prolonged close-up of the cover of his book, *Satan: The Case of Demon Possession and the Rite of Exorcism in Universal Religions under the Light of Modern Perspectives on Mental Diseases*, serving both to introduce the audience to the notion of exorcism while avoiding the problem of having a central character who is questioning his faith.

As we can see in Figures 2.5 and 2.6, the adaptation from Catholicism to Islam further necessitated a number of iconographic alterations. The moment from *The Exorcist* in which Regan defiles herself using the cross is adapted with the use of a Jinn-shaped paper knife (Figure 2.5). In the exorcism ceremony itself, instead of using Christian holy water, the Imam

Figure 2.5 Gul defiling herself with a Jinn-headed knife in *Şeytan* (dir. Metin Erksan, Turkey, 1974)

Figure 2.6 Imam using the Quran to exorcise Gul in *Şeytan*

uses water from the holy well of Zemzem, and reads from the Quran rather than the Bible (Figure 2.6). Significantly, however, these are not simply cosmetic changes but subtly impact the development of the narrative. Most importantly, it is the ending of the film that exhibits the most significant alteration. Rather than ending with the death of Father Karros, as in *The Exorcist*, *Şeytan* adds an extra scene in which Gul and her mother visit a Mosque. In these few moments, Gul spends some reflective time with an Imam while the camera pans the interiors of the mosque, reconfirming the renewal of Islam in these characters' lives. Going beyond the bleak, harrowing ending suggested in *The Exorcist*, *Şeytan* offers a more redemptive conclusion laying emphasis on the religious overtones of the narrative. It is this moment that is the most significant change as the film is explicitly affirming the restoration of community and family through the embrace of religion.

By adapting *The Exorcist* for an Islamic context, the film replaces the notion of possession by the fallen angel Satan with the notion of the Jinn and the spirit Iblis. These changes are evident in the exorcism scene itself:

> Imam: Allah, I find shelter in your holy name. I praise your greatness. Your boundless power will end this torture made by the creature you created from the fires to the one you created from the clay . . . Banish this cruel Iblis from the soul of this innocent servant.

Such expository dialogue points to the emphasis the film lays on explaining the nature of exorcism to the audience, a concept not 'incompatible' but certainly unfamiliar in contemporary Turkish culture. Significantly, at the start of the narrative, neither Father Karros in *The Exorcist* nor Tugrul Bilge in *Şeytan* believes in 'exorcisms', and they attempt to explain away their respective lead girl's troubles in terms of modern, scientific understandings of mental illness rather than seeing it in terms of 'possession' per se. This scepticism about religious dogma forms the core theme of both *The Exorcist* and *Şeytan*, in that the various scientific methods for explaining the girl's illness, which include psychotherapy, shock therapy and a lumbar puncture, fail to clarify what happened to Gul. The key revelation in each character's narrative trajectory is that scientific rationale cannot explain all that happens in the world and that there is a need for a return to religion. Both *The Exorcist* and *Şeytan* deal with the perceived failings of scientific rationalism and propose the continued relevance of religion in the modern world. As William Friedkin states in his introduction to *The Exorcist* DVD,

> *The Exorcist* is a film about the mystery of faith . . . It's a story that can perhaps make you question your own value system. It strongly and realistically tries to make the case for spiritual forces in the universe, both good and evil. (1999)

What is significant is that such an argument had especial resonance in Turkey in the mid-1970s, with *Şeytan* produced at a time when the Kemalist embrace of Western conceptions of modernisation and rationalism was being questioned and Islam was again coming to the fore in Turkish political life. The reforms of Atatürk centred on taking Islam out of public life and moving Turkey towards a more European model of a rationalist, secular culture. To produce a film, then, which highlights the failings of this rationalist, secular discourse, and explicitly celebrates Islam for being able to defeat the 'evil' forces in the world, should be read as an attempt to reconfirm the importance and validity of Islam in the modern world. As Kaya Özkaracalar observes, 'this is by no means a cosmetic issue for Turkey, but on the contrary, one of the major causes of social unrest in this country' (2003: 214).

Moreover, as Savas Arslan notes in his article 'Projecting a Bridge for Youth: Islamic 'Enlightenment' versus Westernisation in Turkish cinema', there were a number of films produced in the late 1980s and early 1990s which more explicitly engaged with the 'enlightenment' of young people who choose to embrace tradition and Islam (2007: 161). Yet, what we find in *Şeytan* is an implicit commentary on the need for a renewed Islam in Turkish public life couched within a remake of *The Exorcist*. In such a way, this form of adaptation allows for a form of political commentary which could be disguised and allegorised in a period when such notions were still being censored by the classification board. It is a 'Turkification' of *The Exorcist* that restructures the imported text in order to affirm the relevance of Islam in contemporary secular Turkey, and offers an insight into the ways in which Hollywood texts were being reworked and put to use within Turkish cinema.

Dünyayı Kurtaran Adam (1982) / *Star Wars*

The fourth and final case study in my analysis is *Dünyayı Kurtaran Adam* (The Man Who Saved the World, 1982). Produced at the tail end of the Yeşilçam boom – leading Nezih Erdoğan to describe it as the 'last stand' of Yeşilçam cinema (2003: 167) – *Dünyayı Kurtaran Adam* may initially seem a strange choice in my analysis of transnational adaptation since the film is not itself a remake or a parody, nor does it use the plot or characters from any prior cultural texts. What it does do, however, is borrow footage from *Star Wars* (1977) along with music from various titles including *Raiders of the Lost Ark* (1981) and *Battlestar Galactica* (1978), and it then utilises these within an unrelated narrative. Through an analysis of the ways in which *Dünyayı Kurtaran Adam* makes use of these elements, I will interrogate what this case study can tell us about the politics of transnational adaptations more broadly.

In his work on convergence culture, Henry Jenkins has discussed the grassroots adaptations of *Star Wars* which surrounded the release of the digitally enhanced original *Star Wars* trilogy in 1997 and the subsequent release of *The Phantom Menace* in 1999. Focusing on fan films such as *Quentin Tarantino's Star Wars* (1998) and *Troops* (1998) which rework characters, situations and material from George Lucas's series, Jenkins argues that their appropriation of elements from the *Star Wars* universe illustrates a democratisation of the means of cultural production in which media fans are 'active participants within the current media revolution' (2003).

For Jenkins, the *Star Wars* fan films represent an intersection between two significant cultural trends: on the one hand, 'the corporate movement towards media convergence' and, on the other, 'the unleashing of significant new tools that enable the grassroots archiving, annotation, appropriation, and recirculation of media content' (2003: 283). What is significant, however, is that much of what Jenkins discusses in terms of a fan-made appropriative form of cinema which bypasses restrictive conceptions of trademark and copyright law is actually present in *Dünyayı Kurtaran Adam* almost twenty years earlier.

The film opens with a long monologue illustrated with stock footage which explains the background to a war that humanity is fighting against an alien race. We are then introduced to our two heroes – Murat (Cuneyt Arkin) and Ali (Aytekin Akkaya) – who are battling the aliens in their space craft. What is significant is that the filmmakers do not create any special-effects footage to illustrate 'outer space' but instead use clips of *Star Wars* which are then back-projected behind the actors, as we can see in Figure 2.7. The scene then cuts between excerpts from *Star Wars* and these images of the actors with the footage projected behind them. During the sequence, the filmmakers also utilise the theme music from *Raiders of the Lost Ark* which had been released the previous year.

As the narrative progresses, our two heroes lose control of their ships and crash onto a nearby planet which is ruled by 'The Wizard'. What follows is a series of battles with The Wizard's henchmen which leads up to a final sequence in which Murat is able to utilise a 'magic' sword to

Figure 2.7 A *Star Wars* X-Wing behind Murat in *Dünyayı Kurtaran Adam* (dir. Çetin İnanç, Turkey, 1982)

eventually defeat The Wizard and free the natives left on the planet. While the film makes a number of interesting allusions to the threat of nuclear war and the need for peace, these are not particularly relevant to the analysis in hand as there is no explicit Hollywood text being used as a source for this material. Instead, what is significant about *Dünyayı Kurtaran Adam* is that this film contains the most explicit use of copyrighted material of all the adaptations I have studied; this is primarily because the filmmakers were not 'recreating' elements but actually physically using the footage and music from the prior films.

As we can see in the following quote, director Çetin İnanc explains this away as being primarily a budgetary consideration:

> A strong wind swept away the spacecrafts we had erected for the film. We couldn't afford to re-build them. We had to make changes in the script. The guys can reconstruct space and everything in their studios . . . Since our budget fell short, we had to use footage from foreign films. (As quoted in Kara 1996: 7)

Yet, in his article, 'Powerless Signs: Hybridity and the Logic of Excess of Turkish Trash', Nezih Erdoğan has argued that the use of *Star Wars* footage is so obvious and transparent in the film that it goes beyond plagiarism and begins to signify something else. By recontextualising the footage into an alternative narrative, Erdoğan argues, the images become imbued with different meanings which reflect the different context of production (2003: 169). Indeed, *Star Wars* was a significant success when it was released in Turkey in the late 1970s so it would not have been difficult for the Turkish audience to recognise where the footage had come from. For Erdoğan, the sequence used in the context of *Star Wars* makes the statement, 'Here is a spacecraft chasing the enemy', but in the case of *Dünyayı Kurtaran Adam* it becomes 'I am a scene taken from a Hollywood science-fiction film which shows a dogfight scene' (ibid.). The effect therefore is a form of double-articulation which takes the viewer out of the interpolated viewing position and potentially evokes what Erdoğan has elsewhere termed an 'unintentional Brechtian alienation effect' (1998: 266) brought about by this kind of juxtaposition.

Moreover, this effect is especially significant in terms of the cult audience that the film has subsequently built up within Turkey. There is much in the film that provokes ironic laughter, including the various logical fallacies, the poor-quality special effects and props (see Figure 2.8), the lack of verisimilitude and the incoherent narrative drive. Yet, as Erdoğan has argued, this is 'an uneasy laughter which also contains pity for the failed challenge of Yeşilçam against Hollywood' (2003: 168). This bears comparison to Joao Luiz Vieira's work on parodies in Brazilian

Figure 2.8 Murat with his lightning bolt sword in *Dünyayı Kurtaran Adam*

cinema – discussed in Chapter 1 – in which he argues that the Brazilian filmmakers try to imitate the technological illusionism of American cinema but ultimately simply provoke laughter at their own expense (Vieira 1995). Perhaps, however, there is a more positive interpretation of this form of appropriative reworking that can help to shed light on this particular mode of filmmaking.

In Henry Jenkins's discussion of fan films, he notes the ways in which theorists of third world cinema have 'described those films as an "imperfect cinema"' (2003: 299) which cannot compete with Hollywood in terms of budget or high-tech production facilities but instead make 'a virtue out of their limitations, often spoofing or parodying Hollywood genre conventions and stylistic norms through films that are intentionally crude or ragged in style' (ibid.). While in the context of third world cinema, this has been read as the basis for an implicit critique of the ideologies and market forces behind the Hollywood blockbuster, Jenkins identifies a much less radical intent in the fan filmmakers who instead 'turned toward parody as the most effective genre for negotiating between these competing desires to reproduce, not to destroy, the special effects at the heart of the contemporary blockbuster and to acknowledge their own amateur status' (2003: 300).

This ties in much more closely with the use of footage from *Star Wars* utilised in *Dünyayı Kurtaran Adam*, which is less of a resistant critique of the Hollywood film but rather an opportunistic attempt to appropriate the special-effects sequences from the film. This is partially explained by the low-budget mode of production in Turkey which could not afford the necessary expenditure to produce those effects sequences itself. This was a period in which films were often being rushed through the production process as quickly and cheaply as possible. It would have been impossible within that production context to reproduce a similar standard of special effects, so the filmmakers simply appropriated existing material and used that instead. Moreover, this film is especially significant in terms of the shifts in copyright law between the film's production and the release of its sequel *Dünyayi Kurtaran Adam'in Oglu* (Son of the Man Who Saved the World, 2006). By outlining the ways in which copyright law shaped the strategies of adaptation in each film, I will now show how recent changes in copyright law have ensured that the Turkish film industry would not have been able today to produce a film that appropriated material to the extent of *Dünyayı Kurtaran Adam*.

It should first be noted, however, that *Star Wars* is notorious for being one of the most tightly regulated corporate franchises in the world. As Jenkins has argued,

> The careful licensing of the *Star Wars* iconography enabled Lucasfilm to form stra-
> tegic alliances with a multitude of corporate partners, including fast food franchises
> and soft drink bottlers, which sought to both exploit and enlarge public interest in
> their forthcoming release. (2003: 285)

In an attempt to minimise the risk of diluting their trademark and copyright holdings, Lucasfilm became notorious in the 1980s and 1990s for issuing legal notices and warnings to fans who had published sexually explicit stories featuring *Star Wars* characters and used material from *Star Wars* in their fan-made films. The question then arises: why was *Dünyayı Kurtaran Adam* not sued for utilising footage and music from *Star Wars* in a much more blatant manner than the fan-produced material which I have outlined? The answer to this question lies in two significant and interrelated contextual factors within the Turkish film industry: the lack of enforcement of international copyright provisions until the mid- to late 1980s, and the primarily domestic market for distribution of Turkish Yeşilçam cinema.

As Temal Nal notes in "Developments in Turkish Copyright Law', the Act on Intellectual and Artistic Works which offered the dominant conception of copyright law within Turkey, came into effect on 1 January 1952 and essentially corresponded to the standards of the Berne Convention. This meant that local copyright protections were extended to works by nationals from all Berne signatories. Nevertheless, these provisions were rarely used in Turkish courts and there was not a specific law to tackle piracy until the Act on Film, Video and Musical Works was passed on 23 January 1986, which required authors to file and register their works in order that they would be protected.

So when *Dünyayi Kurtaran Adam* was produced in 1982 there was little incentive for the filmmakers to request permission to use the footage as they were unlikely to be sued in Turkish courts. Furthermore, because the film was only to be distributed within Turkey, they were also unlikely to be sued in other international forums. While pressure on Turkey to amend its copyright regulations had increased by the late 1980s, it was not until amendments to the 1951 copyright law (Law No. 5846) were enacted in 2001 that Turkey's copyright regime became much closer to the standards set by international treaties and they implemented much of the requirements of the WIPO copyright treaty. This has meant that the sequel *Dünyayi Kurtaran Adam'in Oglu* (Son of the Man Who Saved the World, 2006) does not reproduce any sequences from other films and instead pays homage to other films in a manner more in keeping with prevailing international conceptions of intellectual property law.

As Pete Tombs has argued, *Dünyayi Kurtaran Adam* 'was the swan-song of low-budget Turkish cinema' (1998: 115) with the economic crises of the early 1980s, the rise of television, a concomitant rise in soft-porn cinema, and the various changes in legislation enacted by president Turgat Ozal (1983–93) all contributing towards an industry collapse that meant that most of the production houses centred around Yeşilçam Street in Istanbul had to close down. While popular Turkish cinema has had something of a resurgence with home-grown titles like *G.O.R.A.* (2004) and *Kurltar Vadisi: Irak* (2006) having significant box-office success, we should note that the industry has now changed to such an extent that it is highly unlikely that we will again see the production of films that utilise appropriated material to the extent that we saw in the four films under analysis.

Conclusion

As I have argued in this chapter, these narratives can productively be read through the lens of critical transculturalism. By showing how each of these case studies has reconfigured and recontextualised material from its source texts, I have drawn attention to the ways in which these borrowings mediate the socio-historic periods in which they were produced, and investigated the specific ways in which the industrial conditions of Yeşilçam helped to shape their various forms of transnational adaptation.

Within *3 Dev Adam* (1973), we saw how the borrowing of the characters Captain America, Santo the wrestler and Spider-Man helped draw attention to a relatively generic crime film within an economic market that did not allow for large marketing budgets or expensive promotion strategies.

This primarily commercial impetus lies in contrast to the more explicitly parodic adaptation of *Turist Ömer Uzay Yolunda* (1974) which inserted the character *Turist Ömer* into the world of *Star Trek* and offered a playful engagement with the US media entering the country at the time. Thirdly, I examined the religious politics of *Şeytan* (1974) which translated elements from *The Exorcist* into a different religious context in order to offer a form of political commentary that could be disguised and allegorised in a period when such notions were still being censored by the classification board. Fourthly, and finally, I analysed the use of footage from *Star Wars* in *Dünyayi Kurtaran Adam* (1982) to show how this direct appropriation of special-effects sequences functioned less as a resistant critique than as an opportunistic reworking of available resources to make up for budgetary limitations.

In the following chapter, I will address the forms of transnational adaptation that flourished in the popular film industry of the Philippines between 1978 and 1994. By closely interrogating how these transnational adaptations relate to their specific contexts of production, this will offer a useful comparison to the ways in which material was reworked within Turkey, and take us closer towards a broader understanding of the cultural politics of borrowing material transnationally and the underlying determinant factors that help to shape specific modes of transnational adaptation.

CHAPTER 3

Hollywood and the Popular Cinema
of the Philippines

> Before most Filipinos become aware of Filipino literature, song, dance, history, education and language, the media have already made them alert to American life and culture and its desirability. They sing of White Christmases and of Manhattan. Their stereos reverberate with the American Top 40. In their minds sparkle images of *Dynasty*, *Miami Vice* and *LA Law*.
>
> Doreen Fernandez (as quoted in Lockard 1998: 128)

> The Philippines is not just the site of the largest US military installations in the world. It is also perhaps the world's largest slice of the American Empire, in its purest impurest form.
>
> Pico Iyer (1988: 181)

> Reading too much westernisation into the obvious influences from outside can mislead observers. While many institutions have indeed been inherited from the colonial past, their superficial resemblance to foreign models has usually masked the subtle processes in which they have been domesticated into a unique social fabric.
>
> Craig Lockard (1998: 121)

In 2007, there were two widely publicised intersections between US and Philippine popular culture that can be seen as indicative of wider trends within the transnational relationship between these two nations. First, in mid-July, a video of 1,600 inmates from the Cebu Provincial Detention and Rehabilitation Centre (CPDRC) was posted on YouTube, in which they performed a synchronised dance routine to the Michael Jackson track 'Thriller'. The video became a hugely popular viral success, with over 56 million views to date, and triggered media coverage around the world including articles in *Time* magazine, *Rolling Stone* and *The Washington Post* and a Channel 4 documentary entitled 'Murderers on the Dancefloor'.

The video recreated the dance routine from the music video for *Thriller* with inmate Crisanto Nierre taking the Michael Jackson role and Wenjiel Resane playing Michael Jackson's girlfriend as the other inmates took on the role of the zombie dancers. Part of security consultant Byron Garcia's programme of daily exercise for the CPDRC inmates, this choreographed dance routine was later followed by performances of 'You Can't Touch This' by M. C. Hammer, 'Radio Ga Ga' by Queen, and 'Crank That' by Soulja Boy.

Later in the year, on 5 December, the Filipino singer-songwriter Arnel Pineda was plucked from relative obscurity to become the new singer for the US rock band Journey. Invited to audition for the band after guitarist Neal Schon saw him perform note-perfect renditions of Journey hits on YouTube, Pineda was swiftly flown in from Quezon City to become the lead singer in the band. While he was later acclaimed for his vocal prowess, there were many at the time who criticised his singing style as simply an 'imitation' of the original Journey singer Steve Perry. As Pasckie Pascua notes,

> While the unknown singer's fairytale story fuses inspirational sparks to dreamers all over the globe, many also believe that his 'exact copy' of Perry's vocal charm could be his downfall. Pineda will always be the Filipino who sounded like Journey's Steve Perry. (2008)

Illustrating the ways in which new media technologies are impacting upon transnational cultural flows, both of these episodes point to what has been termed the 'gaya-gaya' syndrome in Filipino culture. Described by the cultural critic and academic Nicanor Tiongson as a trend towards imitation (2001b), this phenomenon is particularly evident in the popular film industry of the Philippines. As Tiongson explains, 'Unable to compete with Hollywood, many Filipino producers or artists have tried to cash in on Hollywood, accepting it as the trend-setter, standard and premise of their own productions' (2001b: 19). This attitude, Tiongson argues, has led to a plethora of localised versions of Hollywood blockbusters which borrow 'plot lines, characters, situations and sometimes even camera angles and movements for their own cinematic take-offs' (2001b: 19).

In this chapter, I will employ my comparative model of transnational adaptation to analyse the specific ways in which popular films produced in the Philippines have adapted and transformed elements borrowed from American popular culture. I will focus my analysis on titles produced during and subsequent to the dictatorship of Ferdinand Marcos (1972–86), a period in which the cinema of the Philippines began to reach out to an international audience both through the development of new institutions such as the Film Academy of the Philippines and through an influx of foreign investment and co-production initiatives. Specifically, I will examine the years subsequent to the Lumauig Bill in 1978 (Parliamentary Bill No. 85) which was one of the major developments in the cultivation of a popular film industry in the Philippines.

As with my case study on Turkish cinema, the cinema of the Philippines is a national cinema that has rarely been tackled in English language criticism so this will initially necessitate a brief historical account of the development of the film industry there. Paying close attention to the ways in which governmental policy and regulation have impacted upon industrial development, this account will attend to the considerable tensions and debates surrounding the notion of a 'popular' film industry in the Philippines. Furthermore, as Nick Deocampo has argued in his book *Cine: Spanish Influences on Early Cinema in the Philippines*, the history of Philippine cinema is very much bound up with the history of colonialism in the country and, while cinema was introduced by the Spanish in 1897, the subsequent transition to the American period saw a 'tension between Spanish and American influences battling over the control of cinema' which came to be seen as emblematic of the larger social tension '*hispanismo* vs *anglo-sajonismo*' (2003: xiv).

Taking these factors into account, I will utilise my comparative model to analyse four specific examples of transnational adaptation within Philippine popular cinema. First, I will consider *Dynamite Johnson* (1978), also known as 'The Return of the Bionic Boy'. Combining elements from various antecedent texts including *The Six Million Dollar Man*, *The Big Boss* and *Dr No*, this was a film – unlike those I discussed in the previous chapter – that was produced primarily for export rather than domestic distribution, and this has shaped the ways in which it makes use of borrowed material. This is also true of my second case study, *For Y'ur Height Only* (1981), a US-Philippines co-production that playfully spoofs both the Bond franchise and the Philippine spy films which followed. I will then move onto films produced primarily for the domestic market with an analysis of *Alyas Batman en Robin* (Alias Batman and Robin, 1993), a film that features the comedy duo Joey and Keempee De Leon as Batman and Robin in a musical pastiche of the US television series *Batman* (1966–8). I will then close this section with *Darna: Ang Pagbabalik* (Darna: The Return, 1994), a film adaptation of the hugely popular 'komiks' series featuring a character dubbed 'The Filipino Wonder Woman'.

Developing the comparative aspects of my broader project, the chapter will utilise my model of transnational adaptation to interrogate how each of these texts specifically reconfigures and recontextualises its source texts. While there are indeed many similarities between the Turkish and Philippine film industries, there are also some significant differences which have helped to mould the particularity of these cultural borrowings. This raises some pertinent questions: how does the country's colonial history affect the modes of appropriation utilised? What is the impact of co-production strategies? How significant is the level of penetration that the American cultural object has achieved in the country? How do films produced primarily for export differ from those produced for the domestic market? In tackling these questions, this chapter will mark out tendencies within the Philippine popular film industry that will offer a useful comparison with my other case studies and will move us closer towards a broader understanding of the cultural politics of borrowing material transnationally and the underlying determinants that help to shape specific modes of transnational adaptation.

Films for the 'Bakya' Crowds

> The hybridity of Philippine cinema is more than just a strategy for economic survival; it is also, in many ways, the result of the complex cultural practices that attend a postcolonial people's mode of existence. In the dizzying mix of permutations, juxtapositions, and combinations that attend the hybridity of Philippine cinema, one discerns the larger patterns of cultural negotiation that operate within its system.
>
> Jose B. Capino (2006: 36)

There is a long history of transnational borrowings between the US and the Philippines, a tradition that is very much tied up with their colonial past. As indicated in the popular saying in which the Philippines is said to have spent '350 years in the convent and 50 years in Hollywood' (Kenny 1995), the transnational impact of American popular culture has a particular resonance for its former colony. This is coupled with the Spanish influences that according to historian Nick Deocampo 'still linger like a waft of breeze, a faint aroma, or a faded image' in the melodramatic forms and even the terminology used to discuss Philippine cinema. Indeed, all three words in the present-day Filipino vocabulary that refer to cinema are derived from Spanish: 'sine' (cine), 'pelikula' (pelicula) and 'sintas' (cintas) (Deocampo 2003: 224). This mixed socio-cultural heritage is what David Steinberg means when he refers to the Philippines as 'both singular and plural' (Steinberg as quoted in Lockard 1998: 115).

However, with the loss of all but four – *Tunay na Ina* (1930), *Zamboanga* (1936), *Giliw Ko* (1939) and *Pakiusap* (1940) – of the approximately 350 films produced before World War II, there is very little textual material available for a study of Philippine cinema in the years under Spanish and US control. As Bienvenido Lumbera has argued, 'this period has become a veritable pre-history of Philippine cinema' (1983: 67). Nevertheless, we do know from records that the Lumière cinematograph was first brought to Manila by Antonio Ramos in 1897, the final year of Spanish rule before control was transferred to the United States. By 1910, American production companies were shooting films on the islands and in 1917, the first Philippine film studio was born. Founded by two brothers, Jose and Jesus Nepomuceno, Malayan Motion Pictures initially focused on producing documentary footage – some of it to be used for newsreels in the US – and then moved into feature film production with *Dalagang Bukid* (A Girl from the Country, 1919), the first Philippine feature film. Based on a popular sarswela (a Spanish-derived form of drama that combines singing and dancing) and written by Hermogenes Ilagan and Leon Ignacio, the film established director Jose Nepomuceno as the first Filipino film director and earned him the title 'The Father of Philippine Movies' (Yeatter 2007: 14).

In this period, the form of production was artisanal and organised through small, often family-based, production companies. This began to change after the advent of synchronised sound in 1933 and the founding of the studio Filippin Films, which by 1938 was producing twenty films a year (Armes 1987: 152). Other production companies including Sampaguita Pictures, LVN and Salumbides Brothers were also founded at this time with the overall national output rising to approximately fifty to sixty films per year. While production was stopped during the Japanese occupation in 1942–5, the immediate postwar period is now considered something of a golden age of Philippine cinema with the early work of Lamberto Avellana, Eddie Romero and Gerardo de Leon earning significant plaudits.

During the 1950s, the local industry was dominated by the studios Sampaguita, Premiere, LVN and Lebran. At the start of the decade, they controlled approximately 90 per cent of Philippine production, distribution and exhibition (Tombs 1998: 50). However, as the decade progressed, a host of smaller production companies were established which began to produce films with much lower budgets and 'quickie' production methods. As director Lamberto Avellana recounts, 'a story is written in two days, shot in eleven and makes money at five days' exhibition, so we make another just like it' (as quoted in Lent 1990: 157). Making films on this basis, it was important to recover production costs quickly so that another picture could be started quickly. According to Bienvenido Lumbera, this encouraged a trend towards 'exploitation' style genre pictures in which 'film companies found it to their advantage to ride on whatever was the audience-drawing trend' (1983: 74). This ranged from secret agent films drawing on the popularity of the James Bond series, such as Tony Ferrer's *Agent X-44* series, through to the popular 'bomba' or 'sexy' film, a form of softcore sex film which came to prominence in the 1960s. This was also the period in which the studios 'tried to outdo one another in developing a new genre, the war/guerrilla film which invariably glorified the underground struggle against the Japanese and celebrated Filipino–American friendship' (1983: 70). These films, such as the Eddie Romero features *The Day of the Trumpet* (1963) and *The Walls of Hell* (1965), were also the beginnings of a long-standing trend for co-productions with American production companies, with these particular films being produced by Kane W. Lynn for the American drive-in market.

For many critics these decades also marked a decline in the general quality of Philippine filmmaking, with Filipino film historian Agustin Sotto noting that in the period 1962–74 'a type of populist cinema directly serving the needs of the lower classes' (Sotto quoted in Armes 1987: 152) came to the fore. Many of these films were imitations of imported films and were heavily criticised for their low budgets, blatant commercialism and appeal to what was referred to as 'bakya crowds'. As Vincente Rafael has explained, the bakya crowd was a term 'coined in the early 1960s by director Lamberto Avellano to describe the type of audience his films were explicitly not meant for' (2000: 171). While the word 'bakya' literally refers to the wooden slippers worn in lieu of shoes by the rural poor, the term came to be used as a description of a certain style and sensibility: in the words of Jose Lacaba, 'anything that is cheap, gauche, naïve, provincial and terribly popular' (1983: 117).

As film criticism and theorisation developed into a professionalised practice in the 1970s, a number of critics and thinkers formed the film reviewers' group known as Manunuri ng Pelikulang Pilipino (MPP). Many of these critics were dismayed at what they perceived as the poor quality of film production in the Philippines. Yet, rather than explicitly criticising the 'bakya crowds', they turned their attention to governmental policy. In the words of Clodualdo Del Mundo, Jr,

> Ninety-seven percent of our yearly movies are trash. These movies flood our theatres – 1,300 theatres throughout the country – and the appalling fact is that 1,200,000 people watch these local movies daily. How can 1,200,000 people go wrong? Well, they are not wrong; they have been wronged by the industry. (1983: 82)

One of the perceived reasons for the poor quality of local production was the lack of a quota on foreign films which were dominating local screens and limiting the opportunities for local production companies, leading one director to bemoan that the country had become the 'dumping ground for rejects shown in US drive-ins' (Brocka as quoted in Lent 1990: 161). In fact, since the 1960s, there had been a number of attempts to push bills through the Philippine Congress which would impose limits on imports and develop a publicly subsidised industry. In his article on the 'gaya-gaya' syndrome in Philippine cinema, the head of the MPP, Nicanor Tiongson, bemoaned the prevalence of derivative imitations of foreign hits and claimed that the fault was not with the producer who 'confronted with the box-office success of Hollywood mediocrities . . . will naturally want to ensure a safe return of profits by sticking to the path already blazed by these foreign hits' (2001b: 33) but with the lack of governmental support for the local industry. While the bill supported by the MPP critics – the Lumauig Bill which proposed to limit the entry of foreign films and the creation of a 'Film Commission to supervise the production, distribution and exhibition of motion pictures' (Torre, Jr 1983: 86) – was again defeated in Congress, their calls for change were eventually heeded under the Marcos administration when several bodies were created to address the perceived problems in the industry. These were the Experimental Cinema of the Philippines (ECP) and its Manila International Film Festival (MIFF), the Film Academy of the Philippines (FAP), the Movie and Television Review and Classification Board (MATRCB), and the Videogram Regulatory Board (VRB).

Despite the imposition of martial law and the oppressive censorship in the period, it was during the Marcos years that cinema boomed in the Philippines. This is at least partly attributable to Marcos's wife, Imelda, who oversaw the creation of the Film Centre in Manila and founded the Manila International Film Festival, and his daughter Imee who became director-general of the Experimental Cinema of the Philippines (ECP). While both of these ventures were tainted with accusations of corruption, not to say nepotism, they each offered support and international exposure to an industry that had been calling out for help for a number of years. Moreover, it was during this period that the directors Lino Brocka, Ishmael Bernal and Mike De Leon came to prominence. Acclaimed as the 'new wave' of Philippine cinema, this younger generation of filmmakers would come to be celebrated both among the highbrow critics in the MPP and at film festivals worldwide. As would be expected, there has been considerable attention paid to their body of work within the few histories of Philippine cinema that have appeared in the English language.

This attention is related to two broader trends which Patrick Campos has identified within Philippine film criticism. On the one hand there are the scholars who have sought to rediscover Philippine folk traditions and to 'assess how these have survived in contemporary mass culture' (Campos 2006: 36). On the other, there are the attempts to systematise the Philippine texts and discourses into 'a unified, continuous and linear national art history' (37). Both of these strands are very much present in the critical work of the MPP who simultaneously seek out the 'authentically' Philippine elements within contemporary cinema and also attempt to position these titles within a coherent history of art cinema in the country. As we saw in the previous chapter on Turkish cinema, however, what has been systematically ignored are the popular cinematic traditions of the Philippines.

By the 1980s, the Philippines ranked in the top ten film-producing nations and yet the vast majority of these productions were left undiscussed in the major publications on Philippine cinema published to date (Guerrero 1983; Lent 1990; Reyes 1989; Vera 2005) which tend to focus their attention on the 'new wave' filmmakers at the expense of the rich traditions of Tagalog action cinema and other popular forms. As Jose B. Capino has argued, however, the hybrid nature of these popular Philippine films could potentially offer us an invaluable insight into the intricate processes of cultural globalisation:

> Strategically repressed in order to emphasise national specificity or to bolster the cultural sovereignty of 'marginalised' or 'peripheral' film traditions, this aspect of national cinema criticism and historiography seems to me both refreshingly pragmatic and particularly instructive in understanding how local cinemas function symbiotically in relation to the foreign films that share the nation's screens. (2006: 33)

Nevertheless, it was not solely cultural elitism that explains the absence of late twentieth-century popular cinema from Philippine film histories. The socio-political context of the 1970s is hugely significant, especially the general disillusionment of the populace after the declaration of martial law by Ferdinand Marcos in 1972. There was a political dimension to the critique of popular cinema, with some critics deriding the low-budget films as 'kiss-kiss, bang-bang, zoom, boo-hoo, song and dance flickers' (Brocka as quoted in Lockard 1998: 130), positioning them as a form of political opiate for the masses. This meant that the key works of Philippine cinema historiography in the period were accentuated by a political climate which saw Marcos as a 'tuta (lapdog) of America' (Campos 2006: 37).

Furthermore, many commentators at the time were characterising the Philippines as 'essentially neo-colonial' (Lockard 1998: 122) strongly shaped by political and socio-cultural influences from the United States, and symbolised by the presence of major US military bases. With this '(neo)colonial' presence under significant debate and discussion, many of the hybrid forms of Philippine popular cinema came to be situated as a capitulation to American influence and a betrayal of Philippine national heritage. It would be tempting, therefore, to read the transnational adaptation of American popular culture in the Philippines as symptomatic of the country's postcolonial status. Yet to portray this phenomenon as a capitulation to American cultural influence or, conversely, as a mode of postcolonial resistance to the former coloniser, would be doing a disservice to the complexity of these transnational processes. As we will find when we come to examine the texts themselves and the contexts in which they were produced, these borrowings should be understood less through the prism of cultural domination and resistance, and more through the lens of local agency and creativity.

To test this assertion, I will now examine my first case study, *Dynamite Johnson* (1978), which reworks elements from various source texts including *The Six Million Dollar Man* and *Dr No*. By analysing the ways in which the film utilises these appropriated elements, I will consider what this can tell us about the phenomenon of transnational adaptation in the Philippines more generally.

Dynamite Johnson (1978) / *The Six Million Dollar Man*

Faster than the SIX MILLION DOLLAR MAN . . .
Deadlier than the BIONIC WOMAN . . .
Mightier and stronger than KING KONG . . .
More powerful than the SUPER SONIC JET FIGHTER
And ATOMIC BATTLESHIP combined!!!
> Poster blurb for *Dynamite Johnson* (1978)

In his article on the Bobby Suarez directed film *Cleopatra Wong* (1978), Tilman Baumgärtel discusses how he initially did not recognise the film as coming from the Philippines and instead could only identify that it came from 'somewhere in Asia' (2006: 204). This wasn't because he didn't care for geographic details, he explains, but rather because the film seemed to come from a 'generic action movie country . . . where people of all races, nationalities and creeds spend their days hunting each other through narrow alleys or abandoned factories' (204). After returning to the film years later, he discovered that this 'nameless never-ever land' (205) where many such films took place was actually the Philippines.

What this anecdote reflects is a particular aesthetic tendency within the popular cinema of the Philippines. Shaped by the nature of pan–Asian collaboration in south-east Asian film production, and the fact that a significant proportion of productions are designed primarily for export rather than for domestic distribution, there is an industrial trend for films to emphasise certain transnational dynamics and downplay elements that indicate national specificity. In this section, I will argue that this geo-spatial vagueness offers a useful way to consider Bobby Suarez's feature *Dynamite Johnson*, and I will show how this relates to the particular mode of adaptation through which the film reworks its source texts. Unlike the Turkish films I discussed in Chapter 2, this is a film produced primarily for export so this will also offer a privileged insight into the ways in which exported films often rely upon differing forms of transnational adaptation to those produced for domestic consumption.

As I argued earlier in this chapter, there is a danger that we read the transnational adaptation of American popular culture in the Philippines purely as symptomatic of the country's postcolonial status. While a significant proportion of films produced in the Philippines are reworkings of US films and television series, it is my contention that this has less to do with colonialism than with certain industrial production factors. Indeed, the industry does not limit its adaptations to titles from Hollywood, but actually reworks popular films from around the world including films produced in Hong Kong, Britain, Japan and others. This has less to do with an attempt to 'resist' the dominance of Hollywood, and more to do with a wider industrial strategy to rework a variety of globally success-ful source texts for the domestic market, and also, crucially, for export. This case study of *Dynamite Johnson*, therefore, allows us to consider what is at stake when these reworkings are designed for the export market – asking how does that impact the mode of transnational adapta-tion that is used?

Turning to the film itself, *Dynamite Johnson* is directed by Bobby Suarez, a prolific director and producer who is better known internation-ally than in his home country. Starting his career at the Philippines branch of Arthur Rank Film Distribution, Suarez always had one eye on the international market, and this is reflected in certain aesthetic choices such as the tendency to emphasise action over dialogue and the fact that his films were generally shot in English rather than Tagalog. Indeed, many of his films gained commercial distribution throughout Europe, the United States and Asia but were not recognised at home. Quite distinct from the Turkish filmmakers discussed in the previous chapter, who were making films primarily for the domestic market, Suarez was making films with the intention of selling them internationally.

Dynamite Johnson was the third production from Suarez's BAS Film Productions, after the success of *The Bionic Boy* (1977) and *Cleopatra Wong* (1978). Both of the earlier films were co-productions with the financial backing of Singaporean producer Sunny Lim, and in many ways *Dynamite Johnson* is an attempt to capitalise on this success by functioning as a sequel to both titles. Significantly, both earlier titles were themselves capitalising on foreign-source texts, with *The Bionic Boy* being a rework-ing of a season 4 episode of *The Six Million Dollar Man* of the same name, and *Cleopatra Wong* being an attempt to capitalise on the popularity of the blaxploitation film *Cleopatra Jones*.

The film tells the story of the young Sunny (Johnson Yap) who arrives in the Philippines for surgery on his broken legs and awakens from the operation with bionic powers, including greater strength, agility, sight and hearing. He then uses these powers to fight crime, first using his enhanced hearing ability to discover that a smuggling operation is taking place at the docks and then single-handedly defeating a number of criminals using his bionically-enhanced skills in martial arts. Structurally the film then cuts between sequences that follow the investigation of Cleopatra Wong into the smuggling operation and Sunny's own battles against the criminal gang. Moreover, these strands function almost as parallel narratives in which Cleopatra Wong and the 'Bionic Boy' are each given space for their own sequel narratives to the earlier films. They soon discover that the criminal mastermind behind the smuggling operation is a Nazi named Kuntz who is portrayed as a slightly camp Bond-style villain complete with eye patch and cane (see Figure 3.1). The film then ends with an extended martial arts sequence in which Sunny and Cleopatra Wong apprehend and defeat Kuntz.

With this example of transnational adaptation, it would be unworkable to go through all the many ways in which the film differs from its source texts since there is actually very little attempt at fidelity. Instead, what is productive is to consider how specific elements from these sources have been utilised. Many of the most memorable aspects of Steve Austin in *The Six Million Dollar Man* are recreated in the character of the 'Bionic Boy' such as his enhanced strength, speed and vision. Most significantly,

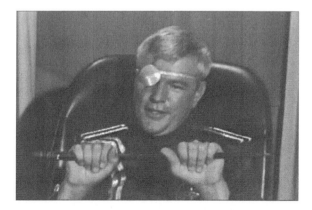

Figure 3.1 The camp Bond-style villain Kuntz in *Dynamite Johnson* (dir. Bobby A. Suarez, Hong Kong/Philippines, 1978)

Figure 3.2 The Bionic Boy showing off his powers in *Dynamite Johnson*

the film also recreates the jittery slow-motion movement and distinctive electronic sound effects when Sunny's bionic powers are activated. This comes explicitly to the fore in the martial arts sequences where this deliberate citation of the earlier series is most apparent (see Figure 3.2). This is clearly intended to be recognisable to the audience and functions more as a homage than as an attempt to parody or critique the US text.

Indeed, there are various citations from other films throughout *Dynamite Johnson* including the moment when the villainous Kuntz employs a 'dragon-tank' which is highly reminiscent of a similar machine from *Dr No*, along with a later explicit evocation of Bruce Lee in *The Big Boss* in a martial arts sequence. This reflects the transnational magpie nature of Suarez's work more generally, as Tilman Baumgärtel has identified, in that his films 'amalgamate Western spy movies, American action films, a Bruce Lee style pan-Asian nationalism and Hong Kong martial arts into a jittery concord' (2006: 225).

This form of transnational adaptation is therefore very much attuned to the international distribution market. In interviews director Bobby Suarez has explained his attempt to tailor his films to the perceived requirements of this market: 'Sometimes I think: Can I sell this (film) to Europe? If I can sell this to Europe, they might not like it in the Middle East. So it has got to be in-between' (as quoted in Baumgärtel 2006: 226). I believe that it is this attempt to cater for different international audiences which best explains the magpie mode of adaptation in *Dynamite Johnson*.

As I have been arguing, the form of adaptation which we find in *Dynamite Johnson* is not an attempt to speak back to its source texts or to localise them for the Philippine national context, but is instead a more opportunistic form which attempts to capitalise on the success of various globally popular films. Furthermore, other examples of transnational adaptation in Bobby Suarez's work include *American Commandos* (1983) which deliberately evokes *Rambo* along with various other Vietnam films, and *Warriors of the Apocalypse* (1985) which reworks the post-apocalyptic world of *Mad Max*. Unlike many of my other case studies, these films are not an attempt to localise an imported source text and tailor it for the domestic market. *Dynamite Johnson* is not an attempt to take elements from *The Six Million Dollar Man* or *Dr No* and make them function for a Philippine audience. Quite the opposite, Bobby Suarez is appropriating elements from various globally popular films as part of an export strategy to make films in the Philippines that will be popular internationally. As Baumgärtel argues, these aesthetic choices take Suarez's films 'out of the trappings of a "national cinema" and into the borderless, never-ever land of international action movies without a defined "country of origin" or a proclaimed "national identity"' (2006: 226). In this case, the borrowed elements are not being adapted for the local context, but are instead being utilised in an attempt to create a form of Philippine cinema that participates in what Simon During terms the 'global popular' (1997) – cultural products that are intentionally designed to circulate beyond the limits of their national context of production. As this example indicates, processes of transnational adaptation are not always about borrowing imported elements and adapting them for a domestic audience. In cases like *Dynamite Johnson*, transnational adaptation is more about producing a local film that will be able to circulate effectively beyond national borders.

For Y'ur Height Only (1981) / James Bond

> One of the most characteristic attitudes of the popular public towards its literature is this: the writer's name and personality do not matter, but the personality of the protagonist does. When they have entered into the intellectual life of the people, the heroes of popular literature are separated from their 'literary' origin and acquire the validity of historical figures.
>
> Antonio Gramsci (as quoted in Bennett and Woollacott 1987: 6)

Throughout the 1960s and 1970s, the Philippines was the location of choice for US film-production companies that wished to achieve high production value on a low budget. Producers such as Roger Corman and companies like A.I.P. would use the Philippines as a shooting location, taking advantage of the relatively cheap cost of living and the fact that English was a commonly spoken second language. Moreover, these productions were actively supported by the Marcos government which enacted legislation to encourage US studios to work in the Philippines.

One man who regularly worked in the Philippines was Dick Randall, a US-born film producer who specialised in a variety of exploitation genres from mondo documentaries to giallo-style thrillers. In this section, I will discuss one of his later feature films, *For Y'ur Height Only* (1981), a US-Philippines co-production that was directed by the Filipino director Eddie Nicart. As with *Dynamite Johnson* this was a film produced primarily for the export market, albeit now with the involvement of an American executive producer. Through this case study, I will explore the impact that co-production arrangements can have on the specific forms of transnational adaptation. Questioning the notion of adaptation as a form of resistance to US film, this particular example allows us to investigate what happens when an American producer funds the transnational adaptation itself.

For Y'ur Height Only is a 1981 spoof of the Roger Moore-era Bond films – specifically, of course, taking off from the film released that same year, *For Your Eyes Only* (1981). What marked the film out from the many international spy films produced in the wake of the success of Bond was the fact that its diminutive star, Weng Weng (real name: Ernesto de la Cruz), was only two feet nine inches tall. Indeed, the film is almost an inversion of the earlier Bond feature *The Man with the Golden Gun* (1974) which starred the similarly statured Hervé Villechaize as Nick Nack, with the humour in *For Y'ur Height Only* mainly derived from switching the roles and having an actor with dwarfism in the Bond role (see Figure 3.3). As I have discussed elsewhere (Smith 2012), Weng Weng has subsequently built up a significant transnational fandom which both celebrates and ridicules his playful reworking of the Bond role. Nevertheless, my

Figure 3.3 The 2 ft 9 in leading actor Weng Weng in *For Y'ur Height Only*
(dir. Eddie Nicart, Philippines, 1981)

focus here is less on the issues raised by this cross-cultural reception than on the specific textual ways in which the film parodies the Bond series.

In terms of the plot, the film very much follows the Bond template which was usefully outlined by Umberto Eco in his essay, 'Narrative Structures in Fleming':

A. M. moves and gives a task to Bond;
B. Villain moves and appears to Bond (perhaps in vicarious forms);
C. Bond moves and gives a first check to Villain or Villain gives first check to Bond;
D. Woman moves and shows herself to Bond;
E. Bond takes Woman (possesses her or begins her seduction);
F. Villain captures Bond (with or without Woman, or at different moments);
G. Villain tortures Bond (with or without Woman);
H. Bond beats Villain (kills him, or kills his representative or helps at their killing);
I. Bond, convalescing, enjoys Woman, whom he then loses.

Eco (1979b: 156)

While this template certainly simplifies what is happening in the Bond novels (and, in turn, the films), and has been justly criticised by Tony Bennett and Janet Woollacott for producing 'an abstract schematisation of the novels which does not adequately encompass the full complexity of either their internal relations or their connections with the cultural and historical processes of which they have formed a part' (1987: 76), the template is very useful for considering *For Y'ur Height Only* precisely because the film is attempting to spoof this recognisable narrative structure. Indeed, director Nicart follows the nine steps almost exactly, right down to the loss of the woman at the end of the film.

Unlike other spoofs of the Bond series such as the *Austin Powers* series, these plot elements are played relatively straight and *For Y'ur Height Only* directly recreates much of the plot and iconography from the Bond series. In this respect, it is similar to *Dynamite Johnson* in that little attempt is made to localise the borrowed elements to fit the Philippines context. Where *For Y'ur Height Only* moves into a more parodic mode, however, is through the performance of Weng Weng in the lead role. Taking on the mantle of the suave, sophisticated secret agent, Weng playfully reworks the recognised conventions of the Bond film and knowingly plays up some of the absurdities of the role. Some well-known Bond moments are also recreated such as the rocket-pack sequence in *Thunderball* (1965) (see Figure 3.4), and one character self-reflexively draws attention to this relationship, telling him, 'You're really a miniature Bond'.

Amit Rai has argued in his discussion of Shammi Kapoor's mimicry of Elvis in Indian cinema that Kapoor could never be an 'authentic' Elvis but that the slippage resulting from the act of mimicry 'acts to dethrone

Figure 3.4 Recreating the *Thunderball* rocket pack in *For Y'ur Height Only*

the Original from its assumed position of Truth' (1994: 66). Similarly, Weng Weng's mimicry of Roger Moore in the Bond films playfully draws attention to the absurdities of the character, recreating the obligatory seduction scenes and fight sequences but now with a lead character who is less than three feet tall. The spoofing of the Bond series therefore relies upon a sense in which Weng could never be Bond, drawing attention to the position of unacknowledged privilege at the centre of the Bond series.

Regarding the nature of this spoofing, it is also worth considering the impact of the co-production relationship between the US and the Philippines. *For Y'ur Height Only* is partly shaped by the transnational nature of its production arrangements, and this is particularly clear in its relationship with the source text. Unlike the Turkish case studies I discussed in Chapter 2, there is no potential copyright issue regarding the utilisation of elements from the Bond series as the parodic nature of the film would be covered by 'fair use' in international law. While a straight reworking of the Bond series which followed the Bond template so exactly could have copyright trouble on the export market, the fact that it spoofs the series allows it cover under the Berne Convention. It would certainly be reasonable to conclude that this helped to shape the particular form of transnational adaptation in this case – especially if we compare it to the films produced for the domestic market which, as I will soon discuss, often did go beyond 'fair use' provision in their use of elements appropriated from Hollywood.

In Tim Bergfelder's book *International Adventures* he quotes the German producer Manfred Barthel on the success of co-productions in Europe:

Co-productions only worked on the level of the adventure genre. Action was inter-national. The perfect karate punch counted more than a subtle gesture, an exploding motor boat had a greater international appeal than the talents of a particular star. (Quoted in Bergfelder 2005a: 146)

This certainly tallies with the phenomenon I have been describing in the Philippines. As I discussed earlier in the chapter, discourses around south-east Asian cinema often focus on national specificities and notions of cultural authenticity and what are left out are those cultural products that transcend or contradict these identity formations. What we find in examples like *Dynamite Johnson* and *For Y'ur Height Only* is a form of cinema which is usually written out of the cinema history books for being insufficiently 'national' in its outlook, but actually tells us a great deal about the transnational nature of cinema. As Andrew Higson has argued, 'The cinemas established in specific nation–states are rarely autonomous cultural industries and the film business has long operated on a regional, national and transnational basis' (2006: 19). This transnational perspec-tive allows us to consider the blurring of cinematic boundaries through international markets and foreign investment arrangements. Such a perspective also allows us to consider the ways in which particular texts are shaped by these conditions, whether through the desire to appeal to a range of different international audiences in the case of *Dynamite Johnson*, or in the emphasis on playful spoofing over straight recreation in the case of *For Y'ur Height Only*.

Alyas Batman en Robin (1993) / Batman

Popular heroes are public property, not in the sense that anyone can produce a Bond film, but in the sense that their images can be reworked, inflected in different direc-tions and to different ends.

Tony Bennett and Janet Woollacott (1987: 283)

In their edited collection, *The Many Lives of the Batman*, Roberta Pearson and William Uricchio (1991) bring together a variety of articles on the cultural life of this iconic figure in American popular culture. Discussing the many different media manifestations in which the character has appeared – from the early DC comics and 1960s TV series, through to the Tim Burton 1989 blockbuster – the book offers a variety of critical lenses through which to approach the multiple incarnations in which the Batman had appeared since his first appearance in Detective Comics #27 in 1939. Nevertheless, one area which was not covered in the book was the many 'transnational' lives of the *Batman* which have appeared in unlicensed films produced around the world. From the Turkish action film *Betmen: Yarasa Adam* (1973) to the Mexican Batwoman film *La Mujer Murcielago* (1968), the character has appeared in a variety of narrative incarnations outside the purview and control of the trademark holders at DC comics.

No other nation – aside from the US – has produced as many Batman films as the Philippines. These adaptations appeared from the 1960s onwards, including *Batman Fights Dracula* (1966), *Alyas Batman en Robin* (1966), and *Fight Batman Fight* (1973), and this continued right through until the most recent incarnation in the 1993 film *Alyas Batman en Robin*. While most of these films have sadly now been lost, one that has survived is *James Batman* (1966) in which the popular screen comedian Dolphy took on the dual role of both 'Batman' and 'James Bond'. Known as the 'king of comedy', Dolphy – real name Rodolfo Vera Quizon – has had a long career running from the 1950s to the present day, appearing in the James Bond spoofs *Dolpinger* (1965) and *Dr Yes* (1965), imitating 'Tarzan' in *Tanzan the Mighty* (1962), and even appearing as a drag-queen Darna in *Darna Kuno?* (1979).

In *James Batman*, he manages to spoof two franchises at once: the Sean Connery incarnation of James Bond and the 1960s Adam West/Burt Ward *Batman* TV series (see Figure 3.5). What is important about this film is that it utilises the music and recreates the recognisable costumes and iconography of both franchises without any form of licensing agreement with any of the rights holders. This was not a licensed part of the *Batman* franchise, paying a fee to DC comics or the TV studio ABC, but an unlicensed appropriation which was taking the characters and music from various antecedent properties and reworking and utilising them in a new film.

Figure 3.5 Bond and Batman teaming up together in *James Batman*
(dir. Artemio Marquez, Philippines, 1966)

This phenomenon continues in the 1993 film *Alyas Batman en Robin* directed by Tony Y. Reyes. The film stars the father-and-son team Joey De Leon (Batman) and Keempee De Leon (Robin), while the villains are played by the comedy duo Rene Requiestas (Joker) and Panchito (Penguin). Indeed, the collaborations between director Tony Reyes and actor Joey De Leon have often dealt with American cultural icons, including spoofs of Tarzan (*Starzan: Shouting Star of the Jungle*, 1989), the Lone Ranger (*Long Ranger and Tonton*, 1989), He-Man (*Sheman: Mistress of the Universe*, 1988), Elvis Presley and James Dean (*Elvis and James*, 1989), and even – in a transvestite narrative – the Barbie doll (*Barbi: Maid in the Philippines*, 1989). What we find again and again is an unauthorised use of characters, music and iconography from these antecedent properties.

To explore how these function within a specific film, I will now discuss the ways in which *Alyas Batman en Robin* utilises the iconography of Batman and how this relates to wider issues of intellectual property and copyright control. I will then move into a discussion of the musical numbers in the film which utilise the melodies from American rock and roll songs. Finally, I will move onto a discussion of the role that language plays in this particular form of transnational adaptation.

As we can see in Figure 3.6, the Batman and Robin costumes familiar from the 1960s TV series are recreated in *Alyas Batman en Robin* (rather than the darker, more gothic costumes used in the contemporaneous Tim Burton film adaptations). Within the narrative of the film, it is further explained that the characters played by Joey and Keempee De Leon are *not* Batman and Robin, nor their alter egos Bruce Wayne and Dick Grayson, but rather they are wearing these costumes in order to capture

Figure 3.6 Recreating the 1960s Batman aesthetic in *Alyas Batman en Robin*

a gang of criminals who have taken on the assumed identity of the Joker and Penguin. As with *3 Dev Adam* in Turkey, the filmmakers are not so much transposing the characters of Batman and Robin to Manila but are rather transposing the recognisable iconography we associate with those characters.

Within the diagesis of the film, then, the costumes function as a form of fantasy roleplay for the characters in which they are able to become crimefighters through taking on the assumed roles of Batman and Robin familiar from the American comics series. On an extra-diagetic level, however, the costumes function as instantly recognisable iconography through which the filmmakers are able to associate their product with the well-known transmedia franchise. It is not simply iconography, however, which is borrowed and adapted in *Alyas Batman en Robin*. The musical numbers in the film also utilise the melodies from popular American rock and roll songs such as the Beach Boys' 1962 hit 'Surfin' Safari'. To take one example, the final musical number takes the melody from the Danny and the Juniors' hit 'At the Hop' and adapts the lyrics to recount how the Joker and the Penguin are going to give up their life of crime.

Lyrics from 'At the Hop'	*Lyrics used in Alyas Batman en Robin*
Well, you can rock it you can roll it	Kung kayo ay isang salbahe
You can stop and you can stroll it at the hop	and you are very naughty, You dirty rat
When the record starts spinnin'	Pwede pa kayo mag bago at
You *chalypso* when you chicken at the hop	hindi pa nahuhuli ang lahat
Do the dance sensation	Let us sing kumpare that the world
that is sweepin' the nation at the hop	means love and not the rot
Ah, let's go to the hop	Let's be good na brod
Let's go to the hop, (oh baby)	Let us not be bad (that's better)
Let's go to the hop, (oh baby)	Let's be good na part
Let's go to the hop	Let's be afraid of God
Come on, let's go to the hop!	Ah, Ah Let's believe in love!

According to Nicanor Tiongson, this form of imitative musical number is derived from the residual tradition of *bodabil*, or 'stage show', which has traditionally 'been the most popular outlet for whatever is fashionable in American pop culture' (1983b: 92). As he explains:

At various times it has featured native versions of American dancers (Bayani Casimiro as the 'Filipino Fred Astaire'), American comedians (Canuplin as the 'Filipino Charlie Chaplin'), singers (Diomedes Maturan still sings as Perry Como no longer does) and singing groups (the Reycard Duet started out as a Jerry Lewis-Dean Martin tandem). (1983b: 92)

This dramatic tradition is certainly evident in the musical numbers in *Alyas Batman en Robin* where the actors recreate the singing group Danny and the Juniors although it is important to stress that this is a hybridised form in which the song lyrics are modified to suit the narrative situation. Unlike in *James Batman*, where the melodies from *Batman* and *James Bond* are simply transposed onto a different narrative, the melodies in *Alyas Batman en Robin* are active reworkings of the American pop songs that playfully modify the lyrics for comedic effect. What further complicates matters is that the song, and indeed much of the dialogue in the film, contains elements of the Tagalog, English and Spanish languages. As Vincente L. Rafael has argued,

> Unlike other Southeast Asian and Latin American countries, the Philippines does not have a national language. Instead, it has a history of state and elite attempts to institute a national language based on Tagalog in the face of the persistence of a linguistic hierarchy, where the last colonial language, English continues to be hegemonic. (2000: 9)

The use of Tagalog, therefore, is implicated within larger state efforts to unify the Philippines under one national language when there are actually over 170 languages spoken on the islands. In spite of this linguistic diversity, however, Tagalog has traditionally served as the language of the commercially driven mass media and especially cinema. It does so, however, only and always in conjunction with those other translocal languages: English and Spanish. Thus, it is in the form of a hybrid language, known as 'Taglish'. This mixing of languages and cultures actually comes to be resonant of transnational adaptation in the Philippine film industry more broadly, whereby imported elements are taken and reworked – adapted and added to – combined and transformed – to create new hybrid forms which are very much embedded in their historical context. As I discussed earlier, the Philippines is a country with a complex relationship with America and so these processes of appropriation are related to differentials in power and status within that dynamic. There is an ambivalence towards the US in titles like *Alyas Batman en Robin* which playfully spoof and comment upon their source while simultaneously attempting to imitate and recreate that same source. As we have seen throughout this book, this is an ambivalence that is shared across the majority of such exchanges, and moreover, this could be said to be the defining characteristic of transnational adaptations of Hollywood.

Darna: Ang Pagbabalik (Darna: The Return) (1994) / Wonder Woman

With a product greatly superior to what local film outfits could offer, Philippine movies were at a disadvantage. For local companies to stay competitive, one resource was to imitate whatever was popular with Hollywood among the local moviegoers. So Philippine cinema developed counterparts for the popular imports – which meant anything from narrative styles to movie stars, a trend which persists today.

Emmanuel A. Reyes (1986: 220)

In his article, 'Philippines: Cinema and its Hybridity', Jose B. Capino describes a scene in the film *Bituing Walang Ningning* (*Fading Star*, 1985) in which a fading diva insults the young upstart who covets her career. After the singer offers a rendition of Steve Wonder's 'I Just Called to Say I Love You', the diva fires back with the insult, 'Those who insist that I have finally found my match must be nuts . . . You'll never make it. You're nothing but a second-rate, trying hard, copycat!'. As Capino asserts, the diva's words 'may very well be directed toward the film's overall plot which, while credited to a serial graphic novel (the vernacular komiks) by Nerissa Cabral, is clearly "inspired" by the 1950 film *All About Eve*' (2006: 32).

This film was part of a larger trend prevalent throughout the industry for drawing on imported sources for plotlines – a phenomenon that was initially attributed to the independent production companies that emerged in the 1960s. As Bienvenido Lumbera observes,

In the 1960s, the foreign films that were raking in a lot of income were action pictures sensationalising violence and soft-core sex films hitherto banned from Philippine theatre screens, Italian 'spaghetti' Westerns, American James Bond-type thrillers, Chinese/Japanese martial arts films, and European sex melodramas. To be able to get an audience to watch their films, the independent producers had to take their cue from these imports. The result was a plethora of films that tried to outdo foreign films in the depiction of sex and violence, giving rise to such curiosities as Filipino samurai and kung fu masters, Filipino James Bonds, and, most notorious of them all, the bomba queen. (1983: 74)

By the 1980s and 1990s, however, the practice of imitating foreign films was not limited solely to the independent production companies. The major studios of the period – Regal Films under 'Mother' Lily Monteverde, Viva Productions under Vic Del Rosario, and Seiko Film under Robbie Tan – were all utilising adapted content in their film productions. One of the most significant of these filmic reworkings of imported characters was the return of Filipino superhero 'Darna' in the Viva films *Darna* (1991) and *Darna: Ang Pagbabalik* (Darna: The Return, 1994); which brought back a character who is 'arguably one of local cinema's most popular and representative figures' (Capino 2006: 33) and had been played by nine actresses (and one actor) in a total of fourteen cinematic appearances by that point. Designed by 'komiks' author Mars Ravelo in 1947, Darna bears considerable resemblance to the character Wonder Woman, created by William Marston six years earlier.

Proposing that the film *Darna: Ang Pagbabalik* can productively be read in terms of a localisation process in which elements were actively translated for the Philippine cultural context, I must first set this up by outlining the contested position of 'komiks' within Philippine popular culture and the position of Darna therein. I will then offer a close textual analysis of the film *Darna: Ang Pagbabalik* in which I locate some of the primary similarities and differences between Darna and the character Wonder Woman. Finally, I will discuss how the question of transmediality impacts upon our understanding of transnational adaptation more broadly.

Emmanuel Reyes, in his article, 'Black and White in Colour: The Lure of the 'Komiks' Movie', has discussed the tensions which underlie the cultural positioning of komiks adaptations in Philippine national cinema. Describing a debate between two critics as to whether an actress who has performed in a komiks adaptation should be included in the roster of 1986's most notable performances, Reyes highlights the two contrasting viewpoints which he sees as typical of the arguments 'that have surrounded the reputation of komiks movies ever since the local film industry discovered their potential to draw people to the box office' (1989: 71).

For one critic, the komiks movie simply exploits the public appetite for fantasy, propagates false values, and lacks any awareness of broader social realities. The other critic does not dispute these criticisms but argues that there must be something intrinsic to the komiks form that means that people can relate to them and that 'these factors should be looked into' (Reyes 1989: 71). Throughout the debates on the positioning of komiks adaptations, this is a theme that constantly recurs: the notion that despite the fantastic nature of the form and its heavy borrowings from imported sources, the Filipino comic book can be seen as something of a 'reflection of the people's collective consciousness' (Reyes 1986: 169). Moreover, some writers go as far as to claim the komiks as the national literature of the Philippines with a readership that has been estimated at 16 million out of a total population of 44 million.

While the notion of a direct 'reflection of the people's collective consciousness' is undoubtedly problematic, it is certainly the case that although the local komiks may appear 'at first glance . . . to be a direct

Figure 3.7 Darna's superhero costume in *Darna: Ang Pagbabalik*
(dir. Peque Gallaga and Lore Reyes, Philippines, 1994)

imitation of American comics' (Reyes 1986: 170) with characters such as
Captain Barbell drawing obvious inspiration from Captain Marvel, they
actually display a more hybridised form in which imported elements have
been mixed with elements from Philippine folklore and culture. With this
in mind, let us turn to the character Darna, who has since her creation
in 1947 become one of the most popular and well-loved cultural icons in
the country. Taking the issues of iconography, narrative and transmedial
storytelling in turn, I will illustrate how Darna's cultural positioning
disrupts any clear sense of linear derivation from Wonder Woman.

First, let us consider the iconographic borrowings from Wonder
Woman. As we can see in Figure 3.7, the character wears a costume that
is highly similar to the Lynda Carter Wonder Woman: a red bustier with
gold accents, gold bracelets for repelling bullets, red boots and a gold tiara.
While there are some aesthetic differences – Darna's costume contains a
strip of loincloth which hangs from her waist, Wonder Woman's costume
covers up her abdomen – the major iconographic difference is that Darna's
costume replaces the stars and stripes of the American flag with the gold
stars of the Phillipines flag.

The question of iconographic borrowings, however, is complicated by
the shifting costume of Darna from the komiks through to these recent
film adaptations. One of the key differences is that the gold bracelets
which in *Darna: Ang Pagbabalik* are used to repel bullets (see Figure 3.8)
were not present in the original komiks character designs of Mars Ravelo.
Viva Films, in adapting Darna for the screen, added this super-ability
from Wonder Woman, giving her a character trait that was not present in
the komiks character. So even if we may reasonably claim that Darna is a

Figure 3.8 Darna repelling bullets with her bracelets in *Darna: Ang Pagbabalik*

distinctive character who is far from a straightforward 'copy' of Wonder Woman, it is nevertheless the case that the screen incarnation of the character borrows further elements from Wonder Woman that were not even present in the komiks. As this example illustrates, discussions of transnational adaptation need to be attentive to this form of transmedial diffusion in which elements from a disparate selection of media incarnations can be present in any single text.

Secondly, we have the question of narrative. Produced against the backdrop of a series of natural disasters which had ravaged the Philippines in the early 1990s – not least of which was the eruption of Mount Pinatubo in 1991 – the film *Darna: Ang Pagbabalik* opens with a volcanic eruption which forces a number of families to leave their homes and seek refuge in Manila. We are then introduced to the character Darna and her alter-ego Narda. There follows a generic narrative in which Darna is pitted against her arch-nemesis Valentina – who it turns out started the volcano – in an attempt to save the city from its impending doom. One noteworthy difference to the Wonder Woman narratives, however, is that whereas Wonder Woman's alter-ego is the fairly affluent Diana, Darna's alter-ego Narda lives in relative poverty. This leads to a narrative that centres on the poor underdog Narda triumphing over the affluent megalomaniacal Valentina and a concurrent emphasis on Darna being the protector and supporter of those in poverty. This adaptation choice reflects what Nicanor Tiongson identifies as a key trend within Philippine cinema where directors symbolically recreate the Philippine sinakulo, a theatrical version of the 'pasyon', in which 'a meek, harmless, suffering Christ is pitted against the minions of darkness, Judas, the kings and priests, the devil and the Jews, with Christ triumphant in the end' (1983b: 85).

What makes this particular case study significant, however, is less to do with the question of iconographic or narrative appropriation but rather the question of how transmediality impacts our understanding of these issues. As Jose Capino has argued in relation to the komiks character Dysebel – a mermaid conceived by Mars Ravelo in 1953 – the story has been retold and remade so many times that it is impossible to establish a comprehensive genealogy of influences; in other words, 'the chain of referentiality that leads to the source has effectively been broken' (2006: 39). So, while the more recent filmic adaptations of Dysebel may draw on various outside inspirations, the Filipino audiences actually '"read" Disney's The Little Mermaid and Splash in terms of the ever-popular Dysebel, not the other way round' (ibid.). The appropriation becomes so deeply sedimented in the host culture that such a relationship complicates any clear understanding of the 'original' and the 'copy'. Indeed, the case of Darna demonstrates how a transnational adaptation can over time become so embedded in the host culture that the adaptation is read less through the prism of the source than the other way round. In the future, rather than asking simply how Darna may function as the 'Filipino Wonder Woman', it may be time to consider how Wonder Woman may also function as the 'American Darna'.

Conclusion

One might say that Philippine cinema's identity as national cinema emerges not from an essential national identity or from a uniquely national film language but from the specificity developed through the unique history and configuration of the local film culture's internal development and its responses to the global film culture and, indeed, to the transnational cultures that surround it.

Jose B. Capino (2006: 43)

By showing how each of these case studies has reworked material from its source texts, I have drawn attention to the ways in which the forms of transnational adaptation in the Philippines mediate the specific socio-historic context in which they were produced, and the ways in which the industrial conditions of Philippine national cinema helped to shape these distinctive modes. First, I argued that the form of appropriation that we find in *Dynamite Johnson* is not an attempt to speak back to its source texts or to localise them for the Philippine national context, but is instead part of an export strategy to make films in the Philippines that could be sold internationally. I then examined *For Y'ur Height Only* and made the case that this appropriation is shaped by the US/Philippines co-production arrangement and the desire to distribute the film internationally, and so playfully parodies the Bond franchise while avoiding any direct bor-rowings that might encounter difficulty with international copyright regulations. Following that, I analysed the form of adaptation in *Alyas Batman en Robin* and suggested that the use of language in the film songs is resonant of the wider processes of cultural globalisation and hybridisa-tion that I have been discussing. Finally, through *Darna: Ang Pagbabalik* I discussed the ways in which a transnational adaptation can become so embedded in its host culture that the adaptation is read less through the prism of the source than the other way round. In the following chapter, I will examine the forms of transnational adaptation that flourished in Bollywood between 1998 and the present day. Through an examination of the ways in which these adaptations relate to their specific contexts of pro-duction, I will argue that the modes of adaptation of Hollywood that we find in India are significantly different from those that we have explored in the previous two case chapters. While Turkey and the Philippines produced a high proportion of films which appropriate and rework the characters and iconography of Hollywood, we find in India a greater emphasis on adapting plotlines with little attempt to produce elements that the domestic audience would recognise as borrowed from Hollywood. As I will argue, this is closely related to the relative market penetration of Hollywood cinema within India.

CHAPTER 4

Hollywood and the Popular Cinema of India

The West may have the biggest stalls in the world's media bazaar, but it is not the only player. Globalisation isn't merely another word for Americanisation – and the recent expansion of the Indian entertainment industry proves it. For hundreds of millions of fans around the world, it is Bollywood – India's film industry – not Hollywood, that spins their screen fantasies.

Carla Power and Sudip Mazumdar (2000)

The present-day Indian commercial film is the end result of a lengthy process of imitation, adaptation, and indigenisation. Confronted with challenges from abroad, Indian society has often responded by indigenising invasive foreign cultural elements and creating a new synthesis that is fundamentally Indian.

Mira Reym Binford (1988: 78)

Tracing Hollywood in India – one of the few remaining places in the world where it plays as a secondary cinema – presents challenges and opportunities for comparative media research. Many of the characterizations that substantiate global Hollywood . . . cannot be uniformly applied in the Indian context.

Nitin Govil (2015: 188)

In my previous chapters, I dealt with boom periods in transnational adaptations of Hollywood in Turkish cinema from 1970 to 1982, and Philippine cinema from 1978 to 1994. In this chapter, I continue the temporal trajectory taking us to the twenty-first century in my study of Indian commercial cinema from 1998 to 2010. As with the historical and spatial conjunctions that I dealt with in the previous chapters, this is a period in Indian cinema with a heightened level of adaptations from Hollywood, and this has much to tell us about the nature of what I have termed 'the Hollywood meme'. These include such diverse reworkings as *Ghulam* (1998) / *On the Waterfront* (1954), *Chachi 420* (1998) / *Mrs Doubtfire* (1993), *Sangharsh* (1999) / *Silence of the Lambs* (1991), *Kahin Pyar Na Ho Jaaye* (2000) / *The Wedding Singer* (1998), *Chori Chori Chupke Chupke* (2001) / *Pretty Woman* (1990), *Mere Yaar Ki Shaadi Hai* (2002) / *My Best Friend's Wedding* (1997), *Humraaz* (2002) / *Dial M for Murder* (1954),

Qayamat (2003) / *The Rock* (1996), *Main Aisa Hi Hoon* (2005) / *I am Sam* (2001), *Black* (2005) / *Miracle Worker* (1962) and *God Tussi Great Ho* (2008) / *Bruce Almighty* (2003).

In this third and final case study chapter, the blurring of the lines between 'original' and 'copy' will come explicitly to the fore. While Sheila Nayar notes that 90 per cent of Hindi films in production in August 1993 were remakes of one kind or another (1997: 74), and the list I have collated above is indicative of how significant this trend has become, this is not to say that sources for these remakes should be considered 'originals'. Indeed, as we will see in the examples I examine later, many of the films that are being remade in Bollywood are actually part of a much longer chain of intertextual reworkings. Furthermore, unlike my other case studies, Indian commercial cinema is far from being a marginal cinema. Bollywood's dominance throughout India, and many parts of the Middle East and Asia, indicates that it is very much a production centre – a net exporter rather than a net importer of cinema. This complicates the dynamics of centre and periphery which so often surround discussions of global Hollywood. In terms of both the number of films and tickets sold, Indian cinema is actually much larger than Hollywood – although it is important to note that this includes the full range of cinematic traditions across the country and these cannot all be subsumed under the banner of Bollywood. Since the late 1970s, the Indian film industry has produced approximately 700 feature films every year, reaching a peak of 948 films in 1990. Of these, approximately 200 are Hindi-language 'Bollywood' films. As Sumita S. Chakravarty argues, 'Indian cinema is too diverse, Indian culture too complex, Indian artistic traditions too varied and eclectic for any one study to encompass their whole range' (1993: 17). It is important, therefore, that before I begin, I delimit which 'Indian cinema' it is that I am studying in this chapter. India consists of a number of culturally diverse regions with films being produced within production centres in Mumbai, Andhra Pradesh, Assam, Kanataka, Kerala, Punjab, Tamil Nadu and West Bengal. Yet the cinema that has long been the dominant force in India both domestically and internationally is the Hindi-language films produced in Mumbai (formerly Bombay) known under the appellation 'Bollywood'. These are also the films that have the strongest tradition of borrowings from Hollywood, especially with regard to plots and narratives. Therefore this chapter is focused primarily on the Hindi-language cinema of Bollywood which, as Mira Binford has noted, is 'generally considered the archetypal commercial cinema of India' (1988: 78).

Finally, as Sheila Nayar has argued in her comparative studies of remakes, it is necessary to keep in mind the particular period in which these films were produced. While India has a long tradition of producing remakes and adaptations of US film and television, some of the issues that I will be exploring throughout this chapter reflect the specific socio-historic context of post-1998 Bollywood cinema. It is worth bearing in mind that, as Nayar has argued, 'A Hindi film from the early 1990s when compared to more recent works will bear some distinct – though perhaps, to nascent eyes, negligible – differences in terms of ideological point of view' (2005: 67). In this chapter, therefore, I utilise my comparative model of transnational adaptation in order to analyse how elements borrowed from Hollywood evolve and adapt to fit these new times and places. Meme transmission is subject to constant mutation as stories are adapted to local contexts, so this study will examine the specific nature of these adaptations and position them in relation to post-1998 North Indian culture. This periodisation is significant as 10 May 1998 was the moment when industry status was granted to the film industry by the right-wing Bharatiya Janata Party (BJP)-led government. According to Nandana Bose, this decision 'marked a watershed in the hitherto fraught relations that had existed between the State and Bombay cinema for over fifty years since independence' (2009a: 23). Under this new regime, the Indian government eased restrictions on foreign involvement with Bollywood cinema, and encouraged the Indian film industry to invite international capital and foreign media investment. This period of economic liberalisation had a marked effect on Bollywood cinema, and this chapter will engage specifically with the impact that this shift has had on relations between 'global Hollywood' and what has now become 'global Bollywood'.

While my previous two case studies dealt with cinemas that have been largely unexplored in English-language criticism, there has actually been a great deal of material written on Bollywood in recent years. Until the 1980s, Indian popular cinema was generally ignored within film histories written in the West – often 'characterised as being meretricious, escapist, mindless drivel and totally irrelevant to the understanding of Indian society and culture' (Dissanayake 2003: 202) – yet in the last two decades there has actually been a significant attempt to engage directly with Bollywood cinema and to position it in relation to older traditions in Indian culture. Even so, there is still relatively little that deals with the relationship between Bollywood and its distant cousin Hollywood. Therefore, rather than trace a narrative that attempts to outline a broad overview of the history of this national cinema for the reader – as was necessary for my chapters on Turkey and the Philippines – I instead focus my attention here on specifically historicising the relationship between Hollywood and Bollywood, attending to the tensions that underlie the dynamics between these two major centres of production. This overview will then be coupled with an industrial account of the various cycles of remakes and adaptations in Bollywood cinema, examining both the strategies employed to adapt Hollywood texts and the assumptions that filmmakers use to think about and construct their audiences.

Building on this historical and discursive account, I will then offer a close textual analysis of four films which adapt elements of Hollywood for diverse purposes. The first example will be *Koi . . . Mil Gaya* (2003), the first large-budget Bollywood sci-fi film, which utilises a range of imported sources including *E.T.: The Extra Terrestrial* (1982), *Close Encounters of the Third Kind* (1977), *The Neverending Story* (1984) and *Forrest Gump* (1994) within a narrative that mediates the ideology of Hindutva. Secondly, I will explore the recent phenomenon of the 'songless' Bollywood film through an examination of a remake of *The Godfather* (1972) entitled *Sarkar* (2005). My third case study will look at the adaptation of gender and sexuality in *Heyy Babyy* (2007), a Bollywood remake of *Three Men and a Baby* (1987) which was itself a remake of the French comedy *Trois Hommes et un Couffin* (1985). Finally, I will examine the adaptation of narrative form in *Ghajini* (2008), a remake of *Memento* (2000), which complicates some of the processes of 'Indianisation' that run throughout this chapter. *Ghajini* is also a remake of an earlier South Indian Tamil film, so this allows for a discussion of the complex transnational and transregional flows of media through and across India.

Ultimately, the aim of this chapter will be to help mark out certain tendencies in the transnational adaptation of Hollywood. This book is engaged in a comparative study of different forms of adaptation in the contexts of Turkey, the Philippines and India, and one key distinction that will be explored in this chapter is between the emphasis on adapting characters and iconography in Turkey and the Philippines, and the emphasis on adapting plots and stories in India. As I will argue, this prevalent mode of adaptation in Indian popular cinema is considerably different from that discussed in my earlier two chapters. Through an analysis of the cultural and industrial factors that influenced these Indian adaptations, I believe that this chapter will move us closer to an understanding of the determinant factors that shape different forms of transnational adaptation, and better help us interrogate the nature of the Hollywood meme.

Bollywood: The Hollywood of the Global South?

[Indian cinema] enjoys a measure of freedom as to what aspects of Hollywood cinema it absorbs and how these are articulated with Indian traditions of representation . . .

There is a relation of imitation, even outright plagiarism, as well as a relation of
uncompromising difference between the two types of cinema.

Paul Willemen and Behroze Gandhy (1980: 25)

In terms of film production and audiences, Bollywood is the world's
largest film industry, employing more than 2.5 million people and
selling over 4 billion tickets every year (1 billion more than are sold for
Hollywood productions). Based in Mumbai, which is the country's commercial centre, the industry has experienced significant growth in export
trade over the past twenty years, with Bollywood becoming one of the
few examples of transnational media flowing from the global South to the
global North (Thussu 2008: 98).

An understanding of its complex and variegated relationship with
Hollywood, however, is only now starting to be addressed in scholarship.
To help interrogate this relationship, therefore, this chapter will explore a
series of dynamics between global Hollywood and global Bollywood. First,
it will consider the appellation 'Bollywood' itself which has been critiqued
for implying a derivative relationship to the so-called 'original' Hollywood
cinema. The chapter will then explore the status of cinema in India as an
imported form, analysing the ways in which cinema has been seen to be
'Indianised' through its relationship with traditional Indian cultural forms.
It will then explore the popular and art cinema traditions in India, with
their competing claims towards representing 'Indianness' through cinema.
The distinctive formal characteristics of Bollywood will then be considered
in relation to notions of 'orality'. Finally, this sub-section will close with an
account of the production context in Bollywood post-1998 with the shift
towards an international market and the increasing presence of Hollywood
studios in India. By historicising this relationship between Hollywood and
Bollywood, I will have built the necessary foundations to allow me to shift
my focus onto the specific modes of transnational adaptation in Indian
cinema in the following section, tracing its distinctive nature through the
various cycles of remakes and adaptations that have been produced.

First, let us consider the name 'Bollywood'. More specifically, let us
consider the name in relation to a rhetorical question posed by Heather
Tyrrell: 'Is Bollywood named in imitation of Hollywood, or as a challenge
to it?' (1999: 260). In other words, does the term hide the complexities
of Hindi popular cinema by positioning it merely as the 'Hollywood of
Bombay', or does the term indicate a more complex dynamic of appropriation and opposition?

The etymology of the term is actually highly contested, with many
claiming credit for its coinage. According to Madhava Prasad, however,

the term came from Wilford Deming, an American engineer, who worked with Ardeshir M. Irani on the production of the first Indian sound film. Writing in *American Cinematographer* in 1932, Deming came up with the term 'Tollywood' to describe films produced in the Indian suburb of Tollygunge, a naming pattern that soon caught on and led to the production centre in Bombay gaining the name Bollywood. For Prasad, this narrative is problematic as it implies that it was 'Hollywood itself, in a manner of speaking, that, with the confidence that comes from global supremacy, renamed a concentration of production facilities to make it look like its own baby' (2003: 17). This plays into domestic criticisms of Hindi-language popular cinema as derivative, in which the 'films are said to be nightmarishly lengthy, second-rate copies of Hollywood trash, to be dismissed with patronising amusement or facetious quips' (Thomas 1985: 117). Such an overt dismissal, however, would overlook the way in which 'Bollywood' actually functions as a heteroglossic term – one that usefully connotes a complex set of material and discursive links between Bombay and Hollywood (Govil 2007: 86).

This is closely linked with the contradictory ways in which critics and academics have discussed the technology of cinema itself. As Amit Rai has argued, cinema was seen in India as a 'foreign technology' that was then being 'used by indigenous elites helping to engender a sense of national identity' (1994: 56). Related to the colonial history of India and the fact that cinema arrived in the country under British rule, the notion of cinema as an imported 'foreign' technology meant that the medium of cinema had to be seen to be indigenised, or more specifically 'Indianised', to be acceptable to domestic audiences post-independence. As Ravinder Kaur has argued, 'Although cinema arrived in India in the colonial setting, it soon became a swadeshi (homegrown) project with Indian images and narratives' (2002: 203). This is actually resonant of the processes of transnational adaptation that I will discuss later in this chapter whereby an imported cultural form goes through a process of 'Indianisation' to adapt to the local domestic context. Or to return to the quote from Mira Binford with which I opened this chapter, the foreign cultural elements are required to be indigenised to such an extent that a new synthesis is created that is seen as 'fundamentally Indian' (1988: 78), even if such a designation runs the risk of lapsing into cultural essentialism.

Reflecting this trend, while the codes and conventions of Hollywood cinema played a major role in the development of cinema in India, there was a push for them to be adapted to suit local tastes and forms. As Wimal Dissanayake argues, 'Makers of commercial cinema in India, very often, took directly from Hollywood films storylines, character types, memorable sequences, and reshaped them to suit local sensibilities' (2003: 208). One of the earliest examples of this phenomenon came in 1913 when Dadasaheb Phalke modelled his mythological film *Raja Harischandra* on a Hollywood Biblical epic. Although the story was taken from Hindu mythology, Phalke drew inspiration from a Hollywood film on the life of Christ. Nevertheless, it was not until the introduction of synchronised sound in 1931 that the Mumbai industry really developed the distinctive local cinematic form which would succeed in both reshaping borrowed plots to suit local sensibilities and resisting domination from other national cinemas. The success of this strategy is demonstrated by the fact that during the silent era, imported films – primarily from the United States – occupied 87 per cent of India's screens while, within a decade of the arrival of sound, the proportion had dropped to less than 10 per cent (Binford 1988: 78).

In addition, Bollywood cinema is far from simply being imitative of Hollywood as the syncretic tradition of popular Hindi cinema actually draws from a range of eclectic sources and influences including 'the celebrated mythological epics; classical, folk, and modern theatre' (Ciecko 2001: 125). These influences have been especially relevant in the processes of Indianisation that are said to be necessary to adapt imported forms for the local context. There is an emphasis on stylised performances, elaborate depictions of emotion and the inclusion of song and dance numbers – elements which Mira Binford has argued can be found as far back as ad 400 in the Sanskrit dramas of Kalidasa (1988: 79). Tejaswini Ganti has even gone so far as to argue that it was the indigenous Parsi theatrical traditions that were the 'immediate aesthetic and cultural antecedent of popular Hindi cinema' (2004: 8) rather than any imported forms.

Such accounts that attempt to identify a 'genuinely Indian cinematic aesthetic' (Binford 1988: 90) in the face of an imported foreign technology often appear in debates around the popular and art cinema traditions in India. As we found in the chapters on Turkey and the Philippines, there has been a disproportionate emphasis within the academic writing on the key auteur figures from the world of Indian art cinema such as Satyajit Ray, Shyam Benegal and Mrinal Sen. Films from these filmmakers – often under the banner of Parallel Cinema – were shown at international film festivals and shown in art-house cinemas around the world, while the popular domestic 'Bollywood' cinema rarely travelled beyond the diaspora in the West. As I have already explored similar debates around the emphasis on art cinemas in national cinema histories in my chapters on Turkey and the Philippines, I will not retread those debates once again here. Suffice it to say that one of the most interesting dynamics in criticism on Indian cinema has been the debate around which form of cinema – popular versus art – gets closest towards representing that elusive notion of 'Indianness'. While the parallel cinema movement is seen to be preoccupied with social problems in Indian society, its form is heavily influenced by international art cinema such as French poetic realism and Italian neo-realism. On the other hand, the commercial cinema, for all its adaptation of plots and themes from Hollywood cinema, is arguably more formally 'grounded in traditional Indian musical-dramatic sources and therefore [it] still speaks most directly to the mass audience' (Binford 1988: 90).

Let us turn then to the formal characteristics of Bollywood which are said to be so distinctive and grounded in Indian traditions. For Sheila Nayar, the key elements of visual narrative in Bollywood cinema are the following:

STRUCTURE & FORM
- Episodic narrative form, including flashbacks and digressions
- Repetition, recycling and formula-privileging
- Spectacle (i.e. flat surface narrative – a 'cinema of attractions')
- Narrative closure (i.e. no ambivalent or open endings)

VISUAL, VERBAL & AURAL TONE
- Agonistically toned (e.g. amplified violence, melodrama)
- Heavy, amplified characters and settings
- Syntagmatic kinaesthesia
- Plenitude and redundancy (e.g. visual, material, and dialogical excess)
- Use of rhetorical devices (e.g. clichés, proverbs)
- Non-interpretive, unambiguous meaning (e.g. privileging of oaths, anti-symbolic)

WORLDVIEW & ORIENTATION
- Manichean worldview (i.e. black and white)
- Non-psychological orientation (i.e. extrospective)
- Non-historical (i.e. synchronic, synthetic, experiential telescoping)
- Non-self-conscious (e.g. parody)
- Fulfilment of audience expectations
- Participatory
- No anxiety of influence (i.e. imitative, no concept of plagiarism)
- Focus on social suturing, on preservation of the status quo
- Collective-social orientation (i.e. 'we'-inflected).

                                                          Nayar (2005: 65)

Nayar traces the roots of these characteristics to the oral traditions of Indian culture, making the case that the lack of a genuine lingua franca across the country necessitated a form of storytelling that could be 'universally applicable' across diverse linguistic regions and to audiences with wildly differing levels of literacy (64). As we will see later in my filmic case studies, these elements form a significant part of the process of 'Indianisation' that the remakes go through when they are adapted for the local Indian context.

The prototypical Bollywood film is generally referred to as a masala, or formula, film which contains a mixture of generic elements. In other words, it cannot be labelled simply as an action, romance or comedy film as it will contain elements of many different genres. As Susanne Gruss has argued, it is this inherent hybridity and ensuing 'anti-naturalism' that 'most people focus on to either explain Bollywood's attractions – or to ridicule them' (2009: 227). Popular Indian films generally do not follow the formal conventions of Hollywood cinema, often departing 'from continuity editing, naturalistic lighting, and realist mise-en-scene' (Ganti 2004: 141), so any appropriation of a Hollywood plot will necessitate some significant changes to adapt to this local cultural form.

Before I turn to the various cycles of remakes and adaptations that have been produced in Indian cinema, and explore the implications of this process of 'Indianisation', I will close this sub-section with a brief account of the production context in Bollywood post-1998. On 10 May 1998, at a national conference entitled 'Challenges before Indian Cinema', members of the film industry were told by Union Information and Broadcasting Minister Sushma Swaraj that the government had decided to grant official industry status to film. This development was followed by a series of other governmental changes to the industry including a reduction in custom duties on cinematographic film, an exemption of recorded audio and video cassettes from excise duty, and various tax incentives for production. This was followed in October 2000 by an allowance in the Industrial Development Bank Act which meant that the film industry became eligible for financial support from 'legitimate' institutions as an attempt to shift the industry away from the criminal underworld. As Monika Mehta has argued, by designating film as an industry and bringing this informal sector of the economy under its purview, the state was 'actively attempting to (re)inscribe its authority in the context of globalization' (2005: 137).

This was a hugely significant shift in governmental policy since, until that point, state policies of taxation and licensing had accorded the film industry the status of a vice trade. From the late 1990s, however, rather than perceiving it as a vice, the Indian state positioned 'commercial film-making as a viable, important, legitimate economic activity that should be nurtured and supported' (Ganti 2004: 50). In fact, this was a process that had started earlier, as economic liberalisation in the industry had been initiated by the Indian government in 1991, while the entry of satellite television in 1992 had significantly shaped the context for subsequent filmmaking. These factors led mid-1990s films to have 'vastly improved production values that include digital sound, foreign locations, extravagant song sequences, and lavish sets' (2004: 37).

Furthermore, the key shift from 1998 onwards was that the 'overseas' market became 'one of the most profitable markets for Bombay filmmakers with certain Hindi films enjoying greater commercial success in Great Britain and the US than in India' (Ganti 2004: 38) and the total overseas market for Hindi films being estimated at around $50 million (ibid.). This was a significant change as Indian filmmakers were no longer targeting their films solely at the indigenous Indian market but were beginning to tailor their work for the lucrative overseas market. Bollywood films were now being released simultaneously in India and abroad with English subtitled and dubbed prints being readied for initial release. As I will demonstrate in the following section, this has had a considerable impact on the ways in which elements borrowed from Hollywood have been adapted in Indian popular cinema.

Finally, while I am primarily focused in this section on the transnational flows of media between Hollywood and Bollywood, there is a further dimension to this relationship that is only recently coming to fruition. As I mentioned above, since the introduction of synchronised sound, India has been one of the few countries in the world where Hollywood has barely got a foothold – currently at only 5 per cent of total film revenues in India as against 70–90 per cent in European markets (Thussu 2008: 99). This situation was heightened by the fact that until 1992, there was a ban on dubbing foreign films into Hindi which thus prevented any significant move by Hollywood into the Indian market. Yet as the Bollywood industry has opened up and increased its global market share, building audiences beyond the south Asian diaspora, the Hollywood studios have begun to take notice.

While attempts to break into the market through dubbing Hollywood films into Hindi have generally failed – with the initial success of *Jurassic Park* (1994) dismissed as an anomaly that could not be replicated – there are now various studios including Universal and Warner Brothers which have set up offices in Mumbai and are getting involved in the production and distribution of Hindi language cinema. As I will argue in the following section, this direct involvement of Hollywood in the Indian market has caused a shift in relations between the two industries and has had a significant impact on the modes of transnational adaptation that can flourish in this new industrial context.

Remakes, Adaptations and Spin-offs within Indian Popular Cinema

I remember once when I was struggling to put an 'original' script together, I. S. Johar, the renowned comedian and Bollywood's first intellectual, laughingly advised me, 'son, why don't you ask your rich producer to buy you a ticket to London, see an American flick, and come back and remake it with Indian actors. It is cheaper, less bothersome and guarantees success'. At the time, I was horrified. Little did I know that in later years, I would take that advice of his too seriously.

Mahesh Bhatt (as quoted in Jess-Cooke 2009: 112)

Mahesh Bhatt is here describing a process which is prevalent throughout Indian popular cinema, not least in his own films which include such titles as *Dil Hai Ki Manta Nahin* (1991) and *Murder* (2004), remakes of the Hollywood films *It Happened One Night* (1934) and *Unfaithful* (2002) respectively. It is interesting to note the commercial imperatives at play here. Rather than positioning the appropriation of Hollywood cinema as a form of homage or resistance, Bhatt describes the process as a pragmatic decision based on the debatable notion that a remake is easier to produce than an 'original' film and less of a risk when it comes to box-office success. This attitude runs through much of the contemporary discourse on Bollywood remakes, although, as I will illustrate, it tends to be rationalised in a variety of different ways. It should also be noted that this is not a new phenomenon. As the US journalist Robert Trumbull described back in 1953:

> Local producers watch imported features with an eagle eye and frankly plagiarise the more popular productions scene by scene. One producer explained that he saw nothing ethically wrong with this, as otherwise the Indian masses who do not understand English, and have few chances to see foreign films anyway, would be denied these masterpieces. (1953: 17)

It is significant how open the Bollywood filmmakers are in talking about these processes. While the English language press often criticises the industry for being derivative of Hollywood – usually in the form of a tell-all expose which will detail a range of titles that are said to be plagiarised – the Bollywood filmmakers themselves are remarkably open about their sources of inspiration. This reflects both a pragmatic perspective on the potential for originality in cinema, a generally relaxed attitude about the copyright of imported texts and, most importantly, an industrial model which necessitates that films be made quickly and cheaply. Like other popular film industries that operate on this model, the Bollywood industry exhibits a 'need to capitalise on any current trend, whether by quickly reworking a Hollywood hit or by quickly producing a sequel to a [local] hit' (Desser 2003: 535).

As this would suggest, it is not only Hollywood films that are being remade in the Mumbai film studios. Remakes of other regional Indian cinemas are prevalent, as I will explore in my case study on *Ghajini* (2008), and there are many recent examples of remakes of earlier Bollywood hits such as *Don* (1978), remade as *Don* (2006), and *Sholay* (1975), remade as *Ram Gopal Varma Ki Aag* (2007). Nevertheless, while it is true that Bollywood directors often borrow elements from other Indian cinemas and earlier Bollywood hits, it is the borrowings from Hollywood that are most significantly reworked to appeal to the contemporary domestic audience. In the words of Tejaswini Ganti, 'While remakes from other Indian languages resemble the original screenplay, adaptations of Hollywood films barely do as they have been transformed, or "Indianised"' (2004: 77). Significantly, it is most often the plotlines from these Hollywood source texts that are the elements that have been borrowed and subsequently 'Indianised'. This is in contrast to the strategies of transnational adaptation that I identified in Turkey and the Philippines, as both of those national cinemas contain a much higher proportion of titles that appropriate and rework the characters and/or iconography from Hollywood. As I will argue in this chapter, this emphasis on plotlines rather than recognisable characters or iconography is closely related to the relative presence, or lack thereof, of Hollywood cinema on Indian screens.

Taking this further, it is worth remembering that while Hollywood does not currently have much of a foothold in the Indian market, this was not always the case. Before the introduction of synchronised sound in 1931, imported films from the United States dominated India's screens and they continued to play a significant role in Indian middle-class viewing habits until the late 1940s (Mishra 2002: 126). This meant that many of the early Hollywood stars had a significant following in India including Charlie Chaplin, Douglas Fairbanks, Sr, Harold Lloyd, Buster Keaton and the Marx Brothers. Moreover, this led many Indian actors to pay homage to these stars and characters in their work, from Raj Kapoor's tribute to Charlie Chaplin's tramp in titles like *Shree 420* (1956), through to Mahipal's imitation of Errol Flynn in *Ali Baba and the Forty Thieves* (1954) and Ranjan's mimicry of Douglas Fairbanks, Sr in films like *Chandredekha* (1948). Not only were these popular with audiences, but some of these homages were themselves hugely influential, with Raj Kapoor's tribute to Chaplin engendering its own tribute thirty years later in Sridevi's performance in *Mr India* (1987). There are also some limited examples of imported popular characters who have managed to flourish in Indian cinema, such as Superman who has appeared in both Telugu (*Superman* (1980)) and Hindi-language (*Superman* (1987)) feature films; James Bond who appears in the Telugu spy film, *James Bond 777* (1971); and Freddy Krueger from the *Nightmare on Elm Street* series who serves as the inspiration for the gloved villains in the Bollywood horror films *Khooni Murdaa* (1989) and *Mahakaal* (1993).

Even so, these films that appropriate and rework recognisable characters and iconography from Hollywood are not so much representative of a larger phenomenon as they are the exceptions that prove the rule. From the 1930s onwards, Hollywood cinema played a relatively small role on Indian screens and there was little incentive to borrow popular Hollywood characters and feature them in domestic titles. Instead, it was plotlines that were most often borrowed and reworked, with the characters and iconography usually changed substantially from their source texts. From Hitchcockian thrillers such as *Woh Kaun Thi* (1964), a loose remake of *Vertigo* (1958), through to horror features like *Zakhmee Aurat* (1988), which reworks *I Spit on Your Grave* (1978), the elements borrowed from the Hollywood source text are almost always the set-up and plotline. This has meant that the Bollywood adaptations feature much less emphasis on recognisable visual motifs, as compared to the examples I discussed from Turkey and the Philippines, and they generally do not draw attention to their status as adaptations. The films, therefore, make little attempt to capitalise directly on consumer knowledge surrounding their source texts.

This phenomenon of Bollywood cinema adapting the set-ups and plotlines from Hollywood is also something that has increased over time. While I would not necessarily agree with Neelam Sidhar Wright that the recent emphasis on remakes is an 'abrupt millennial-phenomenon' (2009b: 197) – since there so many examples that predate the current cycle – I would certainly agree that this is a phenomenon that has shifted from being 'previously something occasional and cursory, to a now much larger-scale investment and cultural trend' (206). Reflecting this trend, various structural factors at play have helped to determine the specific forms of transnational adaptation which we see in this period.

Toby Miller et al. (2005) in their book on the global reach of Hollywood have offered an economic explanation as to why the remaking of Hollywood cinema has become a major part of Indian film production. They suggest that it functions as a form of risk limitation on behalf of the film producer where the proven success of the Hollywood film is seen to diminish their risk (Miller et al. 2005: 239). This is reflected in a series of interviews featured in the Bollywood magazine *Trade Guide* in which filmmakers are asked, 'Do remakes, copies, inspirations of South/English films guarantee success?'. Rajesh Thadani's response is representative in that he explains that although 'everything depends on the subject and the adaptation', the general rule is that 'if the original has been a hit, the chances definitely seem better' (as quoted in Goculdas 1997: 15). This economic explanation, however, is only part of the story. According to interviews published in a later issue of *Trade Guide*, the Hollywood films are rarely selected purely on the basis of box-office success and are instead more often chosen for plots that seem amenable to adaptation. As Sawaan Kumar argues, 'There is no hard and fast rule that a hit English film's copy will be a hit. Sometimes even the fine points of a flop English film, when adapted well, can make a hit Hindi film' (as quoted in Goculdas 1998: 15). Therefore, rather than simply remaking the biggest box-office hits from Hollywood, filmmakers in India are more often searching for plotlines that are easily adaptable to the Bollywood masala form.

Furthermore, as Rosie Thomas has observed, it is not the case that Bollywood filmmakers can simply 'copy' US film and television and expect success. While many filmmakers borrow story ideas and even recreate certain sequences, it has become a truism in the industry that 'borrowings must always be integrated with Indian filmmaking conventions if the film is to work with the Indian audience' (Thomas 1985: 26). To illustrate this argument, Thomas points to various shot-for-shot remakes of Hollywood films – such as *Dirty Harry* (1971), remade as *Khoon Khoon* (1973), and *Irma La Douce* (1963), remade as *Manoranjan* (1974) – which were flops at the box office. This point has also been reinforced by Bollywood blockbuster director Rakesh Roshan who argues that 'a frame to frame copy will not work at all. One needs to adapt to the taste of our Indian audience' (as quoted in Goculdas 1998: 15). As all of this suggests, the source texts will generally go through a localisation process in which the film is adapted for the local Indian audience – a process which Rosie Thomas terms 'Indianisation' and Sheila Nayar terms 'chutneyed' (2003: 73).

Finally, while various scholars have dealt with the Bollywood remake, the scholar who has produced the most useful and productive work is media anthropologist Tejaswani Ganti. Unlike most work on cross-cultural remakes which tends to focus purely on issues of intertextuality, Ganti's writing examines this process not as a 'relationship between texts but as a relationship between filmmakers and audiences' (2002: 282). Shifting focus onto how this process functions in the industry, she explores how 'the act of picking a Hollywood film to adapt is often based on personal cinematic preferences' of the filmmakers themselves, but that they will subsequently 'justify their choices according to what they believe audiences will accept and reject' (2002: 290). The films, therefore, require some elements to be changed and, according to Ganti, the three main elements of 'Indianisation' are 'adding "emotions," expanding the narrative, and inserting songs' (2004: 77). These changes are then rationalised in terms of what the filmmakers believe the audience desire to see. Building on this research, my case studies will explore how Hindi filmmakers act as cultural mediators who 'implicitly delineate a difference between their viewing habits and those of their audiences' (2002: 290). This will allow me to illustrate the ways in which this process of 'Indianisation' cannot be understood as simply reflecting essentialised cultural differences – i.e. that the addition of songs is necessary due to something intrinsic to Indian culture – but instead is mediated through the assumptions of the filmmakers themselves. In other words, transnational adaptation from this perspective is less about localising to cater for intrinsic cultural differences than it is about filmmakers' assumptions regarding those cultural differences.

To explore these issues in more depth, I will now turn to my first case study: *Koi . . . Mil Gaya* (2003), the first major science-fiction film to be produced in India. Through a close analysis of the film and the various source texts it is reworking, I will explore how these sources have been localised for domestic audiences and the implications that this has for our understanding of transnational adaptation more broadly.

Koi . . . Mil Gaya (2003)

If you borrow from just one source, it's called plagiarism; but if you borrow from ten sources, it's called research. And if you succeed in hiding your source, then you're called original . . . I strongly believe that it is better to be an interesting copy than an original bore . . .

Javed Akhtar (1996: 20)

This book has utilised a comparative model of transnational adaptation in order to explore how elements borrowed from Hollywood evolve and adapt in new surroundings. Underpinning this metaphor is the observation that some memes flourish in the new locations, while others fail to adapt, and die out. As I outlined earlier, this does not imply that the memes have agency in themselves, but rather that filmmakers in these new locations are making decisions about which memes to borrow and how best to adapt them to appeal to local audiences. To understand the remake phenomenon in India, therefore, it is necessary to consider which Hollywood memes are flourishing in India, how they are being adapted for Indian audiences, and for what purpose.

As I explained in the previous section, Hollywood films are rarely selected purely on the basis of commercial success. More often they are selected on the basis of whether the plotline is amenable to being localised for Indian audiences. In other words, the films are chosen according to how successfully they could be adapted into the distinctive Bollywood cinematic form. According to Rosie Thomas, there is an attendant assumption among filmmakers that certain genres such as science fiction 'would be outside the cultural reference of the Indian audience' (1985: 26), and would therefore not be chosen. In this section, I will test this assumption through an analysis of the ways in which various Hollywood science-fiction titles were adapted and reworked in the Bollywood blockbuster *Koi . . . Mil Gaya* (I've Found Someone, 2003).

When *Koi . . . Mil Gaya* was initially released, it was promoted as 'India's first science-fiction film' and was celebrated for introducing a genre which had previously been seen as quite literally 'alien' to the Bollywood form. While this was not strictly true – there had been some previous attempts to make science-fiction films in India, mainly B-movies such as *Miss Chaalbaaz* (1961), *Trip to Moon* (1967) and *Wahan Ke Log* (1967) – it is without question that *Koi . . . Mil Gaya* was the first big-budget Bollywood science-fiction film and the first attempt to introduce this genre to the Indian mainstream. The film is also significant for engaging Marc Kolbe, who worked on Hollywood blockbusters such as *Independence Day* (1994) and *Godzilla* (1997), to introduce more complex special-effects technologies into Bollywood cinema.

The film opens with a Hindi scientist named Sanjay Mehra (played by director Rakesh Roshan) who is attempting to contact extra-terrestrial life by sending out a message containing the religious syllable 'Om'. Ridiculed within the scientific community for his use of religion to contact aliens – one scientist asks him, 'Oh, so they believe in your religion as well?' – Sanjay receives a response but tragically dies in a car accident before he can properly make contact with the aliens. His wife, Sonia Mehra (Rekha), who was pregnant when they had the accident, gives birth to their son Rohit (Hrithik Roshan) who has been left with a brain defect caused by the crash. The film follows Rohit as he struggles with his mental handicap and develops a romantic interest in the kindly Nisha (Preity Zinta). At his lowest point, he prays to Lord Krishna for help and is astonished when his prayers are answered by the arrival of an alien spacecraft. It is carrying a blue alien creature who responds to Rohit's 'Om' signal. They come to develop a close relationship and the alien is given the name of 'Jadoo' (meaning 'magic' in Hindi). Taking pity on Rohit's disability, Jadoo is able to grant him greatly increased strength and intelligence. This helps Rohit to build the confidence to propose to Nisha and the films ends with Jadoo returning to his home planet while Rohit and Nisha embark on a happy life together.

As this brief synopsis suggests, while the film is often described in the West as the 'Bollywood E.T', it is actually more like a bricolage of various different intertexts, a conglomeration of influences that is 'more like a rewriting of Hollywood sci-fi than a regurgitation of Spielberg's film' (Jess-Cooke 2009: 117). These intertexts include *Star Wars* (1977) in a homage to the iconic scrolling credits sequence; *Contact* (1997) in Sanjay Mehra's method of contact with extra terrestrials; *E.T.* (1982) in the story of a small alien who is looked after by local children; *Charly* (1968) in Rohit's transformation from being mentally handicapped into a genius; and *Close Encounters of the Third Kind* (1977) in both the use of music to communicate with the aliens and the appearance of their spacecraft when they arrive.

This bricolage of various different intertexts means that the film could be read almost as a compilation of Hollywood science-fiction sequences, adapting and paying homage to many of the most celebrated examples of the genre. While this could arguably be rationalised as a method to avoid claims of plagiarism – evoking Javed Akhtar's claim above that 'If you borrow from just one source, it's called plagiarism; but if you borrow from ten sources, it's called research' (1996: 20) – the more significant outcome was that the film was successful in making the genre of science fiction appealing to Bollywood audiences. It therefore went some way to disproving B. Subhash's argument back in 1998 that *E.T.* was a perfect example to illustrate the notion that 'there are certain English [language] hits which just cannot be copied' (quoted in Goculdas 1998: 15).

Furthermore, while the film draws upon a range of different science-fiction titles, this is not primarily a relationship of imitation. Indeed, unlike the majority of borrowings of characters that I discussed in my earlier chapters on Turkey and the Philippines – such as *3 Dev Adam*'s use of Spider-Man and *Alyas Batman en Robin*'s use of Batman – *Koi . . . Mil Gaya*'s appropriation of E.T., Jadoo, does not closely resemble the character from its source text. In fact, the film does not transpose any recognisable iconography from the Spielberg film. Unlike those other examples of character adaptation I have mentioned, *Koi . . . Mil Gaya* is not utilising the iconography of *E.T.* as an exploitable element to help associate itself with its source text. Consequently, this means that the film does not require audience knowledge of the source text to function. This comparison is even clearer when we compare *Koi . . . Mil Gaya* with an earlier Turkish adaptation of *E.T.* entitled *Badi* (1983). In that film, the character design very closely resembles E.T. and the film relies in part upon recognition of that association. Conversely, *Koi . . . Mil Gaya* borrows from E.T. along with various other science-fiction texts in a localisation strategy where plot elements and character traits are thoroughly adapted and transformed for the local Indian context. In this case, these science-fiction texts are not being evoked to engender recognition from the domestic audience – who, with Hollywood's limited market penetration, could not be expected to have knowledge of the source texts – but rather to adapt the science-fiction generic tropes to appeal to domestic audiences and to reflect contemporaneous domestic issues. As Carolyn Jess-Cooke has argued, the film uses 'the sci-fi genre as an organising structure within which to vocalise Indian identities and ideologies' (2009: 118).

This process of 'Indianisation' is most explicit in the addition of religious themes to the more rationalist depiction of science in the source texts. As described in the synopsis above, the film contains many references to the Hindu religion – from the use of the divine 'Om' syllable to contact the aliens, through to Rohit's prayers to Lord Krishna for help (see Figure 4.1). The successes of both these actions – against the backdrop of various Western scientific failures in the film – represent what Dominic Alessio and Jessica Langer describe as a trend in contemporary Bollywood cinema in which 'Hindu beliefs are deliberately challenging Western conventions by demonstrating the superiority of all things Hindu and Indian' (2007: 225). In such a way, the film is also, to a lesser extent, commenting upon its source texts, playfully highlighting the perceived failings of Western science fiction and asserting the power of Hinduism in contradistinction to a more secular approach. Moments such as the success of the Hindu scientist Sanjay Mehra in contacting extra-terrestrial life using the 'Om' signal, inverting the scientific rationalism of source text *Contact*, put forward an implicit commentary on the neglected role of

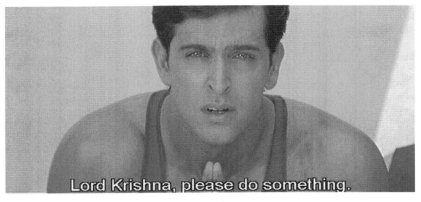

Figure 4.1 Rohit praying to Krishna for help in *Koi . . . Mil Gaya*
(dir. Rakesh Roshan, India, 2003)

Figure 4.2 The alien Jadoo designed to evoke Hindu gods in *Koi . . . Mil Gaya*

religion in these Hollywood texts. While this commentary is fairly limited, not least because the specific source texts are never explicitly referenced, *Koi . . . Mil Gaya* does display the ambivalent tension between oppositional critique and mimetic reverence that I have argued are often central to these processes of transnational adaptation. This trend is continued in the representation of the alien Jadoo who, as we can see in Figure 4.2, looks little like E.T. and was instead designed to evoke the blue skin tone of Lord Krishna and the visage of Ganesh (Colmer 2003). While fulfilling a similar narrative function to the E.T. character, Jadoo has been substantially transformed for the local Indian context. As Neelam Sidhar Wright has argued, Jadoo is presented as 'the cinematic incarnation of the Hindu God Lord Krishna' (2009: 203) with the film containing various moments in which Jadoo is metaphorically linked to Krishna.

The name too is significant as Jadoo is the Hindi word for 'magic' with Jadoo's powers presented less as an extra-terrestrial ability but rather as a divine form of magic – this change fitting in with the traditions of Indian cinema which are generally said to be comfortable with 'characters more magical than scientific' (Srinarahari as quoted in Alessio and Langer 2003). This rooting of science-fiction conventions in the Hindu religion is continued in the film's sequel *Krrish* (2006) where the titular lead character is named in reference to Lord Krishna and various plot points draw on the ancient Indian texts of *The Mahabharata* and *The Ramayana*.

In this 'Indianisation' of the science-fiction genre, therefore, the more overtly scientific elements are combined, or even replaced, with Hindu religious symbolism. In this sense, the film reflects what Arvind Rajagopal describes as the emergence of a 'Hinduised visual regime' (2001: 283) at the close of the twentieth century. Allied with the rise in power of the

Bharatiya Janata Party (BJP), a number of Bollywood films in the late 1990s and early 2000s aligned themselves with Hindu nationalism and *Koi . . . Mil Gaya* is emblematic of this trend. The then BJP prime minister Vajapee even asked for a special screening of the film, and subsequently the film theme music was used for BJP election campaigns (Alessio and Langer 2003: 226). The changes can therefore be read as less about localising the various source texts to fit with Bollywood narrative conventions, and more about adapting the source texts in order to mediate the Hindu nationalist discourse of the period. This has actually come to be something of a problem for those cultural critics who look for moments of resistance to Hollywood in these Bollywood remakes. To take one example, Dominic Alessio and Jessica Langer felt that *Koi . . . Mil Gaya* had potential to be celebrated through a postcolonial framework as a challenge to the hegemony of Western cinematic production but they lament that 'its robust religious and nationalist overtones constitute a postcolonial paradox, for by subverting non-Hindu ideologies it has also manufactured a new kind of colonial order with its assertion of Hindu hegemony' (2003: 218). Moreover, the film is actually much more ambivalent towards Western culture than a purely postcolonial reading would suggest. Quite apart from the borrowings from various Hollywood source texts, it is significant that one of the major set pieces is set around a game of basketball and that the film features some blatant product placement for Coca-Cola. This is transnational adaptation not as a resistant commentary upon Hollywood but primarily as an attempt to localise Hollywood conventions for an Indian audience – transforming various science-fiction tropes through reference to the Hindu religion with an underlying assumption that this would have more local appeal. It is worth noting too that these changes are deeply embedded in their particular historical conjuncture, reflecting the contemporaneous rise of the BJP and the Hindu right in Indian politics. When considering transnational adaptation it is always important to consider the particular historical moment in which the source text is being reworked, and it is clear that the process of 'Indianisation' that this film underwent was very much related to the specific socio-historic context of post-1998 North Indian political culture.

    To conclude, it is worth returning to the notion of *Koi . . . Mil Gaya* as the 'Bollywood *E.T*' as this case study complicates one of the key issues surrounding these transnational adaptations. Such appellations generally lay emphasis on the Hollywood source text as the unquestioned 'original' while defining the specificity of any particular adaptation purely in terms of the national film industry in which it was produced. Aside from the fact that *Koi . . . Mil Gaya* contains a number of different intertexts, and so is therefore as much the 'Bollywood *Close Encounters of the Third Kind*' as it is the 'Bollywood *E.T.*', there are also issues regarding the positioning of *E.T.* as the 'original' source for that film. While this is not universally acknowledged, Spielberg's film was itself accused of being a plagiarism of a script by Bengali filmmaker Satyajit Ray. Novelist Arthur C. Clarke described 'striking parallels' (as quoted in Robinson 2004: 295) between Ray's unmade script entitled *The Alien* and *E.T.*, while Ray himself felt that *E.T.* 'would not have been possible without the script of *The Alien* being available throughout America in mimeographed copies' (ibid.). *Koi . . . Mil Gaya* could therefore be read as an unauthorised adaptation of an unauthorised adaptation, which, ironically, would place its origins back in India rather than Hollywood. This is not to say that the origins should be placed in India – all cultural production rests upon mimesis so it would be problematic to attribute definitive origins to any meme – but rather that this example usefully reminds us that this is not a unidirectional process of adaptation from Hollywood but rather a dynamic back-and-forth process of cultural borrowings with no clear point of origin.

Nevertheless, what we find in *Koi . . . Mil Gaya* is a form of transnational adaptation in which elements from various imported source texts are combined and integrated in order to comment on domestic concerns. While appropriating from the Hollywood science-fiction genre and introducing this global form into mainstream Bollywood cinema, the film functions less as a commentary on its source texts than as an assertion of Hindu nationalism. This process of Indianisation creates a complex form of intertextuality in which plot structures from Hollywood are combined and hybridised with the iconography and symbolism of Hindu mythology. As we will see in the following case studies, this tendency towards localising narratives but retaining few iconographic elements runs throughout contemporary Bollywood cinema and marks an important break from the dominant forms of transnational adaptation we explored in the chapters on Turkey and the Philippines. In the conclusion to this chapter, therefore, I will bring together insights from each of these filmic examples in order to explore the possible determinants that help to shape the specific forms of adaptation prevalent in the Bollywood industry.

Sarkar (2005)

Songs are perceived as the quintessential 'commercial' element in a film. Filmmakers working outside the mainstream treat songs as a way of reaching larger audiences, and this gets characterised by the press as either accommodating or pandering to popular tastes. The omission of songs is interpreted as an oppositional stance; a way of making a statement against the dominant form of cinema as well as circumscribing one's audience.

Tejaswini Ganti (2004: 79)

While scholars and filmmakers occasionally have different views about what is required to 'Indianise' a source text, there is one element that is almost always listed as an essential component: the addition of songs. Indeed, for many scholars it is the song sequence that is 'the quintessential characteristic that distinguishes Indian popular cinema from other cinema traditions' (Bhattacharjya 2009: 53). These musical sequences often circulate as ancillary texts around the release of any Bollywood film and, since the arrival of Indian music video channels, have only increased in visibility over the years.

In fact, while a small number of popular Hindi films have managed to achieve commercial success despite a lack of songs – such as *Kanoon* (1960) and *Ittefaq* (1969) – the musical sequence is still generally considered to be a necessity in order to appeal to Indian audiences. It is significant, therefore, that recent years have seen an increasing number of commercially successful Bollywood features which eschew song sequences, a trend that is generally attributed to the surprise success of the Ram Gopal Varma-directed horror film *Bhoot* (2003). Through an analysis of Varma's subsequent film *Sarkar* (2005), I will now explore the ways in which this reworking of *The Godfather* (1972) breaks with the conventions of the Bollywood narrative form. Furthermore, by interrogating the phenomenon of the songless Bollywood film, I will demonstrate how transnational adaptation can function as part of a strategy to alter local filmmaking conventions more broadly.

Before I move into the analysis of *Sarkar*, it is worth considering the significance of the songless Bollywood film. As Tejaswani Ganti describes above, the omission of songs from an Indian film is generally perceived to be anti-commercial and is usually limited to the Indian art-cinema traditions. As a rule, she argues, 'not having songs communicates that a film is outside the mainstream of the Bombay film industry, possibly even an "art film", and to most people in the industry this means death at the box office' (2004: 84). While there is a long tradition in Indian cinema of songless films, these are generally referred to as 'new' or 'parallel' cinema, and are often seen in opposition to commercial Bollywood filmmaking practices. Many of these filmmakers are influenced by the earlier Bengali filmmakers Satyajit Ray, Mrinal Sen and Ritwik Ghatak, and they are linked as a movement 'primarily by their rejection of the values, both aesthetic and thematic, of the commercial cinema' (Binford 1988: 82). In particular, the films produced under the banner of 'new' or 'parallel' cinema are seen to be 'characterised by their social realist aesthetic, smaller budgets, location shooting, absence of song and dance sequences, lesser-known actors, and a naturalistic style of acting as opposed to the big budgets, elaborate sets, songs, superstars and melodramatics of mainstream Hindi cinema' (Ganti 2004: 50).

What has changed recently, however, is that there has developed a hybrid form of Bollywood cinema which has come to be described as 'commercially successful parallel cinema' (Ferrao 2003). In other words, these movies may not contain song numbers but they are still 'produced with the same commercial intent as Bollywood films', and they are far from being positioned as 'oppositional' (Garwood 2006: 169). This has come to be seen less as a rejection of commercial cinema than an attempt to create a different form of commercial cinema which is closer to the Hollywood form. Ram Gopal Varma, who pioneered the songless Bollywood film with *Bhoot*, describes the process as a way to bring elements of Hollywood formal conventions into Indian filmmaking:

> In Mumbai, we believe every film has to be three hours long, whereas in Hollywood the running time is variable according to the story. Common sense told me to make *Bhoot* only two hours long. I think it will give other filmmakers the courage to go into different areas and use different formats. (Quoted in Jha 2003)

It is worth noting, too, that removing songs can also potentially cut down on the cost of filmmaking, as the song sequences are often the most lavish and costly sequences in a Bollywood feature. So, while Varma positions the removal of songs as part of an attempt to move towards a narrative form influenced by Hollywood, it is also clear that, as Ian Garwood has identified, 'financial considerations motivated the decision to eschew the song sequence in *Bhoot* as much as aesthetic ones' (2006: 171). What we find with *Sarkar* is that this process is taken one step further. Not only is the film formally influenced by Hollywood in its songless narrative and two-hour length, but it is also an adaptation of a specific Hollywood plot, *The Godfather*. Through an analysis of the specific ways in which *Sarkar* reworks its source text, I will now explore the complex relationship with Hollywood cinema evoked by this particular form of transnational adaptation.

It is worth noting that this was not the first Bollywood film to be inspired by *The Godfather*. Among the many Bollywood productions that have taken inspiration from Francis Ford Coppola's adaptation of the Mario Puzo novel are *Dharmatma* (1975), *Aadalat* (1976), *Nayakan* (1987), *Zulm ki Hukumat* (1992), *Aatank hi Aatank* (1995), *Vishwasghaat*

(1996), *Mumbai Godfather* (2005) and *Family* (2005). As this would suggest, the plot is a good fit with the 'collective social orientation' (Nayar 2005: 65) identified by Sheila Nayar as a key characteristic of Bollywood cinema. With its emphasis on familial relationships and codes of honour, it also reflects Kishore Valicha's assertion that 'what is central to the popular Hindi film – and to life in India – is the concern with the values of the family and the extended family' (as quoted in Bisplinghoff and Slingo 1997: 104). Unlike the other Bollywood appropriations of *The Godfather*, however, *Sarkar* is explicitly positioned as an adaptation, with the director acknowledging the influence of the film in a director's note which opens the film: 'Like countless directors all over the world, I have been deeply influenced by *The Godfather. Sarkar* is my tribute to it' (Ram Gopal Varma). Rather than leaving the intertextual relationship implicit, Varma is presenting his film as a direct homage to Francis Ford Coppola's film. Interestingly, however, in the longer version of the director's note which is reproduced on the DVD case, Varma is also at pains to distinguish his film from being merely an imitation: 'Yet at the same time, I would clarify firmly that *Sarkar* is not an imitation or a clone. Its story and screenplay have been located in an Indian milieu, and particularly so in the context of Mumbai's power superstructure'. In order to make the case that *Sarkar* is more than simply an imitation of *The Godfather*, Varma lays emphasis on the ways in which the film embeds these borrowed elements within a new and distinctive cultural context. So, while the plot is certainly heavily influenced by *The Godfather* and *Sarkar* is part of the recent trend towards songless Bollywood features which are influenced by Hollywood, the film has nevertheless been significantly localised to reflect the particular form of organised crime prevalent in Mumbai.

The plot itself centres on Subhash Nagre (Amitabh Bachchan), known as Sarkar or 'overlord', who sees himself as leading a parallel government. In his own words, he is 'working outside the system for the welfare of the people' and the opening scenes show him ordering an attack on a rapist after the law and order system has failed the victim's father. Subhash has two sons, the power-hungry film producer Vishnu (Kay Kay Menon) and the US-educated Shankar (Abhishek Bachchan) who has recently returned to his family. A group of crimelords – the Dubai-based Rasheed (Zakir Hussain), the corrupt Silver Mani (Kota Srinivasa Rao) and the Hindu guru Swami Virendra (Jeeva) – who are jealous of Subhash Nagre's overlord status and constrained by his moral stance on drug smuggling, decide to band together to bring down his empire. After they frame him for murder, Subhash is imprisoned and the unlikely figure of his son Shankar takes over the position of Sarkar temporarily. There are then a series of battles in which the upper hand shifts between Shankar and his enemies, with the film ultimately ending with Shankar winning out and replacing his father as overlord of this 'parallel government'.

As can be seen from this brief outline, the film reworks many elements of *The Godfather*, not least the familial relationships and the rise of the son to take over from the father. What is different, however, is that these plot elements from *The Godfather* are thoroughly integrated with elements from real-life criminal families from Mumbai. So while the character of Subhash Nagre is loosely based on Vito Corleone from *The Godfather*, he is also inspired by Balsaheb Thackeray, the founder of the political party Shiv Sena. Similarly, while Shankar Nagre shares many character traits with Michael Corleone, he is also inspired by Uddhav Thackeray, the son of Balsaheb who took over the mantle of leading Shiv Sena when his father retired. This emphasis on the creation of a parallel government which is passed from father to son, therefore, takes on additional local meanings in the Mumbai context. Furthermore, the depiction of Sarkar as a folk hero loved by his people but functioning outside the law (see Figure 4.3) has resonance with the star image of Amitabh Bachchan himself. As Vijay Mishra has identified, Bachchan was the dominant figure in Bollywood cinema from 1973 to 1990 but was also no stranger to controversy (2002: 127).

Rumoured to have connections with the Mumbai gangster under-world and embroiled in scandal from his short-lived political career in 1985–7, Bachchan's star status functions as a 'parallel text' throughout *Sarkar* lending an extra resonance to his portrayal of a well-loved but morally ambiguous overlord. These intertextual relationships are further

Figure 4.3 Crowds watching the arrival of Subhash in *Sarkar*
(dir. Ram Gopal Varma, India, 2005)

complicated by the passing of the mantle from father to son. As Neelam Sidhar Wright has argued, it is significant that Shankar is played by Bachchan's own son Abhishek, and she argues that the film offers a multiplicity of ways to approach this father/son relationship:

> (1) an allusion to the actors' real life father and son relationship, subject to much discussion in popular widely read Indian media gossip columns, (2) a symbolic depiction of Amitabh Bachchan passing his fame and status as Indian cinema's leading actor onto his son, who has with each film increasingly grown to adopt his father's acting style, image and on-screen persona, (3) an underlying commentary hinting at Bachchan senior's real life political agenda and underworld connections, (4) an analogy of the real life tensions created by the gangster underworld and its power over the Bollywood film industry and its stars and (5) the comparative Bollywood equivalence of Bachchan senior and Bachchan junior, as great actors of their generation, to the original performances of Hollywood legends Brando and Pacino. (2009b: 138)

Taking approach (5) as being of particular relevance to a discussion of transnational adaptation, it is interesting to note that neither Amitabh Bachchan nor Abhishek Bachchan imitate the performance style of their equivalents in *The Godfather*, Marlon Brando and Al Pacino. While director Ram Gopal Varma has positioned *Sarkar* as a tribute to *The Godfather*, the film is not particularly similar beyond the borrowed elements from the plot. Iconography from the film is not recreated or referenced and the characters do not physically resemble their equivalents from the source text. Furthermore, the film – despite calling attention to its intertextual relationship in the opening director's note – makes little attempt to comment upon its source text. As with *Koi . . . Mil Gaya*, this is a form of transnational adaptation that functions less as a commentary on its source text than as a commentary on specific domestic concerns. The film is closer therefore to a model of localisation – localising the plot of *The Godfather* to fit with the context of Mumbai's political corruption.

Reflecting this, the film is significant for the ways in which it comments upon morality and the role of religion in public life. When Sarkar refuses to condone drug smuggling, he explains:

> I concede. I do a lot of things which cannot be considered legal. And that's because I do what I think is right. Even if it goes against God, against society, against police and the law, or even if it goes against the entire system.

This emphasis on a moral code which exists outside of the Mumbai legal system, and even outside of religious conviction, is further bolstered by the depiction of the character Swami Virendra (see Figure 4.4). Loosely

Figure 4.4 The controversial Hindu guru Swami Virendra in *Sarkar*

based on the controversial Hindu guru Chandraswami, the character uses his religious status to manipulate and influence various criminal groups for personal gain. Political corruption is portrayed as endemic in Mumbai public life and it is significant that the most corrupt character is also the only explicitly religious character. Not only that, but Shankar gets the upper hand on him precisely because Shankar is an atheist and is, therefore, shown to be immune to the Swami's manipulations. In stark contrast to *Koi . . . Mil Gaya*, *Sarkar* localises the plot of its source text but ultimately uses this to critique the power of religion in Indian life rather than to affirm it.

As I have outlined so far, *Sarkar* is primarily a localisation of *The Godfather* which adapts the plot to fit with the Mumbai context. From the integration of real-life characters to the depiction of religious corruption, the film takes inspiration from *The Godfather* and then firmly relocates it in a new socio-cultural context. Yet there is a further factor here that complicates such an analysis. While we have this attempt to localise *The Godfather* to reflect contemporary Mumbai and its criminal underworld, this goal actually acts in tension with the attempt to create a songless Bollywood film that is closer to the Hollywood form of its source text. In other words, this form of transnational adaptation is both attempting to localise its source text for domestic audiences and simultaneously attempting to internationalise the Bollywood form through an imitation of Hollywood.

One of the explanations for this latter factor is that Bollywood is increasingly attempting to appeal to a global market. Considering that the audience outside of India accounts for around 65 per cent of the average film's total earnings (Willis 2003: 256), it is accurate to conclude that

Sarkar is 'a hybrid cultural product that fuses the language of Hollywood with the accent, slang, and emotions of India' (Thussu 2008: 107). As Ian Garwood identifies, this is part of a larger strategy to 'tailor Bollywood movies more to the conventions of Western filmmaking, most notably through the reduction or excision of song sequences' (2006: 173).

To conclude, therefore, it is important to recognise the ways in which *Sarkar* challenges Bollywood's formal conventions. As Wimal Dissanayake has argued, 'one of the fundamental tenets of Hollywood filmmaking . . . is the need to cover up the artifice, the constructedness of film articulations of narrative' (2003: 209). This emphasis on verisimilitude is in stark contrast to the Bollywood narratives which rarely attempt to cover up the artificial nature of the set-up. By reworking the *Godfather* narrative as a songless Bollywood film, director Ram Gopal Varma is positioning *Sarkar* as a break with the conventions of the Bollywood narrative form. This evokes a complex relationship with Hollywood in which transnational adaptation functions as a method to introduce Hollywood plots and characters into Bollywood cinema, but also as a way to introduce the more formal characteristics of Hollywood narrative structure. Indeed, Varma himself argues that his experiment with songless Bollywood films 'liberates filmmakers from a lot of restrictions' (as quoted in Jha 2003) within the Bollywood form. In such a way, this form of transnational adaptation functions as a deliberate strategy to introduce alternative narrative forms into local cinema. While the majority of case studies discussed in this book attempt to integrate appropriated elements into a domestic narrative form, this example inverts the process by actually attempting to integrate local elements such as the Mumbai criminal world into a narrative format borrowed from Hollywood.

Heyy Babyy (2007)

Recent popular Hindi films have come to represent culturally hybrid assertions of desi (indigenous) integrity with a millennial fervour, celebrated consumer culture while reaffirming traditional values, resisted and appropriated Hollywood conventions, and recognised the South Asian diaspora – audiences around the globe – even as they remind viewers that, to quote the title of a recent Bollywood film, *Phir Bhi Dil Hai Hindustani*: The Heart Is Still Indian.

Anne Ciecko (2001: 121)

As Anne Ciecko argues, there has been a trend in recent Bollywood cinema for films that celebrate global consumer culture while still reaffirming traditional Indian values. Related to the increasing importance of the non-resident Indian (NRI) audience market, these films often centre on NRI characters living in Europe or Australia and deal with the tensions between Western excess and traditional Indian values in their lives. One recent example of this phenomenon is *Heyy Babyy* (2007), a Bollywood remake of *Three Men and a Baby* (1987), which was itself a remake of the French film *Trois Hommes et un Couffin* (1985). By considering how this narrative has been adapted and transformed in the move from France to the US and then to India, I will demonstrate how the study of transnational adaptations can offer insights into issues of gender and cultural difference.

To begin, it is worth noting that I will build on some excellent academic work that has already been done comparing *Trois Hommes et un Couffin* to *Three Men and a Baby*. A number of academics have found the comparison to be 'fertile ground on which to explore gender and culture' (Durham 1998: 71), and such diverse academics as Raymonde Carroll, Tania Modleski, Carolyn Durham and Lucy Mazdon have offered comparative readings of the films. Indeed, the case study has come to be something of a classic example for exploring the cultural politics of the cross-cultural remake. What has been neglected in academic criticism up to now, however, is the more recent Bollywood remake *Heyy Babyy* which takes these processes of localisation even further. Part of the value in studying processes of transnational adaptation is the insight they can offer into cultural difference, or, more precisely, the construction of cultural difference. This film, therefore, offers us a privileged position in which to consider how stories evolve and adapt to fit new and different contexts.

The film centres on three NRI flatmates, Tanmay (Riteish Deshmukh), Ali (Fardeen Khan) and Arush (Akshay Kumar), who live together in Sydney, Australia. Setting up their debauched lifestyle, the film opens with a voiceover from Arush declaring: 'Love! Affection! Caring! These are such beautiful words. There are many people in this world who believe in these words. The three of us are not among those people'. After a lavish opening song sequence in which they all indulge in the temptations of a decadent Western lifestyle (see Figure 4.5), they each end up in bed with a different woman. After they awake, however, they discover that a baby has been left on their doorstep along with the accompanying note, 'You rascal! Scoundrel! Take care of your daughter!'. Unsure of who is the father, the three men then undergo a radical change of lifestyle as they are forced to collectively look after the baby. The plot then follows the same basic narrative trajectory as *Three Men and a Baby* as the three men 'learn to care for, protect and love the newest member of their household' (Durham 1998: 73).

While this set-up has some slight differences from the source texts – including the fact that all three men are looking after the baby from the

Figure 4.5 Indulging in a decadent Western lifestyle in *Heyy Babyy*
(dir. Sajid Khan, India, 2007)

start – the majority of the early sequences are very similar. Indeed, many of the sight gags from the French and American films are kept intact, with a great deal of the humour coming from the inexperience of the three men in looking after a baby. From the sequence in which Arush must find the correct type of baby milk to all the traumas of the inevitable nappy changing, *Heyy Babyy*, at least initially, resembles its source texts in both narrative structure and humour.

Where the films begin to seriously diverge are in the sequences following the mother's return to collect her baby. Carolyn Dunham has argued, in her comparison of *Trois Hommes et un Couffin* and *Three Men and a Baby*, that the American remake 'reflects the dominant ideology of American feminism' (Dunham 1998: 77) in that gender equality is emphasised over sexual difference, and societal change is emphasised over biological destiny. So, while *Three Men and a Baby* retains the structure of *Trois Hommes et un Couffin* in the recurrent scenes of female characters who reject motherhood, the reasoning behind this rejection depends less on biology than on 'women's own denial of any inherent female ability to mother and their subsequent refusal to continue to substitute for fathers' (ibid.). The reasoning that each mother gives for abandoning her daughter is instructive here. In *Trois Hommes et un Couffin*, the mother has decided to go to the US to work for six months and so is leaving the baby with the father, whereas in *Three Men and a Baby*, the mother declares an inability to cope with the child and a need to simply spend some time alone.

Significantly, what we find in *Heyy Babyy* is that the mother Isha (Vidya Balan) has not actually rejected motherhood at all. When she comes to pick up her baby from Arush, Ali and Tanmay, it becomes clear that it was the child's grandfather who had left the baby with them. Isha had been led to believe that the child had died at birth so, rather than rejecting motherhood, this plot change suggests that she would have held on to the baby if she had known it was still alive. This different handling of the rationale behind the baby being left with three men is revealing in its negotiation of contrasting moral codes.

Furthermore, the drug deal plot, which has been central to many of the comparative studies of these films, has also been removed from the film. In *Trois Hommes et un Couffin* the men come to be aligned with a group of drug dealers after there is confusion over a delivered 'package', whereas in *Three Men and a Baby* the men are very much aligned with the investigating police. For Lucy Mazdon, the different handling of the drug deal signifies a shift from 'ambivalence and gentle derision of authority in the French film to apparently straightforward moral codes and affirmations of authority in the remake' (2000: 54). This whole sub-plot has been removed from *Heyy Babyy*, however, and thereby removes any association in the film between the three men and criminal activity.

These two changes signify a crucially different moral code in the Bollywood remake. Centrally, the role of motherhood is no longer presented as being in crisis and the three men are no longer associated with criminality. This reflects the claim by Tejaswani Ganti that Hindi filmmakers exercise their judgement about how to 'Indianise' a film through an interpretation of what they believe the audience will accept. According to Tarun, 'the term used in story sittings is 'yeh to accept nahin hoga' [This will not be accepted]. Loose moral values are only for the antagonist' (as quoted in Ganti 2002: 288). In such a way, filmmakers portray audiences in India as very sensitive to issues of morality with a judgement being made about whether certain plot elements will be acceptable to the audience. For example, while many films centred on love triangles are thought to have wide appeal in India, the film *Fatal Attraction* has been declared unsuitable since filmmakers 'felt the manner in which marital infidelity was handled in the film would not be acceptable to audiences' (Ganti 2002: 287).

It is my contention that these assumptions about what an Indian audience will or will not accept are the central reasoning for the changes in *Heyy Babyy*. Moreover, I am not making the claim that Indian audiences could not accept the morality inherent in the source texts, but, rather, am claiming that the filmmakers assumed this to be the case. Furthermore, the life of debauchery which opens the film comes to be replaced by more traditional and conservative values as the film progresses. Significantly, the men choose to name the baby Angel because, as Arush explains, 'she

Figure 4.6 The family come together for a traditional wedding in *Heyy Babyy*

taught us the meaning of life and converted us into good human beings'. Later, they decide that they do not want Angel to have any boyfriends when she grows up and, more specifically, they do not want Angel to have boyfriends who are anything like them. In a self-conscious moment of revelation, Tanmay declares that, 'All those girls whose hearts we have broken are also daughters of their parents'. The film then develops a marriage sub-plot in which Arush – who now knows that he is the father – attempts to win the love of Isha so that they can bring up their child in a traditional marriage. Asking to get back into the life of his child, he argues, 'I know a child needs a mother the most, but she also needs a father'. The film then ends with Isha's wedding to Arush (see Figure 4.6) and the restoration of the traditional family structure.

This theme takes on extra resonance when we consider the protagonists' position as NRIs living in Sydney, Australia. As Ravinder Kaur has argued, the Indian diaspora is generally evaluated in cinema 'according to the extent of its interaction with the local society', meaning that 'the less "polluted" it is with Western influences, the more Indian they are in their values' (2002: 206). As I have described, *Heyy Babyy* depicts Tanmay, Ali and Arush as very much in thrall to the perceived debauchery of consumerist Western culture. Depicting the negative moral influence of their lifestyle in Sydney, it is significant that the women that they sleep with (other than Isha) are all Caucasian and English-speaking. Furthermore, all three men fit the stereotype of the 'bad NRI' in that their moral bankruptcy is depicted through 'alcohol consumption, a promiscuous sex-life, love for smoke-filled night clubs, lack of respect for [their] elders, and an absence of spirituality, all of which are understood to be a by-product of [their] Western upbringing' (ibid.). They also represent a globalised and upwardly-mobile middle class in their embrace of Western fashion and consumerism, which reaches almost absurd levels in some song sequences. The ultimately conservative ending, therefore, in which the baby is returned to a traditional family structure reflects a trend in NRI narratives in that the characters' 'redemption comes only after they have realised the hollowness of Western society and returned to their authentic roots' (ibid.). This marks the film out from both its source texts, *Trois Hommes et un Couffin* and *Three Men and a Baby*, in that those films have been read as cultural critiques of their respective countries of production, whereas *Heyy Babyy* functions more as a critique of Western influence and an assertion of traditional Indian values.

In conclusion, it is worth considering the irony of critiquing Western influence from within a remake of a Hollywood film. Structurally this is very much a localisation of *Three Men and a Baby* as it localises the imported plot for the Indian context – reaffirming traditional Indian values even while it reworks a French plot by way of Hollywood. There is an attendant tension, therefore, between the ways in which the film pays homage to the Hollywood source text and, at the same time, laments the pollution of Indian culture with Western influences. The film functions simultaneously as a critique of Western influence while also being a symptom of that very phenomenon, and this is a tension that is never really resolved in the text.

Furthermore, as with *Koi . . . Mil Gaya*, this case study points to the problems with ascribing definitive origins to a particular cinematic meme. Many of these remakes are actually part of a much longer chain of intertextual reworkings, and this is certainly the case with *Heyy Babyy*. Within the critical work on *Trois Hommes et un Couffin*, various critics have cited John Ford's *Three Godfathers*, in which three outlaws save an infant found in the desert, as the structural model for Serreau's film. *Heyy Babyy* can therefore be seen as a remake of a remake of a remake, which is not even to mention the potential intertexts of *Three Godfathers* itself.

Nevertheless, this example demonstrates how studies of transnational adaptation can help to draw out insights into filmmakers' assumptions about cultural difference. The same basic narrative structure is adapted and transformed in each of these cases and the comparisons can therefore be grounded in an analysis of how certain key elements are treated. By studying comparatively how the same basic plot is treated in different countries, we are able to see much more clearly some of the assumptions that underpin cultural production in each of these different contexts. Even when, as in *Heyy Babyy*, some of these assumptions actually work in tension with each other.

Ghajini (2008)

You see our films, it is more difficult to make, twenty times more difficult than the Hollywood film. A Hollywood film can interest their audiences with one track – you can have a bomb in a bus, a girl is driving the bus, and a man has to save the bus driver and the bus passengers. This is the whole film! We can't do a film like that. It could be our climax, only one scene in the film.

Satanu Gupta (quoted in Ganti 2002: 292)

Within the discourse surrounding Bollywood remakes, Hollywood films are frequently described as 'one track' or 'single track'. This is in reference to the high-concept nature of many Hollywood scripts which are said to be reducible to a single line – as in Satanu Gupta's description of *Speed* above. Indeed, Bollywood filmmakers often 'express their amazement and envy at how films can be made on "one line"' (Ganti 2002: 293) when such plots are considered inadequate for audiences in India. The remaking process, therefore, is often positioned as a way of enhancing the narrative through the addition of extra sub-plots or 'parallel tracks'. To explore this process in detail, I will now analyse *Ghajini* (2008), a remake of *Memento* (2000) which supplements the central narrative of a protagonist suffering from anterograde amnesia with a parallel romance narrative told through flashbacks.

As with my earlier example of *Sarkar*, the film opens with a director's note that references the intertextual relationship with its source text but, in this case, the source is only referred to obliquely:

In this film the lead role character suffers from short term memory loss . . . This film has been inspired by some stories and incidents with similar idea [sic] and real life incidents of people suffering from short term memory loss. We acknowledge other stories based on the disease short term memory loss.

Moreover, when star Aamir Khan was asked about whether *Ghajini* was a remake of *Memento*, he declared '*Ghajini* is not a remake or even slightly inspired by Hollywood flick *Memento*, but it is a remake of the Tamil film *Ghajini*' (Anon 2008). As I will discuss in the conclusion to this chapter, this caginess about *Ghajini*'s status as a remake is very much related to the increasing presence of Hollywood studios in India. There is increasing pressure to acknowledge sources and to license remakes from Hollywood, and this has affected the discourse around the type of unacknowledged appropriations that I am analysing. With a film like *Ghajini*, which was the highest-grossing Bollywood film of 2008, increasing pressure is being put on filmmakers to obtain the remake rights from the Hollywood films.

Furthermore, it is significant to note that Aamir Khan dismisses the notion that *Ghajini* is a remake of *Memento* only by explaining that it is actually a remake of a Tamil film, conveniently neglecting the fact that the Tamil film was itself inspired by *Memento*. I will explore this complex relationship with South Indian cinema later in this section but, for the moment, it is worth noting that remakes of South Indian cinema proliferate throughout Bollywood and are at least as prevalent as remakes of Hollywood films. This case study, therefore, allows us to consider these regional borrowings and interrogate the ways in which they can function as a filter for Hollywood plotlines.

Turning to the plot of *Ghajini*, the most significant change from *Memento* is in the narrative structure. It may be technically true that *Memento* fits the description of Hollywood films as containing one-track narratives but that is not to say that this is a conventional storyline. Rather, this is a one-track narrative that is actually told in reverse order. Indeed, for Andrew Kania, this experimental form of narrative is the defining feature of *Memento*, challenging the audience to interpret what is happening in the film:

> There is the initial question of what exactly the structure of the film is and, once this is solved, the much more difficult task of extracting the story –what actually happens in the film, and the chronological order of the fictional events – from the fragmented plot. (2009: 1)

While the DVD for *Memento* has an extra that allows the option of watching the film in chronological order, this is ultimately little more than a gimmick as the film was designed to function in reverse order with the narrative crescendos and reveals built on the lack of knowledge of what has come before. Conversely, *Ghajini* thoroughly reworks the structure of *Memento* so that the central plotline is now designed to function in chronological order, albeit supplemented by a romance-themed parallel track that allows for the inclusion of the requisite song sequences. While retaining many of the conceptual elements of *Memento*, especially those associated with the central character's anterograde amnesia, this is a major change that takes an experimental narrative form and adapts it into the dominant masala form of Bollywood cinema.

Centrally, *Ghajini* tells the story of Sanjay Saghania (Aamir Khan), a hugely successful businessman, who is attacked by the criminal Ghajini (Pradeep Rawat) and left with anterograde amnesia. We are introduced to Sanjay in a violent, baroque opening sequence in which he kills a man while attempting to get vengeance for his lover Kalpana (Asin Thottumkal), following instructions he has left for himself on polaroid

Figure 4.7 Sanjay discovering his tattooed body in *Ghajini*
(dir. A. R. Murugadoss, India, 2008)

photos and tattoos on his body. These elements are actually very close to
the depiction of anterograde amnesia in *Memento*, and the visual iconography of the tattooed body is very similar to the source text, albeit now with
the muscular torso that has come to be a defining feature of the contemporary male Bollywood star (see Figure 4.7).

Where the films diverge, however, is when we start to get flashbacks
to Sanjay's life before the attack and his loss of memory. This sub-plot
explains that Sanjay was the owner of the Air Voice mobile telephone
company and it centres on a developing romance between Sanjay and
the struggling model Kalpana. Interestingly, this parallel plotline is
actually a reworking of romantic comedy tropes which first appeared in
the British musical *Happy Go Lovely* (1951). After an initial misunder-
standing, Kalpana exploits erroneous rumours that link her with Sanjay
to bring her a certain level of kudos at work. However, when they do
actually meet, she fails to recognise him and assumes him to be a struggling model like herself. Their developing romance then rests upon her
not realising that the man she is romantically involved with is actually
Sanjay Saghania since he has decided he wants her to fall in love with him
without knowing about his huge wealth and status. The film then shifts
between this sub-plot and the main plotline, maintaining a gritty realism
for the narrative elements borrowed from *Memento*, but breaking out into
glossy primary colours and song sequences for the sections inspired by
Happy Go Lovely.

These changes mean that one of the key narrative functions of *Memento*
is lost in *Ghajini*. As Noel Carroll has argued, the backwards narration of
Memento

> puts the viewer in a position somewhat like Leonard's. Due to his condition, Leonard has no memory of what has immediately preceded the present moment on screen. Similarly, the audience does not know what has just happened prior to the moment before us, since we haven't seen it yet. So we are dropped into situations in media res, which is, of course, the condition of Leonard's life. (2009: 136)

Of course, we are not quite put in Leonard's situation as we are able to use our own short-term memory to piece together the story from the various fragments – something which Leonard could never do. Nevertheless, *Ghajini*'s change to a chronological narrative removes this puzzle dynamic of the film and marks part of the Indianisation process that the film has undergone.

As Tejaswani Ganti has argued, the three main elements of 'Indianisation' are 'adding "emotions," expanding the narrative, and inserting songs' (2004: 77). What we have in this transnational adaptation is a process of 'Indianisation' which localises the text using all three elements, but these elements are themselves very much inspired by tropes from a 1950s British musical comedy. Furthermore, this romantic sub-plot is actually at odds with the central action-thriller narrative and the shifts between the two create a wildly uneven tone throughout the film. Nevertheless, the addition of this parallel narrative allows for the necessary 'Indianised' elements to be present in the film without affecting the core narrative borrowed from *Memento*. In other words, this means that the film can maintain a dark and gritty tone in its central narrative thread and more importantly, a sense of verisimilitude, while still being able to introduce the requisite amount of song sequences through the parallel romantic sub-plot (see Figure 4.8). In this sense, the addition of a parallel narrative comes to function as a way to supplement an adapted text with the necessary

Figure 4.8 Song sequence from parallel romantic sub-plot in *Ghajini*

local features that an audience expects. Reflecting this, it is significant that Aamir Khan only has song sequences during the flashbacks and never in the central thriller narrative. To explain this, I would contend that the adaptation of certain Hollywood genres requires a level of verisimilitude that cannot be provided in the conventional Bollywood masala form. As a way around this, some films such as *Sarkar* remove song sequences completely. The alternative utilised in *Ghajini* is for the song sequences to be used only in a parallel narrative which is visually and formally kept separate from the main narrative line. While this method is not wholly successful in *Ghajini* as the film ends up tonally schizophrenic, this demonstrates yet another way in which the Hollywood meme can be adapted and transformed for the local cultural context while still fulfilling certain audience expectations.

Finally, it is worth considering the role that the 2005 Tamil film *Ghajini* played in this remaking process. As I described earlier, Bollywood filmmakers often attempt to reduce the chances of box-office failure by remaking films from Hollywood and South India. These are not seen as equivalents, however, with many filmmakers expressing a preference for remaking South Indian films as they are culturally closer to the Bollywood form. Indeed, in a series of interviews for *Trade Guide*, Ashim Samanta argues that:

> English [language] films have a different culture, so one needs to Indianise the subject and incorporate songs too, which may not necessarily be well-received. Whereas remakes, copies or inspirations of South [Indian] films could prove to be safer than tackling a fresh subject altogether. (Quoted in Goculdas 1997: 14)

Manoj Chaturvedi takes this even further in his claim that:

> If you consider the track record in the last 4–5 years, the remakes have fared better in comparison to fresh subjects. English [language] films stand better chances only if they are convincingly Indianised but the South [Indian] remakes are the ones that are definitely safe. There is no question of them being losing proposals! (Quoted in Goculdas 1997: 15)

What we have in *Ghajini* is a film which develops out of an English-language feature, *Memento*, which was experimental in narrative and form and would have required a significant level of 'Indianisation' to directly remake it in Bollywood. What made this a safer proposition for the Bollywood producers, however, was that it had already been remade as a South Indian film and had therefore already proved to be appealing to Indian audiences. In fact, the Bollywood *Ghajini* is actually very similar to its Tamil source text, albeit with a different ending, and this certainly reflects Chaturvedi's assertion that remakes of South Indian films do not need to be 'Indianised' in the same way. Of course, it was the Tamil film that initially took the risk of 'Indianising' the *Memento* plotline and it was the success of this process that convinced the Bollywood production team to invest. Many of the changes that I have described in this chapter (and this book, as a whole) result from an attempt to localise borrowed elements of Hollywood for the particular context in which the adaptation is being produced. Uniquely for Bollywood, the South Indian remakes therefore function as a testing ground to see how successfully these Hollywood features can be localised, ultimately offering the Bollywood producers what they feel is a safer investment.

In conclusion, *Ghajini* reflects some of the key characteristics of contemporary Bollywood cinema. As Rosie Thomas has argued, the emphasis in Bollywood cinema is generally on '*how* things will happen, not *what* happens next [and] on a moral disordering to be (temporarily) resolved rather than an enigma to be solved' (1989: 15). By taking a narrative in *Memento* which is very much focused on what happens next – albeit in the reverse form of 'what happens before' – and also functions as an enigma to be solved, *Ghajini* is an ambitious attempt to translate this into the dominant Bollywood masala form. Supplementing the core narrative with a parallel track that supplies the necessary song sequences and emotional crescendos, the film therefore finds an innovative way to combine the requirements of narrative verisimilitude necessitated by the core narrative with the requirements of the Bollywood form more broadly.

Conclusion

Borrowing ideas, scripts and remaking them in different cultural contexts is a part of international cinema. But there is a right way of going about it. That will be to license the right to use the underlying material. The wrong way is to just take the ideas.

Rich Taylor, MPAA (Quoted in Basi 2010)

Throughout this chapter, I have discussed the ways in which elements from Hollywood films have been adapted and transformed in Indian cinema. Developing an historical account of Bollywood's relationship to Hollywood and then offering a close textual analysis of four case studies, I have drawn attention to the dominant forms of transnational adaptation in India and indicated some of the possible determinant factors which helped shape these specific forms.

Through *Koi . . . Mil Gaya* I explored the ways in which this transnational adaptation drew upon a range of imported sources including *E. T.*,

Close Encounters of the Third Kind and *Contact*. Noting that the film borrowed certain plot points but did not use recognisable iconography from
these sources, I argued that this adaptation functioned less as an imitation
of, or commentary upon, its source texts than as a mediation of the rising
Hindu nationalism at its time of production. I then turned to the phenomenon of the songless Bollywood film, analysing the *Godfather* remake
Sarkar. Showing that this film was integrating the Mumbai context with
a borrowed narrative form, I demonstrated how transnational adaptation
can be used as a strategy to introduce alternative narrative forms into local
cinema. Thirdly, I looked at the adaptation of gender and moral codes in
Heyy Babyy, showing how comparative studies of a series of cross-cultural
remakes can offer a privileged insight into filmmakers' assumptions about
cultural difference. Finally, I examined the narrative form of *Ghajini*,
a remake of *Memento* which supplements the core plot with a romantic
sub-plot complete with song sequences. By exploring how the remaking
process went through a South Indian remake, I was also able to explore
the impact of transregional flows of media on processes of transnational
adaptation.

As I have argued throughout this book, the Hollywood meme is taken
up in very different ways around the world and it is my belief that this
chapter has helped mark out certain tendencies in the transnational
adaptation of Hollywood. One of the key factors that came through in
this analysis was the overwhelming emphasis on the localisation of plots
rather than characters and iconography within the Indian context. Unlike
in Turkey and the Philippines, the borrowed texts are rarely being evoked
to engender recognition from the domestic audience and they are also
rarely being engaged with or commented upon directly. In my concluding chapter, I will utilise my comparative model to reflect upon the
wider factors shaping the different forms of adaptation across these three
contexts; suffice it to say that this lack of emphasis on recognisable iconography in Bollywood borrowings is closely related to the relative lack of
market penetration of Hollywood films on Indian screens. Furthermore,
the fact that these unlicensed borrowings have flourished is partly due to
Indian cinema being seen as 'so far under the radar [that] no Hollywood
executive is aware' of the copying (Amitraj quoted in Desai 2005: 267).

This is all set to change. Since 2000, when the Indian government
allowed the Foreign Investment Promotion Board to approve foreign
investment ventures into filmmaking, studios such as Columbia Tristar,
Paramount and Universal Pictures have all established offices in Mumbai.
The increasing presence of Hollywood studios in India means that there is
associated pressure to acknowledge sources and to license remakes directly

from Hollywood. In addition, the increasing global market share of the Bollywood industry has led Hollywood studios to become interested in co-productions and distribution deals. As Toby Miller et al. have argued, the Indian remakes have 'long been a sore spot for Hollywood, particularly as the Indian industry became the most prolific in the world and domestic protective measures were enacted to ensure its national dominance' (2005: 239). Indeed, it is estimated that in the 1980s, Hollywood major studios lost over $1billion in royalties and remake fees in India.

As a result of this increasing presence and estimated lost revenues, Hollywood studios have started to threaten legal action over these unlicensed adaptations. In 2007, the Will Smith film *Hitch* (2005) was remade as *Partner* (2007), and the Bollywood team soon received a threat of legal action against them from Will Smith's production company. While this threat did not itself come to fruition, it did indicate the readiness of Hollywood studios to start using legal methods to shut down the practice of unlicensed adaptations. One year later, Warner Bros filed a lawsuit against the Bollywood film *Hari Puttar: A Comedy of Terrors* (2008) claiming that the title was too similar to the Harry Potter brand. The plot of the film was actually unrelated to Harry Potter so they could not pursue copyright infringement but instead used trademark law to seek to restrain infringement of the Harry Potter brand name.

Cases such as this have led to a sea change in attitudes towards intellectual property in Bollywood cinema. The production team Nikhil Advani and Mukesh Talreja decided to legally obtain the rights to remake the Warner Bros. comedy *The Wedding Crashers* (2005), marking the first time that a Bollywood production company had legally obtained the rights to remake a Hollywood film. This indicates the impact that an increasing Hollywood presence and the associated threat of potential legal action has had on the Bollywood film industry.

In the following concluding chapter, I will bring together the outcomes of each of my chapters in order to comparatively mark out the dominant tendencies in the transnational adaptation of Hollywood. This book is built around a study of the diverse forms of adaptation in the popular film industries of Turkey, Philippines and India so this chapter will ultimately offer some conclusions as to the determinant factors shaping different forms of transnational adaptation. It will also reflect on the utility of my comparative model for exploring transnational adaptation beyond these case studies.

Conclusion: Reflections on the Hollywood Meme

The [adaptation] of Hollywood reflects a simultaneous chafing at and admiration for at least some aspects of internationally dominant film culture, and it carries distinctive regional and national implications.

Patricia Aufderheide (1998: 192)

More and more rare films are made available in their entirety on YouTube, cut into ten-minute-long segments, while file sharing via BitTorrent has enabled the formation of lively communities that converge around partaking rare material in a variety of languages.

Dina Iordanova (2010: 36)

(American junk) Get it out of my bloodstream
(American junk) Get it out of my system
(American junk) I can only take so much
(American junk) Got to get back to who I am . . .

Apo Hiking Society (1987)

In 1964, Italian film company Alrugo Entertainment produced a film entitled *Italian Spiderman*. Featuring actor Franco Franchetti of *Mondo Sexo* fame, the film was a knowing pastiche of the *Spider-Man* franchise. Thought lost for over forty years, the film was recently discovered in a sunken sea vessel and lovingly restored by Alrugo Studios Milan, who subsequently uploaded the rare theatrical trailer to Myspace, Yahoo and YouTube. Or at least this is what it says on the press release for the film.

In fact, the trailer for *Italian Spiderman* was produced in 2007 by a group of film students based at Flinders University in Adelaide, Australia. Taking inspiration from the kinds of transnational adaptations which I have been discussing in this book, the trailer imagined what a 1960s Italian adaptation of Spider-Man might look like, and was filled with knowing tributes to successful Italian film cycles such as the giallo and eurospy film. After the viral success of the trailer, which has received over 5.9 million views on YouTube to date, the group received funding from the South Australian Film Corporation to produce a series of ten webisodes shown in weekly instalments from 22 May 2008 onwards. The inspiration for *Italian Spiderman* came from the kinds of transnational adaptation discussed in this book – deliberately evoking the aesthetic style of titles such as *3 Dev Adam* and *James Batman* – but it reached out well beyond the limited fandom surrounding these films, and the core creative team Dario Russo and David Ashby have consequently built on this success by producing the highly successful spoof TV series *Danger 5* which pays homage to 1960s and 1970s Euro-cult cinema.

The viral popularity of *Italian Spiderman* is part of a broader shift where the kinds of transnational adaptation that I have been discussing in this book are becoming much more prominent within media discourse. In 2013, Australian filmmaker Andrew Leavold released his documentary *The Search for Weng Weng* which follows his search to find out more about the eponymous 'Filipino midget James Bond', and in the process to investigate the cultural dynamics underpinning the Filipino film industry. Meanwhile, in 2014, Turkish-German director Cem Kaya released his documentary *Remake, Remix, Rip-Off* which investigates the 1960s and 1970s Yeşilçam industry and interviews a number of the cast and crew who produced Turkish reworkings of Hollywood cinema. Together these documentaries have brought attention to the numerous ways in which the Filipino and Turkish industries borrowed from Hollywood cinema, and to a range of films that had been hitherto overlooked beyond their respective domestic spheres. Of course, this is not to say that these kinds of films had been completely neglected within English-language critical discourse. There has been a small but devoted following within Anglo-American cult fandom which can largely be traced back to Pete Tombs' *Mondo Macabro: Weird & Wonderful Cinema around the World* (1998). In the book, he promises to take the reader on a journey through such 'weird and wonderful' cinema as the Brazilian film *Kung Fu Contras As Bonecas* (Bruce Lee versus. Gay Power, 1975) and the Argentinian film *La Venganza Del Sexo* (The Curious Dr Humpp, 1967), and it is notable just how many of the films that he discusses borrow and rework elements from American popular culture. Tombs' book is a pioneering study in many ways, and actually contains a great deal of invaluable research, although it should be noted that the subsequent fandom surrounding the films has occasionally been more focused on celebrating the films simply for appearing 'weird and wonderful' rather than being an attempt to engage with the meaning of these films in any more depth. As Mark Jancovich et al. have argued:

not only are these products celebrated in this new context for their supposed difference from the 'mainstream' (although they may in fact be the mainstream of their
own culture) but this often involves an exoticisation of other cultures. (2003: 4)

This exoticisation process is clearly reflected in a series of online articles
discussing transnational adaptations that have been published over the
last few years. MTV published an article listing the 'Nine Most Random
Movies Ripped Off by Foreign Countries' (D'Arpino 2013), Yahoo
Movies published a list of 'The Strangest Foreign-Language Versions of
Hollywood Movies' (Watkins 2014), Cracked posted a video countdown
of 'Six Insane Foreign Remakes of Famous American Blockbusters'
(O'Brien 2015), and Geek & Sundry published a list of 'Seven Super
Weird Foreign Remakes' (Pinchuk 2016). Nevertheless, while there have
been an increasing number of such lists of 'strange', 'weird' and 'random'
remakes from around the world, there have also been a number of fans and
critics who have gone beyond these more superficial engagements in order
to investigate the complexity of these processes in much greater depth –
Ed Glaser's Deja View video series being a perfect example of how to
investigate such works without lapsing into unthinking exoticisation.

Meanwhile, not only are these transnational adaptations becoming
increasingly well known, but, in a manner that resonates with the broader
argument of this book, they are themselves being taken up as internet
memes. The adaptations of Hollywood that I have written about in this
book are far from being the end-point in this intertextual process. New
media technologies are helping these reworkings gain wider circulation
which, in turn, facilitates further ways in which these borrowings can
themselves be borrowed and reworked. One of the most popular forms of
reworking is when fans add subtitles to construct new narratives such as
in the internet series *3 Dev Adam: The Series* from SJ Cult Movies which
uses footage of the Turkish film *3 Dev Adam* but with subtitles that change
the plot in a manner reminiscent of the acts of détournement in Woody
Allen's *What's Up Tiger Lily* (1966).

As I argued in my case study chapters, the predominant form of
transnational adaptation which I have been dealing with in this book –
adaptations of Hollywood produced for release in Turkey, India and the
Philippines – have slowly died out as industrial changes and alterations to
the legal framework have changed the broader context of production. The
Hollywood meme has become something of a historical phenomenon, at
least in the three industries under consideration. Yet, as examples such
as *Italian Spiderman* and *3 Dev Adam: The Series* demonstrate, this phenomenon has now shifted onto the internet with borrowings continuing to

flourish at the fringes of global copyright law even if no longer in theatrically released feature films.

To conclude, I would like to briefly reflect on my findings during this research project and on the utility of the comparative model I proposed. In Chapter 1, I mapped out the various theoretical frameworks surrounding globalisation, and proposed a move away from models that rely upon notions of dominance and resistance in favour of a more contextual approach that examines the textual strategies through which Hollywood is reworked in specific historical contexts. I then outlined my comparative memetic methodology and explained how I would use this to mark out indicative tendencies in my case study chapters. Significantly, this chapter suggested a number of determinant factors that could play a role in shaping the specific forms of appropriation, such as government policy, industrial conditions, copyright regimes, distribution arrangements, and the relative presence of the source texts in the local film culture. Chapter 2, 'Hollywood and the Popular Cinema of Turkey', then went on to examine the impact of these factors in the case studies of *3 Dev Adam*, *Turist Ömer Uzay Yolunda*, *Şeytan* and *Dünyayi Kurtaran Adam*, specifically highlighting the role of domestic distribution and alternative conceptions of copyright in shaping the predominant forms of transnational adaptation in the Turkish industry. This was then compared to the predominant forms in Filipino cinema in Chapter 3, 'Hollywood and the Popular Cinema of the Philippines'. Analysing four examples that represent the predominant forms of transnational adaptation within that context, *Dynamite Johnson*, *For Y'ur Height Only*, *Alyas Batman en Robin* and *Darna: Ang Pagbabalik*, this chapter examined the ways in which specific industrial conditions such as co-production arrangements or plans for international distribution led to forms of adaptation that differ in significant ways from those outlined in my Turkish case study. Finally, Chapter 4, 'Hollywood and the Popular Cinema of India', complicated the dynamics of the previous chapters by exploring a similar (but distinct) phenomenon within an industry with the financial clout to rival Hollywood itself. Exploring how case studies such as *Koi . . . Mil Gaya*, *Sarkar*, *Heyy Babyy* and *Ghajini* reflect certain commercial imperatives at work, while also being shaped by the relative lack of Hollywood penetration in the country, this chapter demonstrated the distinctive strategies underpinning transnational adaptation in India – strategies that are closer to Hollywood's own attempts to remake foreign-language cinema than the modes present in Turkey and the Philippines.

So what do these tendencies I have identified tell us about the nature of transnational adaptation more broadly? Are we any closer to answering why some traditions favour certain kinds of adaptation? While this can only be tentative and would require further testing to gauge the wider applicability of these claims, my evidence suggests that there is certainly more of a tendency towards the localisation of a borrowed plot where the source text is not well known in the host country, a phenomenon that seems especially pertinent in the four Bollywood case studies but also rings true with *Seytan* in the chapter on Turkey. Indeed, it is notable that in a country like India where Hollywood has relatively small market share, the films are still one of the predominant models for emulation. Conversely, parodic forms of appropriation generally rely upon the notion that audiences recognise what is being borrowed and commented upon, as we saw with *Turist Omer Uzay Yolunda* and *Alyas Batman en Robin*, and therefore necessitate a certain level of market penetration from the host country. Furthermore, the more opportunistic adaptations that attempt to associate themselves directly with the source text through iconographic resemblance – as we saw with *3 Dev Adam* and *For Y'ur Height Only* – utilise this borrowed iconography as exploitable elements through which to draw in an audience who are aware of the source text. Moreover, copyright law plays a relatively small role in determining the particular types of transnational adaptation – the diversity of the adaptations produced within the Turkish industry is a case in point – yet copyright does play a significant role in shaping the level to which the source text is recreated. The Turkish film *Dünyayı Kurtaran Adam*, for example, would not have utilised actual footage and music from its sources if it had been produced in the Filipino or Indian context, for example. There are also considerable differences in the forms of adaptation used between films produced for local audiences and films produced primarily for export. As we saw with *Dynamite Johnson* and *For Y'ur Height Only*, the nature of international distribution, and especially international copyright law, encourages a less overt replication of the source than in films produced for the domestic market. On the other hand, many of the films in the Turkish and Philippines case study that were produced for the domestic market would almost certainly have encountered copyright issues if distributed internationally. Finally, the predominant mode of adaptation in India was a localisation of borrowed plots, and it is my contention that this was due to the relative lack of market penetration of US media in the country. There would have been little point in directly imitating or parodying the source texts if audiences did not recognise them. On the other hand, the adaptations produced in Turkey and the Philippines relied on audience recognition and reflect both an awareness of US media and a desire to self-consciously imitate and comment upon it in those contexts.

To fully test these claims, it would be necessary to use my comparative model to further explore transnational adaptation beyond these case
studies. Certainly my hypothesis based on what I have identified in this
study is that Hollywood adapts foreign-language cinema in a manner that
is much closer to the Bollywood case studies than those from Turkey
or the Philippines. There is little expectation of prior knowledge of the
source texts and little attempt to directly imitate, much less parody, the
material they are adapting. Conversely, the popular cinemas of Brazil and
Italy appear closer to Turkey and the Philippines in the ways in which
they engage with Hollywood, with examples such as *Bacalhau* (1976) in
Brazil and *The Last Shark* (1980) in Italy evoking similar issues to those
raised in my chapters on those contexts. This is, of course, only a hypothesis based on my awareness of certain parallel trends in these countries.
Nevertheless, it is my contention that as more examples of the Hollywood
meme come under the lens of this model, we will have a deeper and richer
understanding of the variety of forms of transnational adaptation, and the
numerous ways in which Hollywood has impacted world cinema more
broadly.

As I hope this book has demonstrated, a comparative analysis of transnational adaptation can tell us a great deal about the way texts circulate internationally and the specific circumstances in which they are received and
reworked. Rather than see the global circulation of Hollywood in terms of
blanket Americanisation, I have argued for a more nuanced model of cultural exchange which pays attention to the tensions and ambivalences in
these processes of globalisation. These borrowings should be understood
less through the prism of cultural domination and resistance than through
the lens of agency and creativity. Furthermore, I have investigated a
wide range of adaptations produced around the world, demonstrating
that the Hollywood meme is adapted and reworked in different ways,
through different methods and to different effects in each case. It is my
hope, therefore, that this work will help point the way towards a greater
understanding of the various forms of transnational adaptation produced
around the world, and the ways in which national cultures interrelate and
exchange with each other.

Ultimately, I hope to have shown that if we are serious about reframing
world cinema as the 'cinema of the world' (Nagib 2006: 35), rather than
seeing it in opposition to Hollywood, then we need to address this history
of syncretism and the factors that shape it. As Ana M. López has argued,
'Rather than a face-off between Hollywood and its others, what we now
seek to understand is a broader zone of cultural debate and economic relationships, in which we can trace the tensions and contradictions between

national sites and transnational processes' (2000: 435). While this book is only my own modest contribution to the broader transnational turn within film studies scholarship, I hope that it helps move us beyond models of cultural globalisation that rely on notions of domination and resistance to instead start engaging with the more complex, interstitial processes through which cultures interact and borrow from each other.

Bibliography

Acland, Charles (2003), *Screen Traffic: Movies, Multiplexes and Global Culture*, Durham: Duke University Press.

Akhtar, Javed (1996), 'Originality . . . What's that?' *Filmfare*, May.

Alessio, Dominic and Jessica Langer (2007), 'Nationalism and Postcolonialism in Indian Science Fiction: Bollywood's *Koi . . . Mil Gaya* (2003)', *New Cinemas*, 5: 3.

Allas, Denise Chou (1983), 'Dolphy: The Way of a Clown', in Rafael Ma. Guerrero (ed.), *Readings in Philippine Cinema*, Manila: Experimental Cinema of the Philippines.

Allen, Graham (2000), *Intertextuality*, London: Routledge.

Allen, Richard (2007), 'Hitchcock and Hindi Cinema: A Dossier', in Sidney Gottlieb and Richard Allen (eds), *Hitchcock Annual 15*, Gambier, OH: Hitchcock Annual Corp.

Alter, Stephen (2007), *Fantasies of a Bollywood Love Thief: Inside the World of Indian Moviemaking*, Orlando: Harcourt.

An, Jinsoo (2001), 'The Killer: Cult Film and Transcultural (Mis)Reading', in Esther C. Yau (ed.), *At Full Speed: Hong Kong Cinema in a Borderless World*, Minneapolis: University of Minnesota Press.

Anderson, Benedict (1991), *Imagined Communities*, London: Verso.

Andrew, Dudley (2006), 'An Atlas of World Cinema', in Stephanie Dennison and Song Hwee Lim (eds), *Remapping World Cinema: Identity, Culture and Politics in Film*, London: Wallflower Press.

Ang, Ien (1989), *Watching Dallas: Soap Opera and the Melodramatic Imagination*, London: Routledge.

Ang, Ien (1996), *Living Room Wars: Rethinking Media Audiences for a Postmodern World*, London: Routledge.

Apo Hiking Society (1987), 'American Junk', on *Made in the Philippines* [CD], Quezon City: Universal Records.

Appadurai, Arjun (1996), *Modernity at Large: Cultural Dimensions of Globalization*, Minneapolis: University of Minnesota Press.

Armes, Roy (1987), *Third World Filmmaking and the West*, Berkeley: University of California Press.

Armes, Roy (1989), 'Twelve Propositions on the Inaccessibility of Third World Cinema', in Christine Woodhead (ed.), *Turkish Cinema: An Introduction*, London: SOAS.

Arslan, Savas (2007), 'Projecting a Bridge for Youth: Islamic "Enlightenment" versus Westernisation in Turkish cinema', in Timothy Shary and Alexandra Seibel (eds), *Youth Culture in Global Cinema*, Austin: University of Texas Press.

Arslan, Savas (2011), *Cinema in Turkey: A New Critical History*, Oxford: Oxford University Press.

Athique, Adrian (2008), 'The Global Dynamics of Indian Media Piracy: Export Markets, Playback Media and the Informal Economy', *Media Culture & Society*, 30: 5.

Aufderheide, Patricia (1998), 'Made in Hong Kong: Translation and Transmutation', in Andrew Horton and Stuart Y. McDougal (eds), *Play It Again, Sam: Retakes on Remakes*, Berkeley: University of California Press.

Bakhtin, Mikhail (1981), *The Dialogic Imagination*, Austin: University of Texas Press.

Banerjee, Kanchana (2003), 'Cloning Hollywood', *The Hindu*, 3 August 2003, available online at: *http://www.hinduonnet.com/mag/2003/08/03/stories/2003080300090400.htm*

Barber, Benjamin (1995), *Jihad vs McWorld*, New York: Ballantine Books.

Barthes, Roland (2001), 'The Death of the Author', in Philip Rice and Patricia Waugh (eds), *Modern Literary Theory*, London: Arnold.

Basi, Hariqbal (2010), 'Indianizing Hollywood: The Debate over Bollywood's Copyright Infringement', in *The Selected Works of Hariqbal Basi*, available online at: *http://works.bepress.com/hariqbal_basi/2/*

Baumgärtel, Tilman (2006), 'Imitation, Indigenisation, Assimilation? No, Globalisation!: The Cinema of Bobby Suarez', in Shin Kim-Dong and Joel David (eds), *Cinema in/on Asia* (Gwangju, 2006), available online at: *http://www.cct.go.kr/data/acf2006/cinema/cinema-Session%203%20-%20 Baumgaertel.pdf*

Beller, Jonathan (2006), *Acquiring Eyes: Philippine Visuality, Nationalist Struggle and the World-Media System*, Quezon City: Ateneo de Manila University Press.

Bennett, Tony and Janet Woollacott (1987), *Bond and Beyond: The Political Career of a Popular Hero*, New York: Methuen.

Berger, Richard (2008), 'Are There Any More at Home Like You?: Rewiring Superman', *Journal of Adaptation in Film & Performance*, 1: 2.

Bergfelder, Tim (2000), 'The Nation Vanishes: European Co-productions and Popular Genre Formula in the 1950s and 1960s', in Mette Hjort and Scott Mackenzie (eds), *Cinema and Nation*, London: Routledge.

Bergfelder, Tim (2005a), *International Adventures: German Popular Cinema and European Co-productions in the 1960s*, New York: Berghahn.

Bergfelder, Tim (2005b), 'National, Transnational or Supranational Cinema?: Rethinking European Film Studies', *Media Culture & Society*, 27: 3.

Berkes, Niyazi (1997), *The Development of Secularism in Turkey*, London: Hurst.

Berry, Chris (2003), 'What's Big about the Big Film?', in Julian Stringer (ed.), *Movie Blockbusters*, London: Routledge.

Bhabha, Homi (2004), *The Location of Culture*, London: Routledge.

Bhattacharjya, Nilanjana (2009), 'Popular Hindi Film Song Sequences Set in the Indian Diaspora and the Negotiating of Indian Identity', *Asian Music*, 40: 1.

Bhaumik, Kaushik (2006), 'Consuming "Bollywood" in the Global Age: The Strange Case of an "Unfine" World Cinema', in Stephanie Dennison and Song Hwee Lim (eds), *Remapping World Cinema: Identity, Culture and Politics in Film*, London: Wallflower Press.

Bhaumik, Kaushik (2007), 'Lost in Translation: A Few Vagaries of the Alphabet Game Played between Bombay Cinema and Hollywood', in Paul Cooke (ed.), *World Cinema's 'Dialogues' with Hollywood*, Basingstoke: Palgrave Macmillan.

Binford, Mira Reym (1987), 'The Two Cinemas of India', in John D. H. Downing (ed.), *Film and Politics in the Third World*, Brooklyn: Autonomedia.

Binford, Mira Reym (1988), 'Innovation and Imitation in the Contemporary Indian Cinema', in Wimal Dissanayake (ed.), *Cinema and Cultural Identity: Reflections on Films from Japan, India and China*, Lanham: University Press of America.

Bisplinghoff, Gretchen and Carol Slingo (1997), 'Eve in Calcutta: The Indianisation of a Movie Madwoman', *Asian Cinema*, 9: 1.

Blackmore, Susan (1999), *The Meme Machine*, Oxford: Oxford University Press.

Bose, Derek (2005), *Bollywood Uncensored: What You Don't See on Screen and Why*, New Delhi: Rupa & Co.

Bose, Derek (2006), *Brand Bollywood: A New Global Entertainment Order*, New Delhi: Sage.

Bose, Nandana (2009a), 'Between the Godfather and the Mafia: Situating Right-wing Interventions in the Bombay Film Industry (1992–2002)', *Studies in South Asian Film and Media*, 1: 1.

Bose, Nandana (2009b), 'The Hindu Right and the Politics of Censorship: Three Case Studies of Policing Hindi Cinema, 1992–2002', *Velvet Light Trap*, 63.

Boyd, David and R. Barton Palmer (2006), *After Hitchcock: Influence, Imitation, and Intertextuality*, Austin: University of Texas Press.

Bozdoğan, Sibel and Resat Kasaba (eds) (1997), *Rethinking Modernity and National Identity in Turkey*, Seattle: University of Washington Press.

Brodie, Richard (1996), *Virus of the Mind: The New Science of the Meme*, Carlsbad, CA: Hay House.

Brooker, Will (1999), 'Batman: One Life, Many Faces', in Deborah Cartmell and Imelda Whelehan (eds), *Adaptations: From Text to Screen, Screen to Text*, London: Routledge.

Burt, Richard (2003), 'Shakespeare and Asia in Postdiasporic Cinemas: Spin-offs and Citations of Plays from Bollywood to Hollywood', in Richard Burt and Lynda E. Boose (eds), *Shakespeare, the Movie, II: Popularizing the Plays on Film, TV, Video and DVD*, London: Routledge.

Campbell, Neil, Jude Davies and George McKay (2004), *Issues in Americanisation and Culture*, Edinburgh: Edinburgh University Press.

Campos, Patrick F. (2006), 'Looming over the Nation, Uneasy with the Folks: Locating Mike de Leon in Philippine Cinema', *Humanities Diliman*, 3: 2.

Capino, Jose B. (2006), 'Philippines Cinema and its Hybridity (or "You're Nothing but a Second-rate Trying Hard Copycat!")', in Anne Tereska Ciecko (ed.), *Contemporary Asian Cinema: Popular Culture in a Global Frame*, Oxford: Berg Publishers.

Capino, Jose B. (2010), *Dream Factories of a Former Colony: American Fantasies, Philippine Cinema*, Minneapolis: University of Minnesota Press.

Carroll, Noel (2009), 'Memento and the Phenomenology of Comprehending Motion Picture Narration', in Andrew Kania (ed.), *Memento*, London: Routledge.

Cartmell, Deborah and Imelda Whelehan (1999), *Adaptations: From Text to Screen, Screen to Text*, London: Routledge.

Cartmell, Deborah and Imelda Whelehan (2007) (eds), *The Cambridge Companion to Literature on Screen*, Cambridge: Cambridge University Press.

Chakrabarty, Dipesh (2000), *Provincializing Europe: Postcolonial Thought and Historical Difference*, Princeton: Princeton University Press.

Chakravarty, Sumita (1993), *National Identity in Indian Popular Cinema, 1947–1987*, Austin: University of Texas Press.

Chan, Kenneth (2009), *Remade in Hollywood: The Global Chinese Presence in Transnational Cinemas*, Hong Kong: Hong Kong University Press.

Chapman, James (2003), *Cinemas of the World: Film and Society from 1895 to the Present*, London: Reaktion.

Chaudhuri, Shohini (2005), *Contemporary World Cinema; Europe, The Middle East, East Asia and South Asia*, Edinburgh: Edinburgh University Press.

Chesterman, Andrew (1997), *Memes of Translation: The Spread of Ideas in Translation Theory*, Amsterdam: Benjamins.

Chhabra, Aseem (2002), 'How Original is Bollywood?', *Rediff*, 31 October 2002, available online at: *http://www.rediff.com/movies/2002/oct/31bolly.htm*

Chow, Rey (1995), *Primitive Passions: Visuality, Sexuality, Ethnography, and Contemporary Chinese Cinema*, New York: Columbia University Press.

Chowdhury, Ayan Roy (2008), 'The Future of Copyright in India', *Journal of Intellectual Property Law & Practice*, 3: 2.

Ciecko, Anne (2001), 'Superhit Hunk Heroes for Sale: Globalization and Bollywood's Gender Politics', *Asian Journal of Communication*, 11: 2.

Ciecko, Anne (2006), 'Theorising Asian Cinema(s)', in Anne Ciecko (ed.), *Contemporary Asian Cinema*, New York: Berg.

Clifford, James (1988), *The Predicament of Culture: Twentieth Century Ethnography, Literature, and Art*, Cambridge, MA: Harvard University Press.

Clifford, James (1997), *Routes: Travel and Translation in the Late Twentieth Century*, Cambridge, MA: Harvard University Press.

Colmer, James (2003), 'The Philosophy of Jadoo', *IndiaFM News Bureau*, 13 August 2003, available online at: *http://www.bollywoodhungama.com/*

movies/news/type/view/id/1179548/sorttype/What/James-Colmer-on-the-phil
osophy-of-Jadoo%3A

Condry, Ian (2006), *Hip Hop Japan: Rap and the Paths of Cultural Globalisation*,
Durham: Duke University Press.

Coogan, Peter (2007), 'The Definition of the Superhero', in Wendy Haslem,
Angela Ndalianis and Chris Mackie (eds), *Super/Heroes: From Hercules to
Superman*, Washington: New Academia Publishing.

Cooke, Paul (2007) (ed.), *World Cinema's Dialogues with Hollywood*, Basingstoke:
Palgrave Macmillan.

Coombe, Rosemary (1998), *The Cultural Life of Intellectual Properties: Authorship,
Appropriation, and the Law*, Durham: Duke University Press.

Cosgrove-Mather, Bootie (2003), 'Is Bollywood a Hollywood Clone?: India's
Bollywood Denies Stealing Shots, Plots, Dialogue', *CBS News*, 4 June
2003, available online at: *http://www.cbsnews.com/stories/2003/06/04/
entertainment/main557012.shtml*

Cowen, Tyler (2002), *Creative Destruction: How Globalization is Changing the
World's Cultures*, Princeton: Princeton University Press.

Craig, Timothy and Richard King (2002), 'Asia and Global Popular Culture: The
View from He Yong's Garbage Dump', in Timothy Craig and Richard King
(eds), *Global Goes Local: Popular Culture in Asia*, Vancouver: University of
British Columbia Press.

Creekmur, Corey (2006), 'Popular Hindi Cinema and the Film Song', in Linda
Badley, R. Barton Palmer and Steven Jay Schneider (eds), *Traditions in World
Cinema*, Edinburgh: Edinburgh University Press.

Cullingworth, Michael (1989), 'On the First Viewing of Turkish Cinema', in
Christine Woodhead (ed.), *Turkish Cinema: An Introduction*, London: SOAS.

D'Arpino, Adam (2013), 'Nine Most Random Movies Ripped Off by Foreign
Countries', *MTV*, 17 October 2013, available online at: *http://www.mtv.com/
news/2817073/movie-rip-offs/*

Davis, Darrell William (2001), 'Reigniting Japanese Tradition with Hana-Bi',
Cinema Journal, 40: 4.

Davis, Rocio (2012), *The Transnationalism of American Culture: Literature, Film,
and Music*, London: Routledge.

Dawkins, Richard [1976] (1989), *The Selfish Gene*, Oxford: Oxford University
Press.

De Castro III, Pio (1986), 'Philippine Cinema (1976–1978)', in Clodualdo
Del Mundo Jr (ed.), *Philippine Mass Media: A Book of Readings*, Manila:
Communication Foundation for Asia.

Del Mundo, Jr, Clodualdo (1983), 'Towards the Development of the Filipino
Film', in Nicanor G. Tiongson (ed.), *The Urian Anthology 1970–1979*, Manila:
M. L. Morato.

Del Mundo Jr., Clodualdo (2002), 'Philippines: 1990s-2001', in Aruna Vasudev,
Latika Padgaonkar and Rashmi Dorasiwamv (eds), *Being and Becoming: The
Cinemas of Asia*, New Delhi: Macmillan.

Dentith, Simon (2000), *Parody*, London: Routledge.

Deocampo, Nick (2003), *Cine: Spanish Influences on Early Cinema in the Philippines*, Manila: National Commission for Culture and the Arts.

Desai, Rachana (2005), 'Copyright Infringement in the Indian Film Industry', *Vanderbilt Journal of Entertainment and Technology Law*, 7: 2.

Deshpande, Manisha (1998), 'Vikram Bhatt', *Trade Guide*, 44: 22.

Deshpande, Manisha (2000), 'Do Remakes of South/English Films Guarantee Success?', *Trade Guide*, 46: 32.

Desser, David (2003), 'Global Noir: Genre Film in the Age of Transnationalism', in Barry Keith Grant (ed.), *Film Genre Reader III*, Austin: University of Texas Press.

Desser, David (2008), 'Remaking Seven Samurai in World Cinema', in Leon Hunt and Leung Wing-Fai (eds), *East Asian Cinemas: Exploring Transnational Connections on Film*, London: I. B. Tauris.

DiPaolo, Marc Edward (2007), 'Wonder Woman as World War II Veteran, Camp Feminist Icon, and Male Sex Fantasy', in Terrence R. Wandtke (ed.), *The Amazing Transforming Superhero! Essays on the Revision of Characters in Comic Books, Film and Television*, Jefferson: McFarland.

Dissanayake, Wimal (2003), 'Rethinking Indian Popular Cinema: Towards Newer Frames of Understanding', in Anthony R. Guneratne and Wimal Dissanayake (eds), *Rethinking Third Cinema*, London: Routledge.

Dissanayake, Wimal (2006), 'Globalization and the Experience of Culture: The Resilience of Nationhood', in Natascha Gentz and Stefan Kramer (ed.), *Globalization, Cultural Identities, and Media Representations*, New York: State University of New York Press.

Dominguez, Virginia and Jane Desmond (1996), 'Resituating American Studies in a Critical Internationalism', *American Quarterly*, 48: 3.

Donmez-Colin, Gonul (2008), *Turkish Cinema: Identity, Distance and Belonging*, London: Reaktion Books.

Dorfman, Ariel (1983), *The Empire's Old Clothes: What the Lone Ranger, Babar, and Other Innocent Heroes Do to Our Minds*, New York: Pantheon Books.

Dorfman, Ariel and Armand Mattelart (1975), *How to Read Donald Duck: Imperialist Ideology in the Disney Comic*, New York: International General.

Dorsay, Atilla (1989), 'An Overview of Turkish Cinema from its Origins to the Present Day', in Christine Woodhead (ed.), *Turkish Cinema: An Introduction*, London: SOAS.

Dorsay, Attila (2002), 'Turkey: On Its Own Terms', in Aruna Vasudev, Latika Padgaonkar and Rashmi Dorasiwamv (eds), *Being and Becoming: The Cinemas of Asia*, New Delhi: Macmillan.

Downing, John D. H. (1987) (ed.), *Film & Politics in the Third World*, New York: Autonomedia.

Drahos, Peter (2002), 'Negotiating Intellectual Property Rights: Between Coercion and Dialogue', in P. Drahos and R. Mayne (eds), *Global Intellectual Property Rights: Knowledge, Access and Development*, Basingstoke: Palgrave.

Dudrah, Rajinder (2006), *Bollywood: Sociology Goes to the Movies*, London: Sage.

Dudrah, Rajinder and Jigna Desai (2008), *The Bollywood Reader*, Maidenhead: Open University Press.

Durham, Carolyn (1998), *Double Takes: Culture and Gender in French Films and their American Remakes*, Dartmouth: University Press of New England.

During, Simon (1997), 'Popular Culture on a Global Scale: A Challenge for Cultural Studies?', *Critical Inquiry*, 23: 4.

Durovicova, Natasa and Kathleen Newman (2009), *World Cinemas, Transnational Perspectives*, New York: Routledge.

Dwyer, Rachel (2000), *All You Want is Money, All You Need is Love: Sexuality and Romance in Modern India*, London: Cassell.

Dyer, Richard (2006), *Pastiche*, London: Routledge.

Dyer, Richard and Ginette Vincendeau (1992) (eds), *Popular European Cinema*, London: Routledge.

Eco, Umberto (1979a), 'The Myth of Superman', in Umberto Eco, *The Role of the Reader: Explorations in the Semiotics of Texts*, London: Hutchison and Co.

Eco, Umberto (1979b), 'Narrative Structures in Fleming', in Umberto Eco, *The Role of the Reader: Explorations in the Semiotics of Texts*, London: Hutchison and Co.

Eleftheriotis, Dimitris (2002), *Popular Cinemas of Europe: Studies of Texts, Contexts and Frameworks*, London: Continuum.

Eleftheriotis, Dimitris (2006), 'Turkish National Cinema', in Dimitris Eleftheriotis and Gary Needham (eds), *Asian Cinemas: A Reader & Guide*, Edinburgh: Edinburgh University Press.

Eleftheriotis, Dimitris and Dina Iordanova (2006), 'Indian Cinema Abroad: Historiography of Transnational Cinematic Exchanges', *South Asian Popular Culture*, 4: 2.

Eleftheriotis, Dimitris and Gary Needham (eds) (2006), *Asian Cinemas: A Reader and Guide*, Edinburgh: Edinburgh University Press.

Elsaesser, Thomas (2005), *European Cinema: Face to Face with Hollywood*, Amsterdam: Amsterdam University Press.

Erdoğan, Nezih (1998), 'Narratives of Resistance: National Identity and Ambivalence in the Turkish Melodrama between 1965 and 1975', *Screen*, 39: 3.

Erdoğan, Nezih (2003), 'Powerless Signs: Hybridity and the Logic of Excess of Turkish Trash', in Karen Ross, Brenda Dervin and Deniz Derman (eds), *Mapping the Margins: Identity Politics and the Media*, Creskil: Hampton Press.

Erdoğan, Nezih (2004), 'The Making of Our America: Hollywood in a Turkish Context', in Melvyn Stokes and Richard Maltby (eds), *Hollywood Abroad*, London: BFI.

Erdoğan, Nezih, and Deniz Göktürk (2001), 'Turkish Cinema', in Oliver Leaman (ed.), *Companion Encyclopaedia of Middle Eastern and North African Film*, London: Routledge.

Erdoğan, Nezih, and Dilek Kaya (2002), 'Institutional Intervention in the Distribution and Exhibition of Hollywood Films in Turkey', *Historical Journal of Film, Radio and Television*, 22: 1.

Evren, Nurcak (2005), *Turk Sinemasi*, Istanbul: Turkish Foundation of Cinema and Audiovisual Culture.

Featherstone, Mike (1990) (ed.), *Global Culture: Nationalism, Globalisation and Modernity*, London: Sage.

Featherstone, Mike, Scott Lash and Roland Robertson (eds) (1995), *Global Modernities*, London: Sage.

Ferrao, Dominic (2003), 'Ramu Hits the Global Highway', *The Times of India*, 18 January 2003, available online at: *http://timesofindia.indiatimes.com/articleshow/34715807.cms*

Forrest, Jennifer and Leonard R. Koos (2002) (eds), *Dead Ringers: The Remake in Theory and Practice*, New York: State University of New York Press.

Francia, Luis (1987), 'Philippine Cinema: The Struggle against Repression', in John D. H. Downing (ed.), *Film and Politics in the Third World*, Brooklyn: Autonomedia.

Francia, Luis (2002), 'Philippines: Beginnings to 1980s', in Aruna Vasudev, Latika Padgaonkar and Rashmi Dorasiwamv (eds), *Being and Becoming: The Cinemas of Asia*, New Delhi: Macmillan.

Frayling, Christopher (2006), *Spaghetti Westerns*, London: I. B. Tauris.

Friedkin, William (1999), 'The Fear of God Documentary', on *The Exorcist*: 25th Anniversary Edition [DVD], Warner Brothers.

Gaines, Jane (1991), *Contested Culture: The Image, The Voice, and The Law*, Chapel Hill: University of North Carolina Press.

Ganapati, Priya (2002), 'Kaante's Identity Crisis', *Rediff*, 26 December 2002, available online at: *http://sports.rediff.com/movies/2002/dec/26kaante.htm*

Garcia, Jessie B. (1983), 'The Golden Decade of Filipino Movies', in Rafael Ma. Guerrero (ed.), *Readings in Philippine Cinema*, Manila: Experimental Cinema of the Philippines.

Ganti, Tejaswini (2002), 'And Yet My Heart Is Still Indian: The Bombay Film Industry and the (H)Indianization of Hollywood', in Faye D. Ginsburg, Lila Abu-Lughod and Brian Larkin (eds), *Media Worlds: Anthropology on New Terrain*, Berkeley and Los Angeles: University of California Press.

Ganti, Tejaswini (2004), *Bollywood: A Guidebook to Popular Hindi Cinema*, London: Routledge.

Garcia-Canclini, Nestor (2005), *Hybrid Cultures: Strategies for Entering and Leaving Modernity*, Minneapolis: University of Minneapolis Press.

Garwood, Ian (2006), 'The Songless Bollywood Film', *South Asian Popular Culture*, 4: 2.

Genette, Gérard (1997), *Palimpsests: Literature in the Second Degree*, Lincoln: University of Nebraska Press.

Geraghty, Christine (2006), 'Jane Austen Meets Gurinder Chadha: Hybridity and Intertextuality in Bride and Prejudice', *South Asian Popular Culture*, 4: 2.

Geraghty, Christine (2008), *Now a Major Motion Picture: Film Adaptations of Literature and Drama*, Lanham: Rowman and Littlefield.

Gitlin, Todd (2002) *Media Unlimited: How the Torrent of Images and Sounds Overwhelms Our Lives*, New York: Picador.

Goculdas, Meena (1997), 'Do Remakes, Copies, Inspirations of South/English Films Guarantee Success?', *Trade Guide*, 44: 10.

Goculdas, Meena (1998), 'What Are the Prospects of English Films Copied by Our Makers?', *Trade Guide*, 44: 30.

Gokulsing, K. Moti and Wimal Dissanayake (1998), *Indian Popular Cinema: A Narrative of Cultural Change*, Stoke on Trent: Trentham Books.

Goodwin, James (1994), *Akira Kurosawa and Intertextual Cinema*, Baltimore: Johns Hopkins University Press.

Gopal, Sangita and Sujata Moorti (2008), *Global Bollywood: Travels of Hindi Songs and Dance*, Minneapolis: University of Minnesota Press.

Gopalan, Lalitha (2002), *Cinema of Interruptions: Action Genres in Contemporary Indian Cinema*, London: BFI.

Govil, Nitin (2007), 'Bollywood and the Frictions of Global Mobility', in Daya Thussu (ed.), *Media on the Move: Global Flow and Contra-Flow*, London: Routledge.

Govil, Nitin (2015), *Orienting Hollywood: A Century of Film Culture between Los Angeles and Bombay*, New York: New York University Press.

Gray, Jonathan (2006), *Watching with The Simpsons: Television, Parody, and Intertextuality*, London: Routledge.

Grigely, Joseph (1995), *Textualterity*, Ann Arbor: University of Michigan Press.

Gruss, Susanne (2009), 'Shakespeare in Bollywood?: Vishal Bhardwaj's *Omkara*', in Sarah Sackel and Walter Gobel (eds), *Semiotic Encounters: Text, Image and Trans-nation*, Amsterdam: Rodopi.

Guerrero, Rafael Ma. (1983), *Readings in Philippine Cinema*, Manila: Experimental Cinema of the Philippines.

Gumperz, John J. (1982), *Discourse Strategies: Studies in Interactional Linguistics*, Cambridge: Cambridge University Press.

Guneratne, Anthony R. (2003), 'Introduction: Rethinking Third Cinema', in Anthony R. Guneratne and Wimal Dissanayake (eds), *Rethinking Third Cinema*, London: Routledge.

Gupta, Chidananda Das (2002), 'India: House Full, No Intermission', in Aruna Vasudev, Latika Padgaonkar and Rashmi Dorasiwamv (eds), *Being and Becoming: The Cinemas of Asia*, New Delhi: Macmillan.

Gürata, Ahmet (2006), 'Translating Modernity: Remakes in Turkish Cinema', in Dimitris Eleftheoritis and Gary Needham (eds), *Asian Cinemas: A Reader and Guide*, Edinburgh: Edinburgh University Press.

Hall, Stuart (1991), 'The Local and the Global: Globalization and Ethnicity', in Anthony D. King (ed.) *Culture, Globalization and the World System*, Minneapolis: University of Minnesota Press.

Halliday, Fred (1996), *Islam and the Myth of Confrontation*, London: I. B. Tauris.

Hannerz, Ulf (1996), *Transnational Connections: Culture, People, Places*, London: Routledge.

Hansen, Miriam (2000a), 'The Mass Production of the Senses: Classical Cinema as Vernacular Modernism', in Christine Gledhill and Linda Williams (eds), *Reinventing Film Studies*, London: Arnold.

Hansen, Miriam (2000b), 'Fallen Women, Rising Stars, New Horizons: Shanghai Silent Film as Vernacular Modernism', *Film Quarterly*, 54: 1.

Hansen, Miriam (2009), 'Vernacular Modernism: Tracking Cinema on a Global Scale', in Natasa Durovicova and Kathleen Newman (eds), *World Cinemas, Transnational Perspectives*, London: Routledge.

Harries, Dan (2000), *Film Parody*, London: BFI.

Hawkins, Joan (2000), *Cutting Edge: Art-Horror and the Horrific Avant-Garde*, Minneapolis: University of Minnesota Press.

Hellier, Chris (1997), 'Turkey: Two Steps Forward, One Back', in Ruth Petrie (ed.), *Film and Censorship: The Index Reader*, London: Cassell.

Herbert, Daniel (2008), *Transnational Film Remakes: Time, Space, Identity*, dissertation, University of Southern California.

Hernando, Mario A. (1986), 'Against All Odds: The Story of the Filipino Film Industry (1978–1982)', in Clodualdo Del Mundo, Jr (ed.), *Philippine Mass Media: A Book of Readings*, Manila: Communication Foundation for Asia.

Hesmondhalgh, David (2000), 'International Times: Fusions, Exoticism and Antiracism in Electronic Dance Music', in David Hesmondhalgh and Georgina Born (eds), *Western Music and Its Others*, Berkeley: University of California Press.

Hesmondhalgh, David (2007), *The Cultural Industries*, London: Sage.

Higbee, Will and Song Hwee Lim (2010), 'Concepts of Transnational Cinema: Towards a Critical Transnationalism in Film Studies', *Transnational Cinemas*, 1: 1.

Higson, Andrew (1989), 'The Concept of National Cinema', *Screen*, 30: 4.

Higson, Andrew (2006), 'The Limiting Imagination of National Cinema', in Elizabeth Ezra and Terry Rowden (eds), *Transnational Cinema: The Film Reader*, London: Routledge.

Hjort, Mette (2009), 'On the Plurality of Cinematic Transnationalism', in Natasa Durovicova and Kathleen Newman (eds), *World Cinemas, Transnational Perspectives*, London: Routledge.

Hoberman, J. (2004), '1975–1985: Ten Years That Shook the World', in Thomas Schatz (ed.), *Hollywood: Critical Concepts in Media and Cultural Studies*, London: Routledge.

Hogan, Patrick Colm (2008), *Understanding Indian Movies: Culture, Cognition, and Cinematic Imagination*, Austin: University of Texas Press.

Horton, Andrew (1998), 'Cinematic Makeovers and Cultural Border Crossings', in Andrew Horton and Stuart McDougal (eds), *Play It Again, Sam: Retakes on Remakes*, Berkeley: University of California Press.

Hoskins, Colin and Rolf Mirus (1988), 'Reasons for the U.S. Dominance of the International Trade in Television Programs', *Media, Culture & Society*, 10.

Howes, David (1996), *Cross Cultural Consumption: Global Markets, Local Realities*, London: Routledge.

Hunt, Leon (2000), 'Han's Island Revisited: Enter the Dragon as Transnational Cult Film', in Xavier Mendik and Graeme Harper (eds), *Unruly Pleasures: The Cult Film and its Critics*, Guildford: FABPress.

Hunter, I. Q. (2002), 'Hammer Goes East: A Second Glance at *The Legend of the Seven Golden Vampires*', in Xavier Mendik (ed.), *Shocking Cinema of the Seventies*, Hereford: Noir Publishing.

Hunter, I. Q. (2009), 'Exploitation as Adaptation', *Scope: Journal of Film and Television Studies*, 15.

Huntington, Samuel (1993), 'Clash of Civilizations', *Foreign Affairs*, 72: 3.

Huntington, Samuel (1998), *The Clash of Civilisations and the Remaking of World Order*, London: Touchstone.

Hutcheon, Linda (1985), *A Theory of Parody*, New York: Methuen.

Hutcheon, Linda (2006), *A Theory of Adaptation*, London: Routledge.

Hutcheon, Linda and Gary R. Bortolotti (2007), 'On the Origin of Adaptations: Rethinking Fidelity Discourse and "Success" Biologically', *New Literary History*, 38: 3.

Hutchinson, Rachael (2006), 'Orientalism or Occidentalism?: Dynamics of Appropriation in Akira Kurosawa', in Stephanie Dennison and Song Hwee-Lim (eds), *Remapping World Cinema: Identity, Culture and Politics in Film*, London: Wallflower Press.

Hutchinson, Rachael (2007), 'A Fistful of *Yojimbo*: Appropriation and Dialogue in Japanese Cinema', in Paul Cooke (ed.), *World Cinema's 'Dialogues' with Hollywood*, Basingstoke: Palgrave Macmillan.

Infante, J. Eddie (1991), *Inside Philippine Movies 1970–1990*, Quezon City: Ateneo de Manila University Press.

Ingham, Mike (2008), 'Following the Dream / Passing the Meme: Shakespeare in "Translation"', *Studies in Theatre and Performance*, 28: 2.

Iordanova, Dina (2010), 'Rise of the Fringe: Global Cinema's Long Tail', in Dina Iordanova, David Martin-Jones and Belen Vidal (eds), *Cinema at the Periphery*, Detroit: Wayne State University Press.

Iwabuchi, Koichi (2002), *Recentering Globalization: Popular Culture and Japanese Transnationalism*, Durham: Duke University Press.

Iyer, Pico (1988), *Video Night in Kathmandu: And Other Reports from the Not-So-Far East*, London: Bloomsbury.

Jameson, Frederic (1986), 'Third-World Literature in The Era of Multinational Capitalism', *Social Text*, 15.

Jameson, Fredric (1991), *Postmodernism, or, The Cultural Logic of Late Capitalism*, Durham: Duke University Press.

Jancovich, Mark, Antonio Lazaro Reboll, Julian Stringer and Andy Willis (eds) (2003), *Defining Cult Movies: The Cultural Politics of Oppositional Taste*, Manchester: Manchester University Press.

Jenkins, Henry (1992), *Textual Poachers*, New York: Routledge.

Jenkins, Henry (2003), 'Quentin Tarantino's Star Wars?: Digital Cinema, Media Convergence, and Participatory Culture', in David Thorburn and Henry Jenkins (eds), *Rethinking Media Change: The Aesthetics of Transition*, Cambridge, MA: The MIT Press.

Jenkins, Henry (2006a), 'Pop Cosmopolitanism: Mapping Cultural Flows in an Age of Media Convergence', in Henry Jenkins, *Fans, Bloggers, and Gamers: Exploring Participatory Culture*, New York: New York University Press.

Jenkins, Henry (2006b), *Convergence Culture*, New York: New York University Press.

Jenkins, Henry (2009), '"Just Men in Tights": Rewriting Silver Age Comics in an Era of Multiplicity', in Angela Ndalianis (ed.), *The Contemporary Comic Book Superhero*, London: Routledge.

Jenkins, Henry, Sam Ford and Joshua Green (2013), *Spreadable Media: Creating Value and Meaning in a Networked Culture*, New York: New York University Press.

Jenkins, Henry, Xiaochang Li, Ana Domb Krauskopf and Joshua Green (2009), 'If It Doesn't Spread, It's Dead: Media Viruses and Memes', available online at: *http://www.henryjenkins.org/2009/02/if_it_doesnt_spread_its_dead_p.html*

Jess-Cooke, Carolyn (2006), 'Screening the McShakespeare in Post-millennial Shakespeare Cinema', in Mark Thornton Burnett and Ramona Wray (eds), *Screening Shakespeare in the Twenty-First Century*, Edinburgh: Edinburgh University Press.

Jess-Cooke, Carolyn (2009), *Film Sequels: Theory and Practice from Hollywood to Bollywood*, Edinburgh: Edinburgh University Press.

Jha, Subhash K. (2003), '"We Know Zilch about Audience Tastes": Ram Gopal Varma', *Rediff*, 9 June 2003, available online at: *http://www.rediff.com/movies/2003/jun/09ramu.htm*

Jun Heng, Wong (2015), 'Eighteen Ways the Force Awakens Ripped Off A New Hope', *Geek Crusade*, 21 December 2015, available online at: *http://www.geekcrusade.com/features/spoilers-18-ways-the-force-awakens-ripped-off-a-new-hope/23988*

Kandiyoti, Deniz (2002), 'Introduction: Reading the Fragments', in Deniz Kandiyoti and Ayse Saktanber (eds), *Fragments of Culture: The Everyday of Modern Turkey*, New Brunswick, NJ: Rutgers University Press.

Kandiyoti, Deniz and Ayse Saktanber (2002), *Fragments of Culture: The Everyday of Modern Turkey*, New Brunswick, NJ: Rutgers University Press.

Kania, Andrew (ed.) (2009), *Memento*, London: Routledge.

Kaplan, Yusuf (1996), 'Turkish Cinema', in Geoffrey Nowell-Smith (ed.), *The Oxford History of World Cinema*, Oxford: Oxford University Press.

Kara, M. (1996), 'Çetin Inanc', *Okuz*, 26: 6.

Katzmann, David and Norman Yetman (eds) (1993), Globalisation, Transnationalism and the End of the American Century [Special Issue], *American Studies*, 34: 1.

Kaur, Raminder and Ajay J. Sinha (2005), *Bollyworld: Popular Indian Cinema through a Transnational Lens*, London: Sage.

Kaur, Ravinder (2002), 'Viewing the West through Bollywood: A Celluloid Occident in the Making', *Contemporary South Asia*, 11: 2.

Kavoori, Anandam P. and Aswin Punathambekar (eds) (2008), *Global Bollywood*, New York: New York University Press.

Kenny, James F. (1995), 'Tagalog Movies and Identity: Portrayals of the Filipino Self', *The Humanities Bulletin* 4.

Kermode, Mark (1997), *The Exorcist*, London: BFI.

King, Anthony D. (ed.) (1991), *Culture, Globalisation and the World System*, Basingstoke: Macmillan.

Klein, Christina (2004), 'Martian Arts and the Globalisation of US and Asian Film Industries', *Comparative American Studies*, 2.

Kooijman, Jaap (2008a), 'Amsterdamned Global Village: A Cinematic Site of Karaoke Americanism', in Jaap Kooijman, Patricia Pisters and Wanda Strauven (eds), *Mind the Screen: Media Concepts According to Thomas Elsaesser*, Amsterdam: Amsterdam University Press.

Kooijman, Jaap (2008b), *Fabricating The Absolute Fake: America in Contemporary Pop Culture*, Amsterdam: Amsterdam University Press.

Kraidy, Marwan M. (2005), *Hybridity: or the Cultural Logic of Globalisation*, Philadelphia: Temple University Press.

Kristeva, Julia (1980), *Desire in Language: A Semiotic Approach to Literature and Art*, New York: Columbia University Press.

Krzywinska, Tanya (2006), 'Narrative Formulas', in Tanya Krzywinska, *Sex in the Cinema*, London: Wallflower Press.

Lacaba, Jose F. (1983), 'Notes on "Bakya": Being an Apologia of Sorts for Filipino Masscult', in Rafael Ma. Guerrero (ed.), *Readings in Philippine Cinema*, Manila: Experimental Cinema of the Philippines.

Lee, P. S. N. (1991), 'The Absorption and Indigenization of Foreign Media Cultures', *Asian Journal of Communication*, 1: 2.

Leeper, Mark R. (2003), 'Review for *Koi . . . Mil Gaya* (2003)', *IMDB*, available online at: *http://akas.imdb.com/reviews/354/35452.html*

Leitch, Thomas (2007), *Film Adaptation and Its Discontents: From Gone with the Wind to The Passion of the Christ*, Baltimore: Johns Hopkins University Press.

Leitch, Thomas (2008), 'Adaptation Studies at a Crossroads', *Adaptation*, 1: 1.

Lent, John A. (1990), *The Asian Film Industry*, Austin: University of Texas Press.

Liebes, Tamar and Elihu Katz (1993), *The Export of Meaning: Cross-Cultural Readings of Dallas*, Cambridge: Polity Press.

Lim, Song Hwee (2007), 'Is the Trans- in Transnational the Trans- in Transgender?', *New Cinemas: Journal of Contemporary Film*, 5: 1.

Lipsitz, George (1997), *Dangerous Crossroads: Popular Music, Postmodernism and the Poetics of Place*, London: Verso.

Livingstone, Sonia (2003), 'On the Challenges of Cross-National Comparative Media Research', *European Journal of Communication*, 18: 4.

Lockard, Craig (1998), *Dance of Life: Popular Music and Politics in Southeast Asia*, Honolulu: University of Hawaii Press.

López, Ana M. (2000), 'Facing Up to Hollywood', in Linda Williams and Christina Gledhill (eds), *Reinventing Film Studies*, London: Arnold.

Lotman, Yuri (1990), *The Universe of the Mind: A Semiotic Theory of Culture*, London: I. B. Tauris.

Lovell, Alan and Gianluca Sergi (2009), *Cinema Entertainment: Essays on Audiences, Films and Film Makers*, Maidenhead: Open University Press.

Lu, Sheldon Hsiao-peng (1997), 'Transnational Film Studies', in Sheldon Hsiao-peng Lu (ed.), *Transnational Chinese Cinemas: Identity, Nationhood, Gender*, Honolulu: University of Hawaii Press.

Lumbera, Bienvenido (1983), 'Problems in Philippine Film History', in Rafael Ma. Guerrero (ed.), *Readings in Philippine Cinema*, Manila: Experimental Cinema of the Philippines.

Lury, Celia (1993), *Cultural Rights: Technology, Legality, and Personality*, London: Routledge.

Lyotard, Jean- François (1984), *The Postmodern Condition: A Report on Knowledge*, Manchester: Manchester University Press.

Maltby, Richard and Melvyn Stokes (eds) (2004), *Hollywood Abroad: Audiences and Cultural Exchange*, London: BFI.

Mann, Harveen Sachveda (1995), '"Being Borne Across": Translation and Salman Rushdie's *The Satanic Verses*', *Criticism*, 37.

Marchetti, Gina and Tan See Kam (eds) (2006), *Hong Kong Film, Hollywood and the New Global Cinema*, London: Routledge.

Martin-Barbero, Jesus (1993), *Communication, Culture and Hegemony: From the Media to Mediations*, London: Sage.

Martinez, Dolores (2009), *Remaking Kurosawa: Translations and Permutations in Global Cinema*, New York: Palgrave Macmillan.

Mazdon, Lucy (2000), *Encore Hollywood: Remaking French Cinema*, London: BFI.

Mazdon, Lucy (2004), 'Introduction', *Journal of Romance Studies*, 4: 1.

McClintock, Pamela (2016), 'Box Office: "Star Wars: Force Awakens" Tops "Avatar" to Become No. 1 Film of All Time in North America', *The Hollywood Reporter*, 6 January 2016, available online at: *http://www.hollywoodreporter. com/news/box-office-star-wars-force-852274*

McMillan, Graeme (2016), 'J. J. Abrams Responds to "Rip-Off" Criticism about "Star Wars: The Force Awakens"', *The Hollywood Reporter*, 8 January 2016, available online at: *http://www.hollywoodreporter.com/heat-vision/ jj-abrams-responds-rip-criticism-853352*

Meehan, Eileen (1991), 'Holy Commodity Fetish, Batman', in Roberta Pearson and William Uricchio (eds), *The Many Lives of The Batman: Critical Approaches to a Superhero and His Media*, London: Routledge.

Mehta, Monika (2005), 'Globalising Bombay Cinema: Reproducing the Indian State and Family', *Cultural Dynamics*, 17: 2.

Mersmamnn, Birgit and Alexandra Schneider (eds) (2008), *Transmission Image: Visual Translation and Cultural Agency*, Newcastle upon Tyne: Cambridge Scholars.

Metcalf, Peter (2002), 'Hulk Hogan in the Rainforest', in Timothy Craig and Richard King (eds), *Global Goes Local: Popular Culture in Asia*, Vancouver: University of British Columbia Press.

Miller, Toby, Nitin Gobil, John McMurria, Richard Maxwell and Ting Wang (2005), *Global Hollywood 2*, London: BFI.

Mills, Jane (2009), *Loving and Hating Hollywood: Reframing Global and Local Cinemas* (Crows Nest, NSW: Allen and Unwin.

Mishra, Vijay (2002), *Bollywood Cinema: Temples of Desire*, New York: Routledge.

Modleski, Tania (1991), 'Three Men and Baby M', in Tania Modleski, *Feminism Without Women: Culture and Criticism in a 'Postfeminist' Age*, London: Routledge.

Molloy, Claire (2010), *Memento*, Edinburgh: Edinburgh University Press.

Mooij, Thessa (2006), 'The New Bollywood: No Heroines, No Villains', *Cineaste*, 31: 3.

Morcom, Anna (2001), 'An Understanding between Bollywood and Hollywood? The Meaning of Hollywood-style Music in Hindi Films', *British Journal of Ethnomusicology*, 10: 1.

Moretti, Franco (1998), *Atlas of the European Novel 1800–1900*, London: Verso.

Moretti, Franco (2000), 'Conjectures on World Literature', *New Left Review*, 1.

Moretti, Franco (2001), 'Planet Hollywood', *New Left Review*, 9.

Moretti, Franco (2005), *Graphs, Maps, Trees: Abstract Models for a Literary History*, London: Verso.

Morris, Meaghan (2004), 'Transnational Imagination in Action Cinema: Hong Kong and the Making of a Global Popular Culture', *Inter-Asia Cultural Studies*, 5: 2.

Morris, Meaghan, Siu Leung Li, and Stephen Chan Ching-kiu (2005), *Hong Kong Connections: Transnational Imagination in Action Cinema*, Durham: Duke University Press.

Mottram, James (2002), *The Making of Memento*, London: Faber and Faber.

Nagib, Lucia (2006), 'Towards a Positive definition of World Cinema', in Stephanie Dennison and Song Hwee-Lim (eds), *Remapping World Cinema: Identity, Culture and Politics*, London: Wallflower Press.

Nair, Kartik (2009), 'Run for Your Lives: Remembering the Ramsay Brothers', in Leanne Franklin and Ravenel Richardson (eds), *The Many Forms of Fear, Horror and Terror*, Oxford: Inter-Disciplinary Press.

Nal, Temal (2001), 'Developments in Turkish Copyright Law', *International Review of Industrial Property and Copyright Law*, 32: 7.

Naremore, James (2000), *Film Adaptation*, New Brunswick, NJ: Rutgers University Press.

Navaro-Yashin, Yael (2002), *Faces of the State: Secularism and Public Life in Turkey*, Princeton: Princeton University Press.

Nayar, Sheila J. (1997), 'The Values of Fantasy: Indian Popular Cinema through Western Scripts', *Journal of Popular Culture*, 31: 1.

Nayar, Sheila J. (2003), 'Dreams, Dharma and Mrs Doubtfire: Exploring Hindi Popular Cinema via its "Chutneyed" Western Scripts', *Journal of Popular Film and Television*, 31: 2.

Nayar, Sheila J. (2005), 'Dis-Orientalizing Bollywood: Incorporating Indian Popular Cinema into a Survey Film Course', *New Review of Film and Television Studies*, 3: 1.

Nayar, Sheila J. (2008), 'Invisible Representation: The Oral Contours of a National Popular Cinema', in Rajinder Dudrah and Jigna Desai (eds), *The Bollywood Reader*, Maidenhead: Open University Press.

Ndalianis, Angela (2004), *Neo-Baroque Aesthetics and Contemporary Entertainment*, Cambridge, MA: MIT Press.

Needham, Gary (2008), 'Fashioning Modernity: Hollywood and the Hong Kong Musical 1957–64', in Leon Hunt and Leung Wing-Fai (eds), *East Asian Cinemas: Exploring Transnational Connections on Film*, London: I. B. Tauris.

Newman, Kim (1986), 'Thirty Years in Another Town: The History of Italian Exploitation', *Monthly Film Bulletin*, 53: 626.

Ng, Stephanie (2005), 'Performing the "Filipino" at the Crossroads: Filipino Bands in Five-Star Hotels throughout Asia', *Modern Drama*, 48: 2.

Nornes, Abe Mark (2007), *Cinema Babel: Translating Global Cinema*, Minneapolis: University of Minnesota Press.

Norton, Christopher S. and Garrett Chaffin-Quiray (2002), '"Jonesing" James Bond: Co-opting Co-optation and the Rules of Racial Subordination', in Xavier Mendik (ed.), *Shocking Cinema of the Seventies*, Hereford: Noir Publishing.

O'Brien, Jack (2015), 'Six Insane Foreign Remakes of Famous American Blockbusters', Cracked, 13 May 2015, available online at: *http://www.cracked. com/video_19390_5-insanely-awful-movie-adaptations-from-around-world.html*

Olson, Scott Robert (1999), *Hollywood Planet: Global Media and the Competitive Advantage of Narrative Transparency*, Mahwah, NJ: Lawrence Erlbaum Associates.

Onaran, Alim Serif (2013), *Muhsin Ertugrul'un Sinemasi*, Istanbul: Agora Kitapligi.

O'Regan, Tom (1996), *Australian National Cinema*, London: Routledge.

O'Regan, Tom (2004), 'Cultural Exchange', in Toby Miller and Robert Stam (eds), *A Companion to Film Theory*, Oxford: Blackwell.

O'Rourke, Dan and Pravin A Rodrigues (2007), 'The "Transcreation" of a Mediated Myth: Spider-Man in India', in Terrence R. Wandtke (ed.), *The Amazing Transforming Superhero! Essays on the Revision of Characters in Comic Books, Film and Television*, Jefferson: McFarland.

Ostrowski, Ally (2007), 'Found in Translation: From Hollywood Hits to Bollywood Blockbusters', *Journal of Religion and Film*, 11: 2.

Özkaracalar, Kara (2003), 'Between Appropriation and Innovation: Turkish Horror Cinema', in Steven J. Schneider (ed.), *Fear Without Frontiers: Horror Cinema Across the Globe*, Guildford: FABPress.

Pang, Laikwan (2006), *Cultural Control and Globalisation in Asia: Copyright, Piracy and Cinema*, London: Routledge.

Pascua, Pasckie (2008), 'Pinoy frontman resurrects glory days of Journey', *Philippine News*, 26 June 2008, available online at: *http://www.gmanetwork. com/news/story/103507/news/pinoy-frontman-resurrects-glory-days-of-journey*

Pearson, Roberta and William Uricchio (1991), 'I'm Not Fooled by that Cheap Disguise', in Roberta Pearson and William Uricchio (eds), *The Many Lives of the Batman: Critical Approaches to a Superhero and His Media*, London: Routledge.

Pendakur, Manjunath (1990), 'India', in John A. Lent (ed.), *The Asian Film Industry*, Austin: University of Texas Press.

Pendakur, Manjunath (2003), *Indian Popular Cinema: Industry, Ideology and Consciousness*, Cresskill: Hampton Press.

Pieterse, Jan Nederveen (1995), 'Globalization as Hybridisation', in Mike Featherstone, Scott Lash and Roland Robertson (eds), *Global Modernities*, London: Sage.

Pieterse, Jan Nederveen (2004), *Globalisation and Culture: Global Melange*, Lanham: Rowman and Littlefield.

Pinchuk, Tom (2016), 'Seven Super Weird Foreign Remakes', Geek & Sundry, 10 February 2016, available online at: *http://geekandsundry.com/7-super-weird-foreign-remakes/*

Pines, Jim and Paul Willemen (1989), *Questions of Third Cinema*, London: BFI.

Porter, Michael E. (1990), *The Competitive Advantage of Nations*, New York: The Free Press.

Power, Carla and Sudip Mazumdar (2000), 'Bollywood Goes Global', *Newsweek*, 28 Feb 2000, available online at: *http://www.newsweek.com/2000/02/27/bollywood-goes-global.html*

Prasad, Madhava (2003), 'This Thing Called Bollywood', *Seminar*, 525.

Pratchett, Terry (2002), *Witches Abroad*, New York: HarperCollins.

Pratt, Mary Louise (1992), *Imperial Eyes: Travel Writing and Transculturation*, London: Routledge.

Punathambekar, Aswin (2013), *From Bombay to Bollywood: The Making of a Global Media Industry*, New York: New York University Press.

Rafael, Vincente L. (2000), *White Love and Other Events in Filipino History*, Durham: Duke University Press.

Rai, Amit (1994), 'An American Raj in Filmistan: Images of Elvis in Indian Films', *Screen*, 35: 1.

Rai, Amit (2009), *Untimely Bollywood: Globalization and India's New Media Assemblage*, Durham: Duke University Press.

Rajadhyaksha, Ashish (2009), *Indian Cinema in the Time of Celluloid: From Bollywood to the Emergency*, Bloomington: Indiana University Press.

Rajadhyaksha, Ashish and Paul Willemen (2002), *Encyclopaedia of Indian Cinema*, London: BFI.

Rajagopal, Arvind (2001), *Politics after Television: Religious Nationalism and the Reshaping of the Public in India*, Cambridge: Cambridge University Press.

Reyes, Emmanuel A. (1986), '1984: Towards the Development of a Nationalist Cinema', in Clodualdo Del Mundo, Jr (ed.), *Philippine Mass Media: A Book of Readings*, Manila: Communication Foundation for Asia.

Reyes, Emmanuel A. (1989), *Notes on Philippine Cinema*, Manila: De La Salle University Press.

Reyes, Soledad (1985), 'Romance and Realism in the Komiks', in Cynthia Roxas and Joaquin Arevalo, Jr (eds), *A History of Komiks of the Philippines and Other Countries*, Quezon City: Islas Filipinas Pub. Co.

Reyes, Soledad (1986), 'The Philippine Komiks', in Clodualdo Del Mundo Jr (ed.), *Philippine Mass Media: A Book of Readings*, Manila: Communication Foundation for Asia.

Ritzer, George (2000), *The McDonaldisation of Society*, London: Pine Forge Press.

Robertson, Roland (1992), *Globalisation: Social Theory and Global Culture*, London: Sage.

Robins, Kevin and Aksoy, Asu (2000), 'Deep Nation: The National Question and Turkish Cinema Culture', in Mette Hjort and Scott Mackenzie (eds), *Cinema and Nation*, London: Routledge.

Robinson, Andrew (2004), *Satyajit Ray: The Biography of a Master Film-Maker*, London: I. B. Tauris.

Saeed, Javaid (1994), *Islam and Modernization: A Comparative Analysis of Pakistan, Egypt and Turkey*, Westport: Praeger.

Said, Edward [1978] (2003), *Orientalism: Western Conceptions of the Orient*, London: Penguin.

Said, Edward (2001), 'The Clash of Ignorance', *The Nation*, 273: 12.

Sanders, Julie (2005), *Adaptation and Appropriation*, London: Routledge.

Sanders, Julie (2007), *Shakespeare and Music: Afterlives and Borrowings*, Cambridge: Polity Press.

Saner, Hulki (1996), *Bu Da Benim Filmim*, Istanbul: Saner Filmcilik Kasetçilik.

Sarkar, Bhaskar (2009), 'Tracking "Global Media", in the Outposts of Globalisation', in Natasa Durovicova and Kathleen Newman (eds), *World Cinemas, Transnational Perspectives*, London: Routledge.

Schiller, Herbert (1992), *Mass Communication and American Empire*, Boulder: Westview Press.

Schneider, Steven Jay, and Tony Williams (eds) (2005), *Horror International*, Detroit: Wayne State University Press.

Scognamillo, Giovanni and Metin Demirhan (1999), *Fantastik Turk Sinemasi*, Istanbul: Kabalc Yaynevi.

Sconce, Jeffrey (1995), '"Trashing the Academy": Taste, Excess and an Emerging Politics of Cinematic Style', *Screen*, 36: 4.

Sconce, Jeffrey (ed.) (2007), *Sleaze Artists: Cinema at the Margins of Taste, Style and Politics*, Durham: Duke University Press.

Segrave, Kerry (1997), *American Films Abroad: Hollywood's Domination of the World's Movie Screens*, Jefferson: McFarland.

Sen, Anubha Mukherji (2004), 'Pictures of Pardes: Imaging the Foreign through Indian Cinema', *Manushi: A Journal about Women and Society*, 140.

Server, Lee (1999), *Asian Pop Cinema: Bombay to Tokyo*, San Francisco: Chronicle Books.

Seton, Marie (1971), *Portrait of a Director: Satyajit Ray*, Bloomington: Indiana University Press.

Shohat, Ella and Robert Stam (1994), 'Syncretism as Artistic Strategy', in Ella Shohat and Robert Stam, *Unthinking Eurocentrism: Multiculturalism and the Media*, London: Routledge.

Simpson, Catherine (2006), 'Turkish Cinema's Resurgence: The "Deep Nation" Unravels', *Senses of Cinema*, 39.

Smith, Iain Robert (2008a), 'Beam Me Up, Ömer: Transnational Media Flow and the Cultural Politics of the Turkish Star Trek Remake', *Velvet Light Trap*, 61.

Smith, Iain Robert (2008b), 'The Exorcist in Istanbul: Transnational Processes of Intercultural Dialogue within Turkish Popular Cinema', *Portal: Journal of Multidisciplinary International Studies*, 5: 1.

Smith, Iain Robert (2011), 'When *Spiderman* Became *Spiderbabe*: Pornographic Appropriation and the Political Economy of the Softcore Spoof Genre', in Xavier Mendik (ed.), *Peep Shows: Cult Film and the Cine-Erotic*, London: Wallflower Press.

Smith, Iain Robert (2012), '"You're Really a Miniature Bond": Weng Weng and the Transnational Dimensions of Cult Film Stardom', in Kate Egan and Sarah Thomas (eds), *Cult Film Stardom: Offbeat Attractions and Processes of Cultification*, London: Palgrave Macmillan.

Smith, Iain Robert (2013), 'Oldboy Goes to Bollywood: Zinda (2006) and the Transnational Appropriation of South Korean Extreme Cinema', in Daniel Martin and Alison Peirse (eds), *Korean Horror Cinema*, Edinburgh: Edinburgh University Press.

Smith, Iain Robert (2015a), 'Batsploitation: Parodies, Fan Films and Remakes', in Roberta Pearson, William Uricchio and Will Brooker (eds), *Many More Lives of the Batman*, London: BFI.

Smith, Iain Robert (2015b), 'Memento in Mumbai: A Few More Songs and a Lot More Ass-Kicking', in Roberta Pearson and Anthony N. Smith (eds), *Storytelling in the Media Convergence Age*, London: Palgrave Macmillan.

Smith, Iain Robert (2015c), 'Tu Mera Superman: Globalization, Cultural Exchange and the Indian Superhero', in Rayna Denison and Rachel Mizsei-Ward (eds), *Superheroes on World Screens*, Jackson: University Press of Mississippi.

Smith, James (2004), 'Karagöz and Hacivat: Projections of Subversion and Conformance', *Asian Theatre Journal*, 21: 2.

Spivak, Gayatri Chakravorty (1999), *A Critique of Postcolonial Reason: Towards a History of the Vanishing Present*, Cambridge, MA: Harvard University Press.

Stam, Robert (1985), *Reflexivity in Film and Literature: From Don Quixite to Jean-Luc Godard*, Ann Arbor: UMI Research Press.

Stam, Robert (2000), 'Beyond Fidelity: The Dialogics of Adaptation', in James Naremore (ed.), *Film Adaptation*, London: Athlone Press.

Stam, Robert (2004), 'Introduction: The Theory and Practice of Adaptation', in Robert Stam and Alessandra Raengo (eds), *A Companion to Literature and Film*, Oxford: Blackwell.

Stam, Robert (2005), *Literature and Film: A Guide to the Theory and Practice of Film Adaptation*, Oxford: Blackwell.

Stringer, Julian (2007), 'The Original and the Copy: Nakata Hideo's *Ring* (1998)', in Alastair Phillips and Julian Stringer (eds), *Japanese Cinema: Texts and Contexts*, London: Routledge.

Stringer, Julian and Qiong Yu (2007), '*Hero*: How Chinese Is It?', in Paul Cooke (ed.), *World Cinema's 'Dialogues' with Hollywood*, Basingstoke: Palgrave Macmillan.

Strong, William S. (1990), *The Copyright Book*, Cambridge, MA: MIT Press.

Taylor, Timothy D. (1997), *Global Pop: World Music, World Markets*, London: Routledge.

Telotte, J. P. (ed.) (1991), *The Cult Film Experience*, Austin: University of Texas Press.

Thomas, Rosie (1985), 'Indian Cinema: Pleasures and Popularity', *Screen*, 26: 3/4.

Thompson, Roger M. (2003), *Filipino English and Taglish: Language Switching from Multiple Perspectives*, Philadelphia: John Benjamins Pub.

Thussu, Daya Kishan (2008), 'The Globalisation of "Bollywood": The Hype and the Hope', in Anandam P. Kavoori and Aswin Punathambekar (eds), *Global Bollywood*, New York: New York University Press.

Tiongson, Nicanor G. (1983a), 'From Stage to Screen: Philippine Dramatic Traditions and the Filipino Film', in Rafael Ma. Guerrero (ed.), *Readings in Philippine Cinema*, Manila: Experimental Cinema of the Philippines.

Tiongson, Nicanor G. (1983b), 'Four Values in Filipino Drama and Film', in Nicanor G. Tiongson (ed.) *The Urian Anthology 1970–1979*, Manila: M. L. Morato.

Tiongson, Nicanor G. (2001a), 'The Filipino Film in the Decade of the 1980s', in Nicanor G. Tiongson (ed.), *The Urian Anthology 1980–1989*, Manila: A. P. Tuviera.

Tiongson, Nicanor G. (2001b), 'The "Gaya-Gaya" Syndrome in Philippine Movies', in Nicanor G. Tiongson (ed.), *The Urian Anthology 1980–1989*, Manila: A. P. Tuviera.

Todorov, Tzvetan (1984), *Mikhail Bakhtin: The Dialogical Principle*, Minneapolis: University of Minneapolis Press.

Tolentino, Rolando B. (2000), *Geopolitics of the Visible: Essays on Philippine Film Cultures*, Quezon City: Ateneo de Manila University Press.

Tombs, Pete (1998), *Mondo Macabro: Weird and Wonderful Cinema Around the World*, New York: St Martin's Press.

Tomlinson, John (1991), *Cultural Imperialism*, London: Pinter.

Tomlinson, John (1999), *Globalisation and Culture*, Cambridge: Polity Press.

Torre, Jr, Nestor U. (1983), 'Lumauig Bill: Pro and Con', in Nicanor G. Tiongson (ed.), *The Urian Anthology 1970–1979*, Manila: M. L. Morato.

Trivedi, Harish (2007), 'From Bollywood to Hollywood: The Globalisation of Hindi Cinema', in Revathi Krishnaswamy and John C. Hawley (eds), *The Postcolonial and the Global*, Minneapolis: University of Minnesota Press.

Trivedi, Poonam (2007), '"Filmi" Shakespeare', *Literature Film Quarterly*, 35: 2.

Trumbull, Robert (1953), 'Movies Are Booming: In Bombay', *New York Times Magazine*, 5 July 1953.

Tulgar, Kunt (2007), 'Director's Interview', on *Supermen Dönüyor* [DVD], Onar Films.

Tumbocon Jr, Mauro Feria (2003), 'In a Climate of Terror: The Filipino Monster Movie', in Steven J. Schneider (ed.), *Fear Without Frontiers: Horror Cinema Across the Globe*, Guildford: FABPress.

Tunstall, Jeremy (1977), *The Media Are American: Anglo American Media in the World*, London: Constable.

Tyrrell, Heather (1999), 'Bollywood Versus Hollywood', in Tracey Skelton and Tim Allen (eds), *Culture and Global Change*, London: Routledge.

Tyrrell, Heather and Rajinder Dudrah (2006), 'Music in the Bollywood Film', in Ian Conrich and Estella Tincknell (eds), *Film's Musical Moments*, Edinburgh: Edinburgh University Press.

Ucak, Tevfik Fikret (2006), 'Director's Interview' on *3 Dev Adam* [DVD], Onar Films.

Vaidhyanathan, Siva (2001), *Copyrights and Copywrongs: The Rise of Intellectual Property and How It Threatens Creativity*, New York: New York University Press.

VanDerWerff, Todd (2015), 'Star Wars: The Force Awakens: Five Ways the New Movie Copies the Original Film', Vox, 21 December 2015, available online at: *http://www.vox.com/2015/12/21/10632690/star-wars-the-force-awakens-spoilers-han-solo-new-hope*

Varma, Rashmi (2004), 'Provincializing the Global City: From Bombay to Mumbai', *Social Text*, 22: 4.

Vasey, Ruth (1997), *The World According To Hollywood: 1918–1939*, Madison: University of Wisconsin Press.

Vasudevan, Ravi S. (1989), 'The Melodramatic Mode and the Commercial Hindi Cinema: Notes on Film History, Narrative and Performance in the 1950s', *Screen*, 30: 3.

Vasudevan, Ravi S. (2000), *Making Meaning in Indian Cinema*, New Delhi: Oxford University Press.

Vera, Noel (2005), *Critic After Dark: A Review of Philippine Cinema*, Singapore: BigO Books.

Verevis, Constantine (2005), *Film Remakes*, Edinburgh: Edinburgh University Press.

Vick, Tom (2007), *Asian Cinema: A Field Guide*, New York: HarperCollins.

Vieira, Joao Luiz (1995), 'From *High Noon* to *Jaws*: Carnival and Parody in Brazilian Cinema', in Robert Stam and Randal Johnson (eds), *Brazilian Cinema*, New York: Columbia University Press.

Vieira, Joao Luiz and Robert Stam (1990), 'Parody and Marginality: The Case of Brazilian Cinema', in Manuel Alvarado and John O. Thompson (eds), *The Media Reader*, London: BFI.

Virdi, Jyotika (2003), *The Cinematic Imagination: Indian Popular Films as Social History*, New Jersey: Rutgers University Press.

Virdi, Jyotika and Corey K. Creekmur (2006), 'India: Bollywood's Global Coming of Age', in Anne Ciecko (ed.), *Contemporary Asian Cinema: Popular Culture in a Global Frame*, Oxford: Berg.

Vitali, Valentina (2006), 'Not a Biography of the "Indian Cinema": Historiography and the Question of National Cinema in India', in Valentina Vitali and Paul Willemen (eds), *Theorising National Cinema*, London: BFI.

Vitali, Valentina (2008), *Hindi Action Cinema*, New Delhi: Oxford University Press.

Wagnleitner, Reinhold and Elaine Tyler May (eds) (2000), *Here, There and Everywhere: The Foreign Politics of American Popular Culture*, Hanover: University Press of New England.

Wandtke, Terrence R. (ed.) (2007), *The Amazing Transforming Superhero! Essays on the Revision of Characters in Comic Books, Film and Television*, Jefferson: McFarland.

Wang, Shujen (2003), 'Recontextualising Copyright: Piracy, Hollywood, the State, and Globalisation', *Cinema Journal*, 43: 1.

Wang, Yimen (2013), *Remaking Chinese Cinema: Through the Prism of Shanghai, Hong Kong, and Hollywood*, Hong Kong: Hong Kong University Press.

Wasko, Janet (2003), *How Hollywood Works*, London: Sage.

Watkins, Gwynne (2014), 'The Strangest Foreign-Language Versions of Hollywood Movies', *Yahoo Movies*, 24 June 2014, available online at: *https://www.yahoo.com/movies/the-strangest-foreign-language-versions-of-hollywood-89778158337.html*

Wells, Alan (1972), *Picture Tube Imperialism: The Impact of US Television on Latin America*, NY: Orbis Books.

Welsh, James M. and Peter Lev (eds) (2007), *The Literature / Film Reader: Issues of Adaptation*, Lanham: Scarecrow Press.

Willemen, Paul (2002), 'Detouring through Korean Cinema', *Inter-Asia Cultural Studies*, 3: 2.

Willemen, Paul (2005), 'For a Comparative Film Studies', *Inter-Asia Cultural Studies*, 6: 1.

Willemen, Paul (2013a), 'The Zoom in Popular Cinema: A Question of Performance', *Inter-Asia Cultural Studies*, 14: 1.

Willemen, Paul (2013b), 'Introduction to Subjectivity and Fantasy in Action: For a Comparative Film Studies', *Inter-Asia Cultural Studies*, 14: 1.

Willemen, Paul and Behroze Gandhy (1980), *Indian Cinema*, London: British Film Institute, in Bronwyn T. Williams and Amy A. Zenger (eds) (2012), *New Media Literacies and Participatory Popular Culture Across Borders*, London: Routledge.

Willis, Andrew (2003), 'Locating Bollywood: Notes on the Hindi Blockbuster, 1975 to the Present', in Julian Stringer (ed.), *Movie Blockbusters*, London: Routledge.

Wirten, Eva Hemmungs (2004), *No Trespassing: Authorship, Intellectual Property Rights, and the Boundaries of Globalisation*, Toronto: University of Toronto Press.

Wright, Neelam Sidhar (2009a), "Tom Cruise? Tarantino? *E.T.*? . . . Indian!': Innovation through Imitation in the Cross-cultural Bollywood Remake', *Scope: Journal of Film and Television Studies*, 15.

Wright, Neelam Sidhar (2009b), *Bollywood: The Postmodern Aesthetics, Scholarly Appeal, and Remaking of Contemporary Popular Indian Cinema*, dissertation, University of Sussex.

Xu, Gary (2008), 'Remaking East Asia, Outsourcing Hollywood', in Leon Hunt and Leung Wing-Fai (eds), *East Asian Cinemas: Exploring Transnational Connections on Film*, London: I. B. Tauris.

Yeatter, Brian L. (2007), *Cinema of the Philippines: A History and Filmography 1897–2005*, Jefferson: McFarland.

Yoshimoto, Mitsuhiro (2003), 'Hollywood, Americanism and the Imperial Screen: Geopolitics of Image and Discourse after the End of the Cold War', *Inter-Asia Cultural Studies*, 4: 3.

Yoshimoto, Mitsuhiro (2006a), 'The Difficulty of Being Radical: The Discipline of Film Studies and the Post-Colonial World Order', in Dimitris Eleftheriotis and Gary Needham (eds), *Asian Cinemas: A Reader & Guide*, Edinburgh: Edinburgh University Press.

Yoshimoto, Mitsuhiro (2006b), 'National/International/Transnational: The Concept of Trans-Asian Cinema and the Cultural Politics of Film Criticism', in Valentina Vitali and Paul Willemen (eds), *Theorising National Cinema*, London: BFI.

Zhang, Yingjin (2007), 'Comparative Film Studies, Transnational Film Studies: Interdisciplinarity, Crossmediality, and Transcultural Visuality in Chinese Cinema', *Journal of Chinese Cinemas*, 1: 1.

Zukin, Sharon (1995), *The Cultures of Cities*, Cambridge: Blackwell.

Index